One Knee
=EQUALS=
Two Feet

(And Everything Else You Need to Know About Football)

One Knee

= EQUALS =

Two Feet

(And Everything Else You Need to Know About Football)

John Madden
with
Dave Anderson

Villard Books • New York 1986

Library of Congress Cataloging in Publication Data
Madden, John, 1936–
One knee equals two feet.
1. Football—Anecdotes, facetiae, satire.
2. Football—Coaching—Anecdotes, facetiae, satire.
I. Anderson, Dave.
II. Title.
III. Title: 1 knee=2 feet.
GV950.5.M3   1986   796.332′0207   86-40099
ISBN 0-394-55328-4

To football's players and coaches, especially those who created and developed the game years ago. They never made much money, but they made the game into what it is today.

Contents

One Knee
= EQUALS =
Two Feet

(And Everything Else You Need to Know About Football)

A
Different
Wavelength

OF ALL THE PLAYERS IN THE NFL today, the one I'd most like to coach is Jim McMahon, the Bears' quarterback. He wakes everybody up. His teammates. His coaches. The media. The fans. When the Bears were about to play the Rams for the 1985 National Conference championship, I'm sure some of his teammates were puking or taking a nervous pee. But he was calmly sitting at his locker with a black pen, printing "Rozelle" on the white headband he likes to wear.

"Hey, do one for me," Walter Payton said.

Walter tossed over his headband and Jim obliged. Remember now, the Bears had to win this game to get to Super Bowl XX, but here was their *quarterback* printing the commissioner's name on two headbands after being fined $5,000 by Pete Rozelle for wearing an adidas headband. Now that's a football player who's on a different wavelength. And to me, that's good. I'd rather have *him* than a player who's half asleep.

Hey, when you play football every week from July to January, it can get boring, just like any other job gets boring. The trick is to do something to keep from being bored. Jim McMahon always finds something, even on an off day.

The following Sunday, before the Bears went to New Orleans, where they would win Super Bowl XX, I invited Jim to be on camera when I did my annual All-Madden team with Pat Summerall on the CBS network. We were doing it from Halas Hall at the Bears' complex in Lake Forest, Illinois, and Jim had his little daughter, Ashley, with him. Somebody had sent me a furry Bear cap to wear on the show. Well, I wasn't about to wear it, so I gave it to Ashley to play with. But when Jim was about to go on, he put on the furry cap. It covered his whole head except for his face.

"Is it okay if I wear this?" he asked.

"I don't care what you wear," I told him.

So he wore it. Hey, he looked silly. But he woke everybody up, especially Ashley.

"My daddy's wearing my bear," she kept saying.

Now, if Jim McMahon did all these things and wasn't a good quarterback, he'd be laughed at. If he did all these things and his teammates didn't like him, he'd be a phony. But his teammates love him, especially his offensive linemen.

"In the huddle, your eyes just glue into him," says Jay Hilgenberg, the Bears' center. "I'd jump out in front of a bus and block it for him."

I don't know if Mike Ditka, the Bears' coach, would go that far. Mike tells me that Jim McMahon is driven to do two things. "To win," Mike says, "and to upset me." Jim disagrees.

"I don't do anything to upset Mike," he says. "I do it to keep my sanity."

That's my kind of football player. And this is my kind of football book. I've tried to make it a book for everyone who's interested in football. For all those fans who watch NFL and college games. For anybody who plays football. For the guy who once played football, and for the guy who didn't. For the woman who isn't too knowledgeable about football, and for the woman who is. For the person who didn't know what football was until arriving in this country. Even for the football coach who, I hope, might learn a thing or two.

Football books have been done before, usually with too many X's and O's that a lot of people don't understand. But this is not a high-tech training manual. This is a book about my kind of football, the fun and the famous and the not-so-famous.

In writing about how to play a position, I've written how the best quarterbacks or the best cornerbacks have played their positions. In writing about coaching, I've tried to show how other coaches think, not just how I coached. I also list "The Best I've Ever Seen" among players and coaches. If some of your favorite players aren't on my lists, maybe it's because I haven't had a chance to watch them play enough to rate them. And if you think I've named too many of my Raider players, you're probably right. But hey, they were *my* players.

As you go along, I hope opening and closing this book will be as much fun for you as opening and closing a refrigerator. Or enjoying The Refrigerator himself.

William "The Refrigerator" Perry, the Bears' defensive tackle who sometimes lines up at fullback, is what football is supposed to be all about: blocking, tackling, running with the ball, catching the ball, and, more than anything else, having fun. As an American folk hero, The Refrigerator is a reminder that when people watch football, they're looking for fun things. More than anybody else, the National Football League should have learned a lesson from The Fridge's popularity.

For too long, the NFL tried to legislate sterility. No celebrations by the players. No shirttails hanging out. No characters.

But in all the headlines and TV highlights created by The Fridge, football fans were really saying, Hey, let's have some fun again. Let's get away from that faceless image, let's have some characters in the game. After all, that's what football is supposed to be—a game.

More than most, I related to The Refrigerator instantly. I'm just an older model.

When a big baby is born, that's the last good day he or she ever has. As that baby grows into a big person, all he or she ever hears is, "You're really big." The people who say that don't mean big as in tall, they mean big as in fat. Or to be polite, big as in heavy. I know. On occasion, I've been over 300 pounds myself. In all those years before The Fridge made fat fun again, I knew what he had to put up with—America's passion for beautiful bodies.

Trim, slim, that's all we big folks ever heard or saw. Mr. America, Miss America.

But hey, there aren't as many of those trim slims as there are of us, the bad bodies. On an "NFL Today" show a few weeks after The Fridge was plugged into America's psyche, I joked about forming the Brotherhood of United Bad Bodies Association—BUBBA for short. I even announced that its phone number would be 1-800-YO-BUBBA. Some people took me seriously and dialed it.

"We're sorry," that familiar computerized voice answered, "but your call cannot be completed as dialed. Please check the number and dial again."

If you dialed that number, my apologies. But when that computerized voice answered, you probably laughed. That's the beauty of what The Fridge has done for pro football. He has people laughing. Not at him, *with* him. The Fridge is pro football's Santa Claus—when somebody dresses up as Santa Claus in that red suit, red hat, and white beard, it's never one of those trim slims. To be a good Santa Claus, you need a big jolly guy.

If we ever get BUBBA really organized, The Fridge would be honored as the first member. He knows what it is to be big. Not being able to keep your shirttail tucked in. Not being able to look down and see your toes. Not being able to wear any of those one-size-fits-all bathrobes. In the mirror, that bathrobe looks like a bib.

It's not easy being big, but The Fridge keeps smiling. And long before he was famous, he enjoyed being big. As a Clemson freshman, William weighed 290, not bad for him. But when he showed up as a sophomore at 330, he was put on a diet of bananas and milk. Dan Benish, the Falcons' 265-pound defensive tackle who was at Clemson then, remembers that The Fridge would sit in the college cafeteria with stacks of bananas and cartons of milk on his table.

"He hadn't been given any limits on the amount of bananas and milk he could have," Dan says. "He just kept eating bananas and drinking milk. And he kept gaining weight."

But no matter how much The Fridge weighs, he's an athlete. He can dunk a basketball. He can hop up and down from the floor to a three-foot-high table. And not many people know that at Clemson, he enjoyed going to the swimming pool and diving. Dale Hatcher, his classmate at Clemson who is now the Rams' punter, remembers that whenever The Fridge went to the pool, he drew a crowd.

"Everybody would come over to watch the diving board bend and then to watch the splash," Dale says. "When he got out on the end of the board, it would bend down so far it looked like it was going to break. And when he dove, half the water would come out of the pool."

In visualizing The Fridge on a diving board, all I can see is him wearing one of those slim trim bathing suits that Greg Louganis wore at the Los Angeles Olympics when he won his two diving gold medals. But when William showed up at the Bears' training camp weighing 336 pounds as their first-round draft choice, Buddy Ryan, their defensive coordinator then, obviously would have preferred he had stayed on a diving board.

"He's a wasted draft choice," Buddy said. "He's a nice kid, but so's my son, and my son couldn't make our team."

You couldn't blame Buddy for thinking that way. When The Fridge arrived in Chicago after the draft weighing 318, the Bears told him to lose weight. But when he returned for a minicamp, he was up to 328. Now the Bears got tough and put him on a diet. When he gained eight more pounds by training camp, the Bears invoked the clause in his contract that says he can't weigh more than 310 pounds. Just inside the front door of Halas Hall is a big Toledo scale, the kind you usually see in a warehouse. The arrow goes all the way up and around and down to 500 pounds. That's where The Fridge weighed in twice a week.

"My whole rookie year," he says, "I only missed being under three-ten once."

The nation knows William Perry as The Refrigerator, but among his Bear teammates, he's known as Biscuit. During the ups and downs of William's weight, Dan Hampton, one of the Bears' defensive ends, who goes 267 himself, put him in perspective.

"William," said Dan, "is just a biscuit away from three-fifty."

The rest is history: how The Fridge scored on a 1-yard smash against the Packers, how two weeks later against the Packers he caught a 4-yard touchdown pass, how against the Falcons he scored on another 1-yard plunge, how he scored in Super Bowl XX on another 1-yard smash. His nickname was perfect, even if he wasn't always. In a goal-line situation against the Cowboys, he hurried onto the field, hunched into the huddle, hopped out of the huddle, and lined up. Then he realized he hadn't lined up in the correct formation. He hurried to another spot, then to another spot.

"Well, the Bears got The Refrigerator delivered," I said in the TV booth, "but they don't seem to know which wall to put him on."

By then, The Fridge had his picture on the nation's wall. Including the Super Bowl, he carried the ball only six times for a total of 8 yards. Plus his 4-yard pass reception. Nobody has ever gotten more mileage out of 12 yards. His popularity has turned them into a million dollars in commercials, endorsements, and appearances. But what impressed me was that his teammates didn't resent his popularity. If anything, Walter Payton appreciated it.

Throughout most of his career, Walter Payton had been the only Bear who attracted the media. Especially when he was approaching Jim Brown's career rushing record, which he broke during the 1984 season. But The Fridge has taken some of the media heat off Walter.

The Fridge's presence as a fullback alongside Walter Payton was inspired by the 49ers having used an offensive guard, Guy McIntyre, a substitute guard, as a fullback against the Bears during the 1984 National Conference championship game. During the week before that game, I was at the 49ers' training complex in Redwood City, California. One of their players told me about their plans to use what they called the "Angus" play. As a 264-pound guard, Guy McIntyre's nickname was Angus.

Sure enough, Bill Walsh, the 49ers' coach, used McIntyre as a blocking back for Wendell Tyler, their halfback. When the 49ers won, 23–0, the Bears felt they had been insulted by the Angus play.

When the Bears were preparing to play the 49ers early in the 1985 season, Mike Ditka, the Bears' coach, decided to use William Perry as a fullback—and as a payback. The difference was, William carried the ball. On the Bears' last possession in a 26–10 victory, he carried the ball twice, gaining 2 yards each time. Back in Chicago the next day, Mike was asked if he planned to use The Fridge as a ballcarrier again.

"You have to think about him on the goal line," Mike said.

When The Fridge scored his first touchdown against the Packers in the Bears' next game, other NFL coaches started thinking. Joe Walton, the Jets' coach, used his two All-Pro defensive linemen, Joe Klecko and Mark Gastineau, in the backfield. In a third-and-goal situation at the Dolphins' 3-yard line, the two linemen lined up as blockers for Freeman McNeil, but Gastineau missed his assignment. McNeil was stopped for a 1-yard loss. Raymond Berry, the Patriots' coach, used an offensive tackle, Steve Moore, as a blocking back.

Other than The Fridge, only one NFL lineman carried the ball during the 1985 season: Bruce Smith, the Buffalo Bills' 280-pound defensive end. In a late-season game with the Jets, he carried once near midfield in a third-and-one situation. No gain. And no role as a folk hero despite a good nickname: The Snowplow.

In my ten years as coach of the Raiders, it never occurred to me to use a lineman as a fullback. But now that The Fridge has turned on a light inside my head, I think the next step will be to take that defensive or offensive lineman and use him in the backfield as a pass blocker, especially in an obvious passing situation. Probably a backup offensive guard. He's trained to be a pass blocker. Uh-oh, I'm starting to sound like a coach. But don't worry, you won't need an interpreter for coach talk. To understand this book, about all you have to know are a few football terms, which you probably already know anyway:

Strong side—the side of the offensive line with the tight end

Weak side—the side of the offensive line without the tight end

4-3 defense—four defensive linemen and three linebackers (plus four defensive backs)

3-4 defense—three defensive linemen and four linebackers (plus four defensive backs)

Nickel defense—a fifth defensive back replacing one linebacker; *dime defense*—a fifth and sixth defensive back replacing two linebackers; *quarter defense*—a fifth, sixth, and seventh defensive back replacing three linebackers

Zone defense—defensive backs and linebackers are responsible for covering an area rather than a specific player

Man-to-man defense—defensive backs and linebackers are responsible for covering a specific pass receiver

Hey, if you didn't know that before, you do now. In football, you're always learning. Doing a Jets-Bengals preseason game in 1983, Jerome Barkum, the Jets' tight end, caught a pass from Richard Todd in the end zone and rolled across the sideline. In the booth, Pat Summerall and I weren't sure if Barkum had scored.

"He has to have *both* feet in bounds *and* he has to have possession," I said. "That's the rule."

When we saw the replay, we clearly saw Barkum's right knee hit in bounds. But not his feet.

"One knee," I said. "But the left foot never hit."

After a commercial, we looked at the replay again. Barkum's right knee definitely was down in the end zone but as he rolled across the sideline, his left foot was in the air.

"The right hits," I said, "but the left never does."

According to what Pat and I were saying, it appeared that the official had blown it, ruling that Barkum had scored when he really hadn't. Hearing that at home, Art McNally, the NFL's supervisor of officials, phoned our CBS truck in Cincinnati. Then our people in the truck informed us over our earplugs of Art's explanation.

"Art McNally has just called us," Pat announced, "and he says that one knee down is as good as two feet down."

"One knee equals two feet," I said, laughing. "They ought to give that one to Pat McInally [the Bengals' punter]. Let him take it back to Harvard. It'd be a new physics thing on that chart. You know that chart. You always go into that phys. ed. class, they have that chart up on the wall—one knee equals two feet. Explain that one."

That's what I mean when I talk about how in football, you're always learning. I think the game gets better all the time, both in the NFL and in college. The athletes keep getting better— faster, bigger, stronger.

If you get the impression that I love football, you're right. But hey, I don't love everything about it. For years I've been push- ing to protect the quarterback after he throws a pass. Nobody in the NFL office seems to have heard me, even though their most valuable properties, the quarterbacks, keep getting hurt unnecessarily. Some of those injuries can't be prevented, but some can—especially those that occur after a quarterback has thrown the ball. If the NFL rules can protect a punter and a placekicker from being roughed in that split second after he gets the ball away, the rules should also protect a quarterback in that split second after he gets the pass away.

My solution is to provide the referee with a horn that, when blown, produces a different noise than a whistle. The horn should have an *ooonnnkkk* sound. Once the quarterback has thrown the ball, the referee should use his horn. If a defensive player hits the quarterback after the *ooonnnkkk*, it's a 15-yard penalty.

Some, if not all, of the NFL coaches might disagree, arguing that a pass rusher has too much momentum to stop in time. But I don't buy that. Nobody has more momentum than those punt rushers and placekick rushers. But those rushers have learned how to avoid hitting the punter and the placekicker. If a punter or placekicker is roughed, it's a 15-yard penalty. If a pass rusher roughs a quarterback after he gets the ball away, it should also be 15 yards. But the penalty should apply only to a quarterback who stays in the pocket. Once a quarterback starts to scramble, he's on his own.

I know, some punters and placekickers are great actors, falling and writhing when touched as if they had been shot. With my rule, some quarterbacks might be candidates for an Oscar, but that's better than being candidates for an ambulance.

As a group, quarterbacks are the NFL's toughest players. On a pass play, the quarterback takes the snap from the center, hurries back into his pocket of blockers, and stands there searching for an open receiver with those huge pass rushers swarming toward him. When he throws, his body is completely exposed to the pass rushers. But after he throws, just about everybody watches the ball. Complete, incomplete, interception—everyone's eyes are on the ball.

Next time watch the quarterback after he throws the ball. Watch him get blasted in that split second after the pass is on its way. Watch him get slammed down—and watch him get up, slowly sometimes. He has a tough job, and to endure it a quarterback has got to be a tough guy.

Several years ago the NFL put in what is known as the "in the grasp" rule: If a passer is in the grasp of a tackler, he is ruled to have been tackled. That's a good rule. But when a passer is in the grasp is not when he gets hurt. When he's in the grasp, he usually can protect himself. It's after he's thrown the ball that he usually gets hurt—when his arm is up and his body, especially the rib area, is exposed. When a punter gets the ball off, he has the same problem. With one leg in the air, he's defenseless. If he gets hit, it's a penalty. I've never understood that double standard.

Another rule I'd like to see changed is the return of the 2-point conversion after a touchdown—passing or running from the 2-yard line for 2 points instead of placekicking for 1 point.

In 1969, when I took over as the Raiders' head coach in the last year of the American Football League, before the 1970 merger realignment, we had the option in the AFL of going for the 2-point conversion. Some coaches didn't like it but I did; it gave me another way to win a game. If we were 7 points behind and then scored a touchdown, we had a chance to win by passing or running instead of settling for the 1 point that would create a tie. If we didn't make the 2-point conversion, well, then we had a chance to lose. And that's why some other coaches didn't like it.

When the 2-point conversion was possible, the 1-point conversion wasn't that big a play. I preferred it that way.

The way it is now, if your placekicker misses an extra point or has it blocked, all that work for a touchdown isn't worth any more than two 3-point field goals. But to me, a touchdown should be worth more. With the 2-point conversion, if you happen not to get your 1-point conversion after one touchdown, you have an opportunity to get it back after another touchdown. That's when I usually went for the 2 points.

I always thought the AFL fans liked the 2-point conversion. Going or not going for the 2 points created another second-guess situation. That's another reason why some coaches didn't like it.

The second guess is part of the fun of football for fans. And the fans deserve all the fun they can get. That's why The Refrigerator has been so appealing. On a train ride to Chicago not long after The Fridge arrived, I was sitting in the club car near a white-haired lady who had lived in Chicago all her life. We got talking and she told me about how she had always been a baseball fan, a Cubs fan, but had never followed football until The Fridge came along.

"That young man," she said, "makes football fun."

And this book, I hope, will make football even more fun for you.

My
Favorite
Guys

IN MY YEARS WITH THE
Raiders and, before that, as an assistant coach at San Diego
State, every so often I would let my offensive linemen beat the
stuffing out of a tackling dummy. One by one.

"Take it into the weight room," I'd tell them. "Punch it.
Wrestle it. Kick it. Bite it. Do anything you want to it."

They loved it. There's nothing like fighting something that
you know isn't going to fight back. I'd put a watch on 'em. I'd
let 'em fight that big bag for three minutes, like it was a round
of boxing. Some people thought I was crazy. But I've got a
theory about offensive linemen, who happen to be my favorite
guys on any football team, probably because I was an offensive
lineman once myself. My theory is that most offensive linemen
were big when they were kids, whereas most defensive players
were tough little kids who became big when they grew up. That
might not sound significant, but in football it is. Big kids have
a hard time being aggressive. Wherever they go, they're told,
"Hey, don't pick on that little kid." If a big kid does anything

aggressive to a smaller kid his own age, then he's a bully. If he's a big brother, he's not allowed to pick on his little brother or, worse, his little sister. But if a tough little kid does something aggressive to a big guy, he's cute.

"Hey, look at that tough little kid," people will say. "What a cute little kid."

The big kid has to live with not being allowed to be aggressive. I know. I was a big kid. When the big kid starts playing football, usually as an offensive lineman, all he hears is his coach telling him about some tough little kid. The coach is saying, "If he was only as big as some of the other guys I've got here, he'd be All-Everything someday." Or the coach is saying, "If some of my big guys were as tough as that little kid over there, you couldn't stop 'em." You hear that in high school, in college, even in the NFL.

As a coach, I realized that you can't take the tough little kid and make him bigger, but you can take the big guy and make him aggressive. And that's why I had my offensive linemen beat the stuffing out of a tackling dummy: to teach them to be aggressive.

One of my pet peeves is hearing people say that offensive linemen should be passive, especially pass blockers trying to stop an opposing defensive lineman or linebacker. Those people don't understand what it is to be an offensive lineman. Yes, pass-blocking is passive in that you have to accept the other guy's charge and keep yourself between him and your quarterback. And an offensive lineman has to be thoughtful, whereas a defensive player is more animalistic. But that doesn't mean an offensive lineman can't be aggressive.

As a coach, I had always preached that philosophy to my offensive linemen. And when Bob Brown joined the Raiders in 1971, he proved it to them.

As an All-Pro tackle, Bob had a boxer's instincts. He believed in punching a defensive end in the solar plexus—*boom*, with both fists. That's not as bad as it sounds because it has to be a perfect punch, just under the shoulder pads and above the hip pads, and that's a pretty small area. But when a defensive end put his hands up to grab Bob's shoulders, sometimes he was vulnerable.

"Anytime I got a good one in there," Bob used to say, "it'd take a quarter out of the guy."

Bob didn't mean twenty-five cents, he meant the next fifteen minutes of the game. And when Bob got his shot in, his man would be floating around for the next fifteen minutes like a boat with no wind in its sails. I never considered that dirty football; to me it was aggressive football, aggressive pass-blocking. Don't let that defensive guy knock you back. Instead, you knock him back. That's what run-blocking has to be—aggressive. Pass-blocking has to be the same way. But some passing teams practice their passing so much, their offensive linemen forget how to be aggressive. Those teams usually don't run the ball well, especially in short-yardage situations.

The 49ers were that way years ago. Their offensive linemen spent so much time going backward as pass blockers, they forgot how to fire out as run blockers.

By nature, some offensive linemen are more aggressive than others, but I love 'em all. They're my guys. Anytime I felt bad about something, like if I had just cut some players in training camp, I always went over to where they were warming up at practice. We would always warm up in groups—offensive linemen here, wide receivers there, running backs over here, defensive linemen over there, linebackers somewhere else, defensive backs over there. Somehow, just being with the offensive linemen always made me feel better. Maybe it was because they were such solid guys—solid as rocks.

Not everybody on a football team is that way. Wide receivers are like artists. Linebackers are like caged tigers. But offensive linemen are the foundation of your offense and, to me, of your whole team. They have to be solid. And they are. I'm thinking mostly of the Raiders that I had—Jim Otto and Gene Upshaw and Art Shell—but also of those I had in the Pro Bowl from other teams—John Hannah and Jim Langer—and those I've gotten to know from the broadcast booth—Russ Grimm, Joe Jacoby, Jim Covert, Jay Hilgenberg, Jackie Slater, and Dennis Harrah.

Not enough people appreciate those guys, mostly because not enough people watch them. But if you want to know what's happening, offensive linemen will tell you.

Throughout my whole football career, I've heard people say they never know where the ball is at the start of a play. That's because they're trying to watch the ball.

At the start of a play, anybody trying to watch the ball *shouldn't* know where the ball is. With a good team, if you try to watch the ball, you'll almost always be looking the wrong way. When the quarterback hands off on a running play, he's going to reverse-pivot in order to hide the ball—not from you, from the other team. And if he succeeds in fooling the other team, chances are he's fooling you, too.

The best way to know what's happening is to watch the guards and the center.

Learn to watch one guard first, then both guards at the same time. Once you've got that down, watch the center as well. After that, try to watch the fullback, too. You'll find that your vision expands. As a coach, I knew what all twenty-two players did on a play—offense and defense. In the TV booth now, it's even easier to see all twenty-two than it was on the sideline. But when a play begins, I still watch what I call the "triangle" of those four players: the center, the two guards, and the fullback.

Nothing happens on a play until the center snaps the ball. But as soon as he does, everything starts.

By watching that triangle, it's easier to know what's happening. Unless it's an obvious passing situation, I always look for the run. If the center and two guards fire out to block, you know it's a run, probably up the middle or off-tackle. If the left guard pulls and goes to the right, you know it's probably a running play to the right, what is known as a sweep. Of the two guards, the left guard pulls the most. More plays are run to the right, more sweeps are run to the right. For that reason, the right guard is usually bigger and stronger than the left guard, who is usually faster and quicker. Kent Hill of the Rams is fast and quick. He's a left guard who can get out there all the way to the right to block for Eric Dickerson on a sweep.

As a rule, if both guards pull and take off to one side, it's a sweep. If one guard pulls and the other guard fires out straight ahead, it's an off-tackle run. If one guard pulls short, it's a trap —the runner won't be sweeping wide. If both guards fire out, it's a straight-ahead run. If both guards and the center drop back to block for the passer, it's obviously a pass play—unless it's a draw, where the quarterback drops back as if he's going to throw, then hands off to a running back. You don't know if it's a pass until the quarterback moves back beyond the running back. On a pass, you have plenty of time to see what's going on. You have time to watch the quarterback; you also have time to look downfield at the wide receivers to see if they're open.

By watching certain players instead of the ball, you should know where the ball is.

Another way is to watch the middle linebacker in a 4-3 defense or the two inside linebackers in a 3-4 defense. It's their job to know where the ball is. If they drop back, you know it's a pass. If they move up, it's an inside run. If they hurry to the right or left, it's a run to that side.

While everything starts with the center's snap, it's not always as mechanical as it looks.

When another offensive lineman fires out in his run block or steps back in his pass block, he just lifts his body out of a three-point stance with both hands up to protect himself. But before a center can get up, he has to snap the ball to the quarterback. As soon as a center moves his right arm, he's fair game. Worse, he can't protect himself with that right arm. Against a team that uses a 4-3 defense, it's not too bad. In that defense, the middle linebacker is a step away from the ball. But in the 3-4 defense that most teams use now, the nose tackle is eyeball to eyeball with the center, just waiting for that arm to move so that he can blast the center.

Knowing he's going to get blasted as soon as he snaps the ball, a center needs more mental discipline than anybody at any other position.

A good center hangs in there and takes the shot, then lines up and does it again. Does it for ten or twelve seasons, sometimes longer. That durability is what has always impressed me about the best centers: Jim Otto, Mick Tingelhoff, Jim Langer, Mike Webster, Jack Rudnay, Jeff Van Note. They're all big, strong, farmer-type guys who look as if they should be carrying a calf on their shoulders. Not only did they hardly ever miss a game, they hardly ever missed a practice. Only a coach understands how important it is to have your center at every practice. The snap to the quarterback has to be the same every time. No surprises. The quarterback has enough to think about without wondering about the snap.

A good center also knows how to snap the ball and still get his other hand up quick on the nose tackle or the linebacker. His other hand should be up there flat, to keep the nose tackle or the linebacker from crashing into the shoulder of the hand he's snapping the ball with.

Once the nose tackle gets that shoulder turned, the center has lost his leverage. If your center can't get his other hand up quick enough, you've got to use one of your guards to double-team that nose tackle. That's why a center who can block a nose tackle by himself is so important. Dwight Stephenson of the Dolphins has been the All-Pro center in recent years. I'm sure he's good, but in my TV travels, I just haven't seen that much of him. The best I've seen lately is Joe Fields of the Jets, along with Jay Hilgenberg of the Bears, who has the perfect approach for an offensive lineman, especially a center.

"The thing I like about football," Jay says, "is that you don't have to take a shower before you go to work."

The center position changed in the sixties, when the Bears put their middle linebacker, Bill George, over the center and the Chiefs moved one of their tackles, either Buck Buchanan or Ernie Ladd, over the center.

Year by year, more teams would put a defensive lineman or a linebacker on the center's nose until today's nose tackle evolved. Some teams still use the 4-3 defense, which usually leaves the center without anybody to block in pass protection. One of the smartest centers against a four-man line was Mike Webster of the Steelers. In that situation, some centers miss the linebacker blitzing up the middle, or they slide over to help a blocker who doesn't need help. Not Mike. He always picked up the blitzer, or he helped the blocker who needed the most help.

The Best I've Ever Seen

Centers   Joe Fields
Jim Langer
Jim Otto
Mick Tingelhoff
Jeff Van Note
Mike Webster

Guards   Russ Grimm
John Hannah
Gene Upshaw

Tackles   Bob Brown
Joe Jacoby
Henry Lawrence
Ron Mix
Art Shell

Another smart center was John Schmitt of the Jets back when Joe Namath was their quarterback. Nobody ever talked about John, maybe because he didn't look like a good athlete, but he did smart things. If somebody got by him, he'd grab a foot and get away with it.

Maybe the strongest center I've ever seen was Jim Langer on the 1972 Dolphin team that had the perfect 17–0 record. Jim probably looked like a center the day he was born—wide shoulders, big legs, low center of gravity. But not all the good ones were big. I always thought Jack Rudnay of the Chiefs was too small. He weighed only about 230 pounds—a little puny for a center—but nobody ever seemed to get by him. And that's the real test.

Another test for a center is whether he's anxious, or whether he gets that way as he gets older.

In my TV travels, I once visited a team with one of the NFL's most celebrated centers. He was a Pro Bowl choice, a starter for a decade, but his new coach was considering cutting him.

"This guy," his coach told me, "is giving me an early snap."

That center finished out the season, but he was gone the next. When a center is gun-shy, he tends to snap the ball a split second early in order to provide himself with that split second of extra protection. But the quarterback isn't ready for that early snap. Neither are the other offensive linemen. Say the snap count is "three," meaning the ball should be snapped when the quarterback yells, "Hut one . . . hut two . . . hut three." If the center snaps the ball on "two," the defensive players get a jump on the offensive linemen who are still in their stance, waiting to hear "three."

With that early snap, the anxious center might make himself look better, but he makes his teammates look bad. They're getting whipped. And pissed off. So is his coach.

Being anxious can also create a fumble on the snap. When the quarterback crouches behind the center, he puts his right hand firmly under the center's butt, with his left hand back a little. On the snap count, the center lifts the ball into the quarterback's right hand, then the quarterback uses his left hand to guide it up. If the center is anxious, his snap might hit the left hand instead. Sometimes an anxious center doesn't even bring the ball all the way up, forcing the quarterback to reach down for it. Either way, a fumble is possible.

Conversely, a center can be so eager to get into his block that he botches the snap. That's what caused Phil Simms, the Giants' quarterback, to fumble several snaps from Bart Oates during the 1985 season.

After putting together film of each of the fumbles, the Giants' coaches realized that whenever Bart was blocking to his left, he would take his first step with his left foot, which meant his right leg was leaning across to the left. When that happened, Bart was snapping the ball up into his right thigh instead of into Phil's hands. *Blap,* a fumble. To prevent that from happening when Bart had to block to his left, the Giants' coaches had him take a short step to his right, then go left. That kept his right thigh out of the way of the snap.

Even without a fumble, the hesitation involved in a quarterback having to search for the ball can mess up his timing with the running backs or the wide receivers.

Of all the positions, center is not the toughest to play skill-wise, not the toughest to play physically. It's the mental discipline that makes it tough, even to the extent of remembering the snap count. In the huddle, the center will hear the quarterback call, say, "Full right, eighteen bob odd O on three." When the center turns out of the huddle, he's thinking about the play so much that he forgets the snap count. Hey, he's human. He forgets things like everybody else. But if the center does it too often, he's gone.

Obviously, the center is the only player who can snap the ball. So if he forgets the count, when does he snap it?

When in doubt, the center should always snap the ball early. If he's not sure if the count was "three" or "two," he should snap it on "two." That way none of his teammates will be offside. If the count is "two" and he waits to "three," his teammates will have made their move on "two." Then everybody's offside.

Sometimes a center is only as good as the guards on each side of him. I've always liked guards, maybe because I was a rookie guard with the Philadelphia Eagles in 1959, before a knee operation finished me as a player. Wherever I see young players, I always check out the guards. After the Raiders got knocked out of the 1972 AFC playoffs by Franco Harris' "immaculate reception" for the Steelers, I went to Honolulu to see the Hula Bowl workouts. One day I was standing on the sideline with Dan McGuire, at the time the sports columnist for the *Honolulu Advertiser*, when I noticed a big guard out of the University of Alabama.

"There's the best player out here," I said. "John Hannah."

I was half talking to myself, half talking to Dan. It never occurred to me that he might quote me. But the next day the headline on his column was HANNAH BEST PLAYER—MADDEN. When people asked me about it, I backed off. I was there to rate players for the Oakland Raiders, not for the readers of the *Honolulu Advertiser*. But when John Hannah was named to the All-Rookie team after his first year with the Patriots, I took credit for having spotted him at the Hula Bowl.

"John Hannah, yeah, I knew he was going to be great the first time I saw him at a Hula Bowl workout," I said. "Look it up."

Not that I had found a needle in a haystack. If anything, I had found a haystack. John Hannah had the look and the build of a guard: natural size, huge legs, thick arms, wide neck. *Boom*, he just went out and bowled people over. The type of guy you put in there for fifteen years. Just watching him work out that day, I knew he could run-block. And I knew he would learn to pass-block. At 6 foot 3 and 265, he developed into as good a guard as there is in the NFL, maybe the best ever. People still talk about how Jerry Kramer and Fuzzy Thurston were great pulling guards for Vince Lombardi's great Packer teams, but Jim Ringo was the center between those guards. And early in John Hannah's career with the Patriots, Jim Ringo was their offensive coordinator.

"John Hannah," Jim said, "has better pulling speed than either Kramer or Thurston, even though he's twenty pounds heavier than either one."

That's enough of a tribute for me. John Hannah, of course, was a left guard. As I've said, the quicker of your two guards usually is. With the tight end usually lined up next to the right tackle, the strong side of your basic offensive formation is usually the right side. To balance that, you put your quicker guard on the left side. In the history of football, just as the power usually has flowed through the right side of the offensive formation, the tricks have come on the left side.

Gene Upshaw was my left guard on the Raiders, big at 6 foot 5 and 255, but quick and fast enough to pull and get out in front of a running back on a sweep to the right.

My big right guard on the Raiders for several seasons was George Buehler, who looked like a 275-pound silo. He hardly ever had a holding penalty called against him. Which proved to be his undoing in a 1976 game against the Packers in Oakland. The night before, Dave Rowe, one of our defensive tackles, got together with his friend Mike McCoy, the Packers' defensive tackle who would be going against George.

"Mike," Dave said, "you're really going to enjoy playing against George; he's the cleanest guard in the league. He never holds."

Before the game the next day, Dave got George aside and told him, "I told Mike McCoy how much he'll enjoy playing against you because you're such a clean player." When the game started, I'm sure Mike McCoy enjoyed himself. In our previous six games, our quarterback, Kenny Stabler, had been sacked a total of only seven times. But that day Mike sacked him three times, once forcing a fumble. We won, 18–14, but George was never worse. At the Tuesday meeting, I chewed him out. Later on, Dave Rowe came to my office to confess.

"George's bad game," he said, "I think that was my fault."

Dave told me how he had told George what he had told Mike, and then about how George later acknowledged being so conscious of not holding Mike, he hardly blocked him at all.

"From now on," I told Dave, "if you talk to a player on another team, make sure it's not the guy playing against George Buehler."

As seldom as George had been called for holding, he had been psyched out by Dave Rowe's description of him as a guard who never holds. To justify Dave's endorsement, George didn't dare hold. And a guard or any offensive lineman can't go into a game thinking he's not going to hold. If he does, he can't get the job done. In pass protection, you've got to use your hands on the defensive man, you've got to ride him outside. You've got to keep him away from your quarterback as long as necessary. Some coaches tell their pass blockers that their quarterback needs three seconds to get his pass off. But when I was coaching, I didn't want time to be a factor.

"You have to protect the passer until he gets rid of the ball," I always told my offensive linemen.

I wanted them to protect the quarterback, to push the pass rushers around, to hold if they had to. Whenever I hear people talk about how this or that offensive lineman holds, I just laugh to myself. Hey, they all hold. Any offensive lineman who has ever played in the NFL has held. If he's out there, he's holding.

On a routine pass play, when the quarterback drops back to throw, at least one of the offensive linemen will be holding. As the game gets tight, on some pass plays *all* the offensive linemen will be holding. And the best offensive linemen are the best holders. They hold, but they don't get caught—at least not too often.

In the *NFL Digest of Rules,* holding is not defined as such. What is defined is the "use of hands, arms and body" in pass blocking:

> During a legal block, hands (open or closed) must be inside the blocker's elbows and can be thrust forward to contact an opponent as long as the contact is inside the frame. Hands cannot be thrust forward above the frame to contact an opponent on the neck, face or head. (Note: The frame is defined as that part of the opponent's body below the neck that is presented to the blocker.) Blocker cannot use his hands or arms to push from behind, hang onto, or encircle an opponent in a manner that restricts his

movements as the play develops. By use of up and down action of arm(s), the blocker is permitted to ward off the opponent's attempt to grasp his jersey or arm(s) and prevent legal contact to the head.

If that sounds like the pass blocker is in a fight with the pass rusher, you're right. That's exactly what it is—a fight.

Even better, that's what it's *supposed* to be. That's why a guard is a guard. That's why he's down there in the dirt and the mud—except that in stadiums with artificial turf and, worse, stadiums with domes, there is no dirt and mud anymore, just that green carpet that turns football into a video game. But some players always will be throwbacks to the days when there was dirt and mud, players like Russ Grimm and Joe Jacoby, the Redskins' left guard and left tackle. They remind me of offensive linemen who played in the sixties, guys who would yank off their helmets in the heat of training camp, dip a scooper into a bucket, and splash water over their heads.

I never see pictures of players doing that now. Not sanitary enough, I guess. But an offensive lineman doesn't worry about sanitation any more than a hog does.

By the time the Redskins won Super Bowl XVII, their offensive line had earned the nickname The Hogs. One day at training camp, Joe Bugel, the Redskins' offensive line coach, kept staring at Russ Grimm, the left guard at 6 foot 3 and 292.

"Russ," he said, "you are a prototype hog."

When the other linemen heard that, they wanted to be hogs, too. And they all qualified: Joe Jacoby, the left tackle, 6 foot 7 and 311; Jeff Bostic, the center, 6 foot 3 and 258; Mark May, the right guard, 6 foot 6 and 295; George Starke, the right tackle, 6 foot 5 and 270.

Notice that their biggest, strongest tackle, Joe Jacoby, is on the left side, not the right side where I would put him. There's a reason. Joe Gibbs, the Redskins' coach, often uses two tight ends. Which means Jacoby seldom has to pass-block without a tight end alongside him. On most teams, the best pass rusher is the right end on defense, who lines up against the left tackle on offense. Without a tight end next to him, that left tackle is truly on an island. Without a tight end there, that defensive right end can line up wide, which makes it tougher for the left tackle to keep him away from the passer.

You can't play offensive tackle in the NFL if you can't pass-block. You can get by at guard and center without being a great pass blocker, but not at tackle. Not where you have to handle those defensive ends.

You have to keep your body square between the passer and the pass rusher. And you do this with footwork as much as with strength. You can bench-press 450 pounds, but if your feet aren't in the right place, it doesn't mean a thing. Especially your inside foot. If you're the left tackle, that means your right foot. Art Shell, my left tackle on the Raiders, developed his footwork as a basketball center at Maryland State, and as big as he was, 6 foot 5 and about 300, he never lost that footwork.

For an athlete, having good feet isn't that much different from having good hands. In reaching for a ball, your hands should move together. In stepping, your feet should move together, usually at shoulder width. If your feet are too close to each other, you can get pushed over easily. If they're too far apart, you can't get anywhere quickly.

But no matter how good a tackle's footwork is, he still has to keep his inside foot up. Stand up and I'll show you. I'm the defensive right end and you're the offensive left tackle. You should have your left foot back a little, that's your outside foot. If you keep your right foot up, your inside foot, I can't go inside you. I can go outside you, but that's what you want me to do. You'll just keep riding me to the outside away from the quarterback. By keeping his inside foot up, the offensive tackle blocks the pass rusher's inside route to the passer.

I'm not saying it always works. Sometimes the pass rusher will simply overpower the tackle. Sometimes he'll feint the tackle out of position. But by keeping his inside foot up, the tackle has the best possible chance of pass-blocking effectively. If his inside foot is not up, he'll always get beat by an inside move.

If he's not strong enough, the tackle probably has no chance either. One of the strongest tackles was Dan Dierdorf of the Cardinals, now a CBS broadcaster. When he came out of Michigan in 1971, I wanted to draft him for the Raiders, but Al Davis, our managing general partner, and I were committed to bolstering our defense that year. In the first round, we took Jack Tatum to play safety. But when the second round began, Dan was still available.

"How about Dierdorf?" I asked.

"Not if Villapiano is there," Al said. "He's the guy we want next."

"Yeah, but Dierdorf should've been a first-round pick."

"I know," Al said, "but we've got to get that linebacker."

As it turned out, the Cardinals, who were drafting two teams ahead of us, took Dan in the second round. Then we took Phil Villapiano, a linebacker I really wanted. But when Dan had still been available after the first round ended, I had to say something. Dan turned out to be a great offensive tackle, but I would have played him at guard. He fit my mold for a guard on a team that played most of its games on grass: wide butt, good feet, strong, heavy.

I would've had some fun with Dan Dierdorf, and he would've had some fun fighting that tackling dummy.

The Most Important Position

ALL THE GOOD QUARTER-
backs I've been around seem to have one thing in common:
They don't worry. And when you think about it, a quarterback
can't be a worrier. He can't worry if the coach or his teammates
or the fans or the media are going to second-guess him. He can't
worry what the commissioner will say if "Rozelle" is on his
headband. He can't even worry about the weather. Don Shula
tells about a rainy day in Baltimore in 1983 when Dan Marino
was awaiting his third start as the Dolphins' rookie quarterback.
Before the game, Shula called Marino into his office to tell him
not to use some of the plays in the game plan.

"How come?" Dan asked.

"It's raining too hard," Don explained.

"That doesn't make any difference."

It didn't. In a steady rain, Dan Marino completed eleven of
eighteen passes for 157 yards and two touchdowns in a 21–7
victory. I had a similar experience with George Blanda in 1968,

when I was still a Raider assistant. We had a game in Denver when Daryle Lamonica couldn't play. George was forty-one years old that season, but he didn't worry about his age. And when a November snowstorm swirled through the Rockies the Saturday we arrived in Denver, everybody began to worry about the weather. Everyone except George.

"I like throwing in the snow," he said.

"You what?" somebody said. "You like throwing in the *snow?*"

"It's easier to throw."

"How can it be easier?"

"There's no pass-rush," he said. "In the snow, pass rushers are like cars, they can't get any traction. And the defensive backs don't know where the wide receivers are going. If the wide receivers stay under control in the snow, the defensive backs will fall down trying to cover them."

By the next day, the storm had stopped. Snow was piled along the sideline and the field was dry, but it was cold and windy. George didn't worry about that either. He sent Warren Wells out on a post pattern and hit him for a 94-yard touchdown. We won, 43–7.

Joe Montana doesn't worry. In the weeks before the 49ers won Super Bowl XIX, some sportswriters were wondering if he had a sore arm. He hadn't been throwing deep. Over the years I've gotten to know Joe, and I've found him to be one of the most knowledgeable quarterbacks I've ever talked to. Anytime I've asked him how he was going to attack an opposing defense, he's told me his thinking. So when the stories appeared in the Bay Area newspapers about his not throwing deep, I visited him at the 49ers' complex in Redwood City.

"Are you going to start throwing deep?"

He never batted an eye. "No," he said.

"Why not?" I pressed. "Is your arm sore?"

"No, my arm's not sore; I can throw deep," he said. "But we don't have any plays to throw deep. We never practice throwing deep."

"How come?"

"Look at our practice field here," he said. "Most teams have two full hundred-yard fields, one grass and one artificial turf. But we only have one field that's half grass and half artificial turf. When it rains in December here, the receivers have to wear either artificial turf shoes or grass shoes, depending on which half of the field we're practicing on. If we practice on the grass half, the receivers don't want to run out on the artificial turf with cleats. If we practice on the artificial-turf half, the receivers don't want to risk falling on the wet grass with their artificial-turf shoes. When we practice plays, we put the ball on what would be the twenty-yard line, so I've got only about thirty yards to work with. You can't throw deep in thirty yards. Even in the pregame warmup, it's the same situation. You only have half the field to work with. That's why I don't throw deep."

"Have you told anybody else this?" I asked.

"I don't worry about those things," he said.

That's only one reason why I think Joe Montana is the NFL's best quarterback today. He can throw. He also can move around back there. He can set up quickly. If he's chased out of the pocket, he can roll out to throw or he can run for yardage. When the 49ers won Super Bowl XIX, he burst through the defense and dove into the end zone for a 6-yard touchdown. Against the Giants in the playoffs three weeks earlier, he took off up the left sideline for 53 yards. When a quarterback is that dangerous, a defense doesn't know what to do. Even when a defense is playing the pass, he can zip the ball in there to a receiver who doesn't appear to be open. On a 20-yard pass, he throws darts.

In the NFL, quarterback is still the most important position. If you don't have a good quarterback, your team won't be a winner. For that reason, it's still the toughest position to play. But as good as Joe Montana, Dan Marino, Jim McMahon, and a few others are now, quarterback is not as tough a position as it used to be.

The way coaches send in plays these days, a quarterback just plays his position the way his teammates play theirs. Years ago, a quarterback had to be a strong leader who was a good play caller. He had to select the right play at the right time. In the NFL today, most quarterbacks don't call the plays anymore. Their coaches do, and as a result, you seldom see quarterbacks chewing out their receivers or their blockers. They're no longer in a position to. In a sense, their leadership has been eroded.

All a quarterback really has to do now is throw. Years ago it usually took about five years for a quarterback to develop to where an NFL coach would trust him to be his starter. But with Dan Marino, it took about five weeks. Partly because all he had to do was throw.

Dan had a better situation than most rookie quarterbacks do. He joined a team that had been to the Super Bowl the season before. He had a good offensive line, good receivers, and, most important, he had Don Shula coaching him. Dan had everything going for him, plus his great talent. Most young quarterbacks need time to develop because their teams need time to develop. By the nature of the NFL draft, where the worst teams get the early choices, a touted quarterback usually joins one of the worst teams. As gifted as Jim McMahon is, he had to wait until the Bears developed before he really developed. The day the Bears drafted Jim in the first round in 1982, he arrived at Halas Hall in a limousine. And when he stepped out of the limo, he was wearing sunglasses and holding a can of beer.

"Right then," Mike Ditka has said, "I knew we had a different guy."

Notice that Mike didn't say that Jim was bad or goofy. Just *different.* Jim showed everybody just how different when he wore that "Rozelle" headband during the NFC championship game.

"I thought if I got Pete a little publicity, he might not fine me for my adidas headband," Jim explained.

Pete laughed, but Jim's fine stood. By then, his fourth season, he had grown as a quarterback—as the Bears had grown as a team around him. By the time they swept through Super Bowl XX, he had an offensive line to protect him and wide receivers to catch his passes. Phil Simms of the Giants took longer than

Jim did, mostly because he kept getting hurt: two shoulder separations, knee surgery, a fractured thumb on his passing hand. He kept getting hurt because he didn't have an offensive line that could protect him properly. Then the Giants put together an offensive line and got him better pass receivers. Suddenly he was ready to go. At the same time, his team was ready. And he had confidence because he knew his coach, Bill Parcells, and his team had confidence in him. Some quarterbacks are like that. If nobody *shows* any confidence in them, they don't *have* any themselves. But as soon as they feel others have confidence in them, it rubs off. In Phil's case, that confidence even rubbed off on his little boy, Christopher. After a Saturday practice at Giants Stadium, I noticed Christopher, who was four at the time, throwing a football with Lawrence Taylor's son and Jim Burt's son. Every time I've seen a kid throw a football, he always tells the other kids to run out for a pass. But not Phil Simms' boy.

"Blitz me," he yelled. "Blitz me."

Ken O'Brien of the Jets developed pretty much the same way Phil Simms did, but without the injuries. His rookie year Ken stood on the sidelines. His second year he lost a lot of time testifying in a New York–disco assault case (he was acquitted). But by his third year he was ready to take over at the same time the Jets were ready to roll into the playoffs.

With coaches calling the plays, a quarterback can rise as fast as the talent around him rises. In a way, a quarterback nowadays isn't that much different from a running back or a guard or a middle linebacker or a cornerback. He's told what to do and he tries to do it. He really doesn't have to think like the old quarterbacks did. To some football people that may be progress, but I don't like it. The way it's developing, football is going to be just another video game: too robotic. My computer against your computer instead of people against people.

Back when I was the Raiders' coach, I would send in maybe a dozen plays a game, usually in short-yardage and goal-line situations. But mostly I let my quarterback call his plays. That phrase "his plays" is important. I always believed that if a quarterback is calling his plays, then they are exactly that: his plays. If his coach is sending in the plays, they're the coach's plays, not the quarterback's. I think any quarterback would rather use *his* plays—those he thinks will work, those he has confidence in.

But that's not the case today, and that's why quarterbacks are different. That's why John Elway of the Broncos is going to be a great NFL quarterback. All he has to do is throw—and he's got the arm to do that.

Not that John Elway couldn't develop into a good play caller. But since he doesn't have to, he never will. When a coach sends in a play, he's really saying, "According to the computer, this play should work in this situation." Sometimes, if not most of the time, it does. But coaches who do that are what I call "system" coaches. I preferred to be a "people" coach. On the sideline, I always liked to look in a player's eyes. Anytime we needed a touchdown near the goal line, I would look in Pete Banaszak's eyes.

"I'll get it," Pete would say.

We didn't use a computer, but if we had, it probably would not have agreed that Pete would score in that situation. Too slow, too old. But if Pete ran to the left side behind Art Shell and Gene Upshaw, he would get into the end zone. Whenever I looked in Kenny Stabler's eyes, I had the same good feeling. In the huddle, his teammates also had the same good feeling—even when he called a play that wasn't supposed to work in that situation against a certain defense.

"Snake," somebody would say, "we can't run that."

"Easy to call, hard to run," he'd say. "Let's go."

Snake didn't listen. If he had listened, if his teammates had been able to talk him out of calling a certain play, they wouldn't have had any respect for any other play he called. Easy to call, hard to run. But when Snake called that play, the Raiders ran it. Usually they made it work.

"Just the way Snake called it," Art Shell once told me, "you'd think, 'Yeah, it'll go.' "

That sense of command in the huddle is something all the

best quarterbacks have. "Being in the huddle with John Unitas," the Colts' tight end of that era, John Mackey, once said, "is like being in the huddle with God." Well, almost. But the more confident a quarterback sounds in calling a play, the more confident his teammates will be in running that play. If he's hesitant, his teammates will be hesitant. That's another reason why I wanted my quarterback to call his own plays. If he calls it, presumably he believes in it. If the coach sends it in, he might not sound as if he believes in it.

In the huddle, a quarterback who calls his own plays doesn't have time to think about what he's going to call. He's got to know right away.

In calling a play, a quarterback considers several factors: his field position, the down and distance to a first down, the opposing defense, the score, and the weather. But it's not as complex as some football people like to make it sound. Back in 1940, when the Bears popularized the modern T-formation by trampling the Redskins, 73–0, in the NFL championship game, George Halas talked about how his quarterback, Sid Luckman, had to know 350 different plays. If you want a big number, that's also true today. It all depends on how you count. One basic play can be run from several different formations. If you run the same play from a strong-right formation and then from a strong-left formation, technically you can count that as two different plays. If you run the same play with the running backs and the wide receivers in, say, four different formations, technically you can count that as four different plays.

In a specific game plan, a quarterback usually has only a few dozen plays—say, six running plays and six pass plays for first down, another six and six for second down, six running plays for third down and short-yardage (2 yards or less), six pass plays for third down and 2 to 7 yards to go, and another six pass plays for third down and 7 or more yards to go.

From the referee's ready-to-play signal to the snap, a quarterback has only thirty seconds. To make the most of those thirty seconds, in the huddle a quarterback uses numbers mixed with a few one-syllable words—as few numbers and words as possible. That takes less time. In the Raider huddle, my players might hear: "Eighteen bob odd O." And that's all my quarterback needed to say to tell everybody what to do.

In our playbook, "eighteen" meant the halfback would carry the ball on a sweep around right end; "bob" told our fullback to block the linebacker outside our right end (back on 'backer); "odd" told our offensive linemen which way to block—the tight end blocked down on the defensive end, the right tackle blocked down on the defensive tackle, the right guard pulled to lead the interference for the halfback; and "O" told the left (or offside) guard to pull and follow the right guard.

In our huddle, a pass play might have been: "Ninety-one out flare seven." Any call in the nineties was a pass play; "ninety-one" and "out" told our three pass receivers what to do. The two wide receivers would run 15 yards downfield, then run a square-out pattern to each sideline. The tight end would run a hook pattern toward the middle. "Flare seven" told our two running backs to run 10 yards downfield, then hook on the yard-line numbers chalked inside the sidelines. Since the backs line up 5 yards behind the line of scrimmage, they would be running a total of 15 yards—the same distance as the wide receivers. Ideally, the two wide receivers, the tight end who had to battle his way past a linebacker, and the two running backs would be breaking open at about the same time. As for the linemen, they know that on any play in the nineties series, they pass-block.

After calling the play in the huddle, the quarterback has to call something else: the snap count.

The quarterback will say "on one," or "on two," or "on three," sometimes even "on four." When he's up at the line of scrimmage, he will yell, "Hut . . . hut . . . hut." If the snap count had been "on three," the center will snap the ball on the third "hut." Some quarterbacks prefer to yell "hut-hut" quickly, but that usually counts as one "hut," not two. As simple as a snap count is, players occasionally forget it. That's why a lineman jumps offside. Sometimes the center forgets it. Sometimes even the quarterback forgets it, as Bob Griese of the Dolphins did in the first quarter of Super Bowl VIII on the Vikings' 5-yard line.

"In the huddle," Bob remembers, "I called the formation, the play, and the snap count: Brown left, eighteen straight on one."

Simple enough. But after the huddle broke, Bob walked up behind his center, Jim Langer, and drew a blank. In studying the Vikings' goal-line defense to see if he should call an audible to change the play, he realized he had forgotten the snap count. He turned to Larry Csonka and Jim Kiick, lined up as running backs.

"I asked Zonk, 'What's it on?' and he told me, 'On two,' " Bob says. "But then Kiick yells, 'No, it's on one,' and Zonk yells back, 'No, it's on two.' "

Here were the Dolphins, hoping to win their second straight Super Bowl, debating on the 5-yard line what the snap count was. But if the Dolphins were confused, so were the Vikings, who were listening to all this.

"I yelled, 'It's on two,' " Bob says, "but I'm still not sure and by now nobody else is either."

Bob began calling signals. But Jim Langer, remembering that Bob had instructed in the huddle that the snap count was "on one," snapped the ball on the first hut.

"When I turned with the ball," Bob remembers, "Zonk was still in his stance. But when he saw me, he took off. I handed him the ball and he went in."

That's one way to confuse a defense. Another is for a quarterback to be a good ball handler. To pretend to hand off to one running back, then to toss a pitchout to the other. To hide the ball on his hip. To have a little magician in him. Sad to say, it's a dying art. You never hear people talk about a quarterback being a good ball handler anymore. Back when I was a kid, Frankie Albert of the 49ers was considered to be the best ball-handling quarterback. Joe Montana and Bob Griese are the best I've seen in recent years. Joe Namath, Ken Stabler, and George Blanda were good ball handlers. So was Fran Tarkenton, who also had great footwork. Bad ball handlers show you the ball all the way, but a good ball handler confuses the defense, as well as the spectator in the stands and the TV viewer at home. That's why you're better off watching the guards.

Before the quarterback takes the snap at the line of scrimmage, he's barking signals. He's either *calling* an audible, meaning a different play than the one he called in the huddle, or he's *faking* an audible.

If he calls an audible, it's because he thinks the opposing defensive alignment will stop the play he called in the huddle. By yelling a word, usually a color, and a number as he crouches behind the center, a quarterback can tell his teammates what the new play will be.

Audibles sound mysterious but they're not. If they were that mysterious, the players wouldn't understand the new play.

When a quarterback is at the line of scrimmage, the first thing he yells is a color, then a number. Turning his head to one side, then to the other side, he might say, "Red, eighteen . . . red, eighteen." If red is the live color for that game or that half or maybe even only that series, it alerts his teammates to pay attention to the number that will signify the new play. If red is not the live color, it alerts his teammates that he is *not* calling a new play.

If red was the live color and my Raider quarterback yelled, say, "Blue, thirty-two . . . blue, thirty-two," that meant the play he called in the huddle was still on. But if he yelled, "Red, eighteen . . . red eighteen," that meant he was changing the play he called in the huddle to the play he was calling now at the line of scrimmage—eighteen, the audible for one of our running plays. If he yelled, "Red, twenty-seven . . . red, twenty-seven," the twenty-seven was the audible for one of our pass plays.

All this is rote stuff for the players. Certain numbers mean certain plays. It's just a matter of studying that playbook and paying attention in meetings until it's second nature.

With an audible, a quarterback has to be careful not to tip off the other team by the way he yells it. Not that the opposing defense will know the actual play, but if a quarterback yells loudly and slowly, "Reeeeeddd, twenty-seven . . . reeeeeddd, twenty-seven," that might mean he wants to make sure his wide receivers hear him. Listening to that loud call, a free safety who had expected a running play might adjust to pass coverage.

If a quarterback is calling a live audible, he sometimes pauses between the time he yells, "Reeeeeddd, twenty-seven . . . reeeeeddd, twenty-seven," and the snap count. He uses that pause to give his teammates a moment for the twenty-seven to sink in. But if it's a dummy audible, he might yell, "Blue, twenty-seven . . . blue twenty-seven," like he's ordering a cup of coffee.

Ideally, a quarterback should yell his live audibles and his dummy audibles the same way. But that's easier said than done. In a critical situation with a game at stake, a quarterback doesn't want a mix-up. It's only natural for him to yell the live audible louder and slower than the dummy audible. In calling the snap count in the huddle, a quarterback also can get in a rut. He'll call a play and without thinking, he'll say, "On three." Play after play after play. If he does that too much, the opposing defense will get into the same rhythm. Those defensive linemen will be taking off on the third "hut," which takes away the offensive lineman's advantage. Knowing the snap count is about all an offensive lineman has going for him. He operates on timing. The defensive lineman operates on reaction to the offensive lineman's movement. If the defensive lineman can anticipate the snap count, *he* has the advantage.

On a running play, the quarterback hands off to a running back. Then the quarterback should fake the bootleg, looking to see if the defense took off after the ballcarrier. If it did, he knows he can run the bootleg later on.

If the safety moves up on a running play, a smart quarterback knows that the option pass might work. That's why Walter Payton of the Bears has been so effective as a passer on the option. As soon as Walter takes a handoff or a pitchout, everybody on the defense moves up. That leaves the deep area open for a pass receiver.

But in the NFL, a quarterback isn't in there to hand off or toss a pitchout. He's in there to pass.

Pro football is a quarterback's game; college football, on the other hand, is a running back's game. Look at John Elway of the Broncos—the first player selected in the 1983 NFL draft, and rightly so. In his senior year at Stanford, his team had a 5–6 record. As good as John was in college, he couldn't turn his team into a winner the way running back Herschel Walker did at Georgia that season. In the NFL, even a great running back like Eric Dickerson hasn't lifted the Rams to a Super Bowl championship. Some teams have won the Super Bowl with adequate running backs, but no team has ever won the Super Bowl without an outstanding quarterback, often a Hall of Famer. Consider this game-by-game list of Super Bowl champions and their quarterbacks:

> I—Packers (Bart Starr)
> II—Packers (Bart Starr)
> III—Jets (Joe Namath)
> IV—Chiefs (Len Dawson)
> V—Colts (Johnny Unitas, Earl Morrall)
> VI—Cowboys (Roger Staubach)
> VII—Dolphins (Bob Griese)
> VIII—Dolphins (Bob Griese)
> IX—Steelers (Terry Bradshaw)
> X—Steelers (Terry Bradshaw)
> XI—Raiders (Ken Stabler)
> XII—Cowboys (Roger Staubach)
> XIII—Steelers (Terry Bradshaw)
> XIV—Steelers (Terry Bradshaw)
> XV—Raiders (Jim Plunkett)
> XVI—49ers (Joe Montana)
> XVII—Redskins (Joe Theismann)
> XVIII—Raiders (Jim Plunkett)
> XIX—49ers (Joe Montana)
> XX—Bears (Jim McMahon)

To win the Super Bowl, you need a quarterback who has a strong arm, can spot his receivers, can find the open receiver, and, more than anything else, can whip a pass to that open receiver. That's what a quick release is: finding the open receiver and getting the ball to him before he can be covered. With that pass rush thundering at him, a quarterback doesn't have much time. Only a second or two to set up, sometimes only a split second to get that pass off. That's why he needs a quick release—the time from the moment his brain signals his arm that the receiver is open to when the ball is on its way.

Joe Namath had it. Terry Bradshaw had it. Roger Staubach had it. Kenny Stabler had it. Joe Montana, Dan Marino, Jim McMahon, and Dan Fouts have it now.

Of all those quarterbacks, I always thought Joe Namath had the quickest release. As the Raiders' coach, I feared Joe more than any other passer, especially in his early years. My first year as the Raiders' linebacker coach, in 1967, we went to Shea Stadium with several new blitzes that I had designed. Quick blitzes that would get our linebackers to Joe before he could get rid of the ball.

"He won't get away this time," I said.

Joe had trouble. He completed only nine of twenty-eight passes for 166 yards with two interceptions and two sacks, but the Jets still won, 27–14. No matter how quickly our linemen and linebackers got there, he got the ball away before they got him. As good as the Jets were in those years, Joe didn't have the weapons that, say, Terry Bradshaw had with the Steelers later on, but Joe had that great arm and that great release. Because of his bad knees, you didn't worry about his running, but in his first few seasons, that's just when he would hobble out there on a bootleg for a first down, maybe a touchdown. If he hadn't needed two operations on each knee, no telling what he would've done. Yet for all his knee problems, he had the quickest feet I've ever seen. He could skip back there to set up faster than most quarterbacks with good knees. In the warmup, I always checked to see how Joe was moving on those knee braces that made his white pants bulge.

"He's slowing down," I'd tell my players. "We can get to him."

Wrong. And if we played the Jets at Shea, in that wind tunnel there, I would check to see which way the wind was blowing when they had the ball.

"He can't throw against that wind," I'd say.

Wrong again. Joe threw the ball right through the wind. Just like Dan Marino didn't worry about the rain in Baltimore that day in 1983, Joe Namath didn't worry about the wind at Shea any day. It didn't make any difference whether the wind was with him or against him. Joe just threw the ball. And he didn't throw high-percentage passes to his running backs. He threw the ball up the field—20, 30, 40, 50 yards, more if he had to. When he rallied the Jets to beat the Raiders, 27–23, in the 1968 AFL championship game, the big play was Joe's pass to Don Maynard for a 52-yard gain to our 6-yard line that set up their winning touchdown. Figuring the distance from where Joe threw the ball at about his own 30 across the width of the field to where Maynard caught it at the sideline near our 10, it covered about 75 yards in the air.

By the 1972 season, Joe's knees were a little slower but his release wasn't. We played the Jets at Oakland in a Monday night game that turned into a shootout: Joe hit twenty-five of forty-six passes for 406 yards; Daryle Lamonica hit ten of seventeen for 202 yards and two touchdowns. We won, 24–16, but after that game I went into the Jets' locker room to congratulate Joe on his performance, the only time during my coaching career I ever did that.

"We had all our pass coverages lined up knowing you were going to throw," I told him, "and you still tore us apart."

I had learned to respect Joe Namath back in 1967, my first year as a Raiders' assistant. Before our game with the Jets in Oakland that year, I was leaving the house when my wife, Virginia, called to me.

"Get Namath," she said.

"We'll get him," I said.

Believe me, we weren't trying to *get* Joe that day, we weren't trying to hurt him. But on a pass rush in the second half, one of our defensive ends, Ike Lassiter, happened to break Joe's left cheekbone. Not that it stopped him. He finished the game, completing twenty-seven of forty-six passes for 370 yards and three touchdowns, but we won, 38–29. When I came out of our locker room, Virginia was waiting for me.

"You shouldn't have done that," she said.

"I shouldn't have done *what?*" I asked.

"You shouldn't have gotten Namath, that was the worst thing I ever saw."

"Didn't you tell me to *get* Namath?"

"But he's such a nice young man," she said.

"How do you know he's so nice?"

"He just came out of the Jets' locker room," she said. "He was holding an ice bag on his cheekbone, but when a little kid asked him for an autograph, he put the ice bag down and signed the kid's program. Now that's a nice young man."

Two years later, in New York at his Bachelors III restaurant, Virginia thought Joe was even nicer. Our charter landed in New York on Friday to give us extra time before Sunday's game to get over the jet lag. That night I was busy with my coaches, so Virginia went to Bachelors III with Wayne Valley, then one of the Raider partners; his wife, Gladys; and a few other Raider people. Joe stopped by Wayne's table.

"Join us," Wayne said.

Joe sat down, talked with Wayne and Gladys, with Virginia and everybody else. But then Virginia had a question for him.

"Do you know of any big men's clothing stores here?" she asked.

Joe got up and walked away, rejoining some of his Jet teammates. Virginia thought maybe Joe was bored by the conversation or bored by her. But a few minutes later, he returned with a slip of paper with the addresses and phone numbers of three big men's clothing stores.

"I told you two years ago," she said to me later, "that Joe Namath was a nice young man."

That's how Virginia remembers Joe Namath, but I think of him as the best pure passer I ever saw. Terry Bradshaw could really throw, but as strange as it sounds, I always worried more about his running than his passing. Not his rollouts, not his scrambles, but his *running*. If we got him backed up without an open receiver, he would just take off and run for a first down. Most quarterbacks who run, you think of them as scramblers or rollouters—Fran Tarkenton and Roger Staubach years ago, Joe Montana now. They scoot around, slip between tacklers, and slide to a stop rather than try to bull an extra yard.

But when Terry Bradshaw ran, he picked his legs up like a running back. Tacklers bounced off him. Most of the time, if a linebacker gets an arm around a quarterback, sometimes even a hand, *whap*, that quarterback goes down. But not Bradshaw—he ran right through an arm or a hand.

In our games with the Steelers, we got to the point where we preferred to keep Bradshaw in the pocket. Let him pass and take our chances. When he passed, our defense knew its coverages. But when he ran, it seemed like nobody knew what to do. Not that letting him pass was a bargain. He had a strong arm, he could drill the ball. That's why he was so dangerous, even in his first few seasons. In those years, he didn't really know what he was doing. His arm was a little wild, but that wildness kept you guessing. Playing defense against Terry Bradshaw then was like batting against Nolan Ryan in his early years.

Some people think Terry threw the ball too hard, but I don't agree. Unless you're talking about a really short pass of maybe 5 yards, I don't think a quarterback can throw the ball too hard.

The harder the ball is thrown, the less time the pass is in the air. The less time it's in the air, the less time there is for it to be intercepted. That was always my philosophy—no matter how much some of our pass receivers complained. Some thought Daryle Lamonica threw the ball too hard. And when Kenny Stabler was breaking in, some thought that a ball with a left-handed spin was too hard to catch. I never bought either excuse.

"If you can't catch the ball," I always told them, "I'll get receivers who can."

No matter how hard a quarterback throws the ball, a good pass receiver will adjust to the speed. It might take him a few days, maybe even a week or two, but he'll adjust. That's why he's a good receiver. Those Steeler receivers didn't have any trouble adjusting to Terry Bradshaw's hard passes. They caught enough against us. They caught enough to win a record four Super Bowl games. Terry Bradshaw was 4–0 in the Super Bowl, that's good enough for me. He was a winner in the biggest game you can win. Four times. Without a loss.

Another winner was Roger Staubach, the Cowboy quarterback on two Super Bowl championship teams. He also was on two Super Bowl teams that lost to the Steelers and Terry Bradshaw, but hey, both teams couldn't win. And even when Roger's team lost, he was never *defeated*.

Roger was like that the first time I saw him. It was a rookie game in 1969, the Raiders against the Cowboys, my first game in my first year as head coach. Roger had won the Heisman Trophy as a junior at the Naval Academy in 1963, then he fulfilled his military commitment, some of it in Vietnam as a supply officer. Now he was finally joining the Cowboys the same year we had drafted Eldridge Dickey, a quarterback out of Tennessee State, in the first round and when Kenny Stabler was still a virtual rookie. The year before, after we drafted Kenny out of Alabama, he had a bad knee. To display all these quarterbacks, Al Davis and I talked about having a formal scrimmage with the Cowboys, who were training in Thousand Oaks outside Los Angeles.

"Never mind the scrimmage," Al said. "With those two quarterbacks, we'll put on a rookie game in Oakland and sell tickets."

More than thirty-two thousand tickets were sold and we won, 33–0, but Roger Staubach wasn't *defeated*. Battered and confused maybe, but not defeated. In the AFL in those years, we played tight man-to-man coverage, tough bump-and-run coverage. Bump that receiver all the way. Not only were the Cowboy receivers unaccustomed to that type of coverage, but Roger was looking at a pro pass defense for the first time. He thought he was back at the Naval Academy, where if you threw the ball over the defender's head, his receiver would run and catch it. Our defenders bumped those receivers so hard, Roger's passes were sailing 10 yards over their heads. And if that wasn't bad enough, his ribs got banged up.

"I couldn't complete a pass, I couldn't breathe," he told me years later. "I realized this was going to be a tough career."

Tough, but Roger was tougher. During his Cowboy career, he put together one of the most amazing football statistics I've ever heard: In twenty-three games he brought the Cowboys from behind in the fourth quarter to win, and fourteen of those comebacks were in the last two minutes or in overtime. He knew how to get it done, how to win. Until he joined the Cowboys, they had a reputation for not being able to win "the big one." I always thought that was a cheap shot, maybe because I was accused of it myself as the Raiders' coach. Some people just waited until we finally lost each season, then they called that final game the big one. What they forgot was that we had to win several big ones to get to the conference championship game or into the playoffs. Hey, tell me what the big one is *before* we play it, not after.

When the Cowboys had Don Meredith and Craig Morton at quarterback, they couldn't win the Super Bowl, but with those Cowboys in the playoffs every year, those two must've won a big one somewhere.

All that talk about the big one is what Roger had to put up with before the Cowboys finally won Super Bowl VI in his first season as the starting quarterback. So he knew how I felt when the Raiders finally won Super Bowl XI, 32–14, over the Vikings. Not long after our win, I went to the Washington (D.C.) Touchdown Club dinner, where I was to be honored as the NFL Coach of the Year. At the cocktail reception, Roger, who was there as the NFL Player of the Year, walked over and we shook hands.

"Congratulations," he said. "Of all the things you get out of

winning the Super Bowl—the money, the ring, the notoriety—
the biggest thing you have now is that nobody can ever say as
long as you live that you can't win the big one. No matter what
happens from now on, you've *won* the big one."

That was typical of Roger, a very aware guy. Aware of how
things affect other people. Aware of how things affect him.
When he was a CBS football analyst, we had to do a bunch of
network promos that were to be shown during the holidays. For
Thanksgiving Day, several of us sat around a table, each holding
a wine glass, as Brent Musburger passed a platter of turkey. For
Christmas Day, we sat around with glasses of eggnog. When we
sat down to do the promo for New Year's Day, we were supposed to be holding a drink.

"No, no," Roger said, "I don't want to be associated with
drinking hard liquor. I'll have a glass of milk."

Everybody else laughed, but Roger wasn't laughing. He was
serious. As serious as if he were talking to Tom Landry on the
sideline. Roger was the ideal quarterback for Tom's system.
Tom sent in virtually all the plays, so he needed a quarterback
who wouldn't question the coach. After four years as a navy
lieutenant, Roger knew how to take orders from his command-
ing officer. Roger also knew how to give orders to the enlisted
men, so to speak—his Cowboy teammates. Roger was so ideal
in Tom's system, some people have wondered if he would have
developed into a Hall of Fame quarterback with another team
and another coach in another system.

To me, Roger Staubach would have been a Hall of Famer
with any good team, with any good coach, in any good system.
When he joined the Cowboys, he was able to adjust to Tom
Landry's system. Tom didn't have to adjust his system to Roger.

Joe Namath, Terry Bradshaw, and Ken Stabler could have
been plugged into any coach's system, just as Dan Marino could
now. Joe Montana would be good in any system, but maybe not
as good as he is in Bill Walsh's system.

Not every coach is fortunate enough to have a quarterback
who can adjust to his system. Sometimes it works the other way

around, which is usually a tribute to the coach as much as to the quarterback. Joe Theismann, for example, wasn't able to adjust to Joe Gibbs' system, so the Redskins' coach adjusted to his quarterback. Gibbs took over as the Redskins' coach in 1981 after having been the Chargers' offensive coordinator for two years. He tried to use the same plays with Theismann that he had used with Dan Fouts, but they are two different quarterbacks. Fouts is a pocket passer with a short drop, a quick release. And at 6 foot 3, he's tall; he can spot his receivers easier than a shorter quarterback. Theismann is listed at 6 feet even, but he looks shorter to me. Whatever he is, he couldn't make Gibbs' system work the same way Fouts did.

His first few weeks, Gibbs started out 0–5, so he adjusted his system to what Theismann could do best—what I call the "organized scramble." His blockers slide to the right, Theismann slides to the right and throws.

The next season, Gibbs and Theismann won Super Bowl XVII, 27–17, over the Dolphins with that adjusted system. The following season they again got to the Super Bowl with that adjusted system, though they lost to the Raiders, 38–9. But hey, at least they got there. When they did, Theismann went out of his way to cooperate with the media. In addition to the hour-long interview sessions that every player was required to attend on Tuesday, Wednesday, and Thursday that week in Tampa, he scheduled several special interviews, usually early in the morning. One morning, he was up and talking to me for CBS by 6:30.

"No problem," Joe told me. "I'm always up early."

Maybe so, but to me, doing a TV interview at 6:30 in the morning was above and beyond cooperation. All week Joe was like that. As soon as he saw a microphone or a notebook, he started spouting. Everybody loved him. But when the Redskins lost, I heard some people criticizing him for having been *too cooperative* with the media. Hey, he deserved a trophy for being cooperative. If he hadn't been, they would have knocked him for that. Now he was being knocked for having been too cooperative, ostensibly because all that time he spent doing interviews disrupted his concentration on the game. I've always believed the Raiders disrupted his concentration, not the interviews. Just as the Raiders disrupted the system, Joe Gibbs had adjusted to Joe Theismann.

Adjusting a system to a quarterback isn't new. Vince Lombardi did it with Bart Starr, then Don Shula did it with Bob Griese. As talented as both quarterbacks were, I don't think either one would have been nearly as good with another coach in another system.

Just as Lombardi was the perfect coach for Starr, Bart was the perfect quarterback for the Packers' coach. As the son of an army master sergeant, Bart knew how to take orders, how to be happy without headlines. He didn't mind Paul Hornung, Jim Taylor, and Ray Nitschke being more popular than he was. As a quarterback, he was the best I've ever seen at the play pass, where you try to fool the defense by faking a handoff as if it were a running play, then drop back to pass. One reason was the design of the play, another was his faking ability. But the biggest reason was that he had Hornung and Taylor as his running backs. In the Lombardi years, the Packers were a running team. When teams run, you tighten your defense. You bring your linebackers up tight. Even your defensive backs, especially your safeties, move up tight.

When the Raiders lost to the Packers, 33–14, in Super Bowl II, one of Bart Starr's play passes broke our backs.

On the sideline, as the Raiders' linebacker coach, I saw Bart appear to hand off. But then I saw Boyd Dowler, the wide receiver on their right side, running down the field, wide open. Bart's fake handoff was so good, Dowler was all alone when he caught Bart's pass for a 62-yard touchdown and a 13–0 lead. In the confusion of our other defensive backs, our strong safety, Roger Bird, was our closest defensive back. Roger chased Dowler into the end zone, which made it appear as if Roger had been beaten on the play.

Actually, as soon as Roger realized Dowler was all alone, he hustled over to try to catch him. Roger had no chance, but to this day most people believe Roger was beaten for that touchdown.

That's what Bart Starr could do to a defense with a play pass. I didn't know him in those years, but later on, when he was coaching the Packers, we got to know each other. I found him to be as classy a man as he had been a quarterback. Quiet, thoughtful, sensitive. With his personality, I wondered how he had reacted to Lombardi's reputation for yelling at his players.

"Coach Lombardi would yell at the guys he thought needed it," Bart told me. "But he wasn't that way with me and he wasn't that way with some of our other players."

In general, I don't think any coach yells at his quarterback as much as he yells at other players. Any coach is only as good as his quarterback. If he's got a good one, a coach is going to treat him with tender loving care. If anything, a coach might yell at his quarterback when the team is winning, but not when it's losing. When his team is losing, a quarterback gets enough heat without having his coach put him on the griddle. Don Shula has been known to yell at players occasionally, if not often. But he doesn't yell at Dan Marino and he didn't yell at Bob Griese.

When the Dolphins won Super Bowl VII with their perfect 17–0 record and also won Super Bowl VIII, they had as ideal a situation as any team ever had, beginning with Bob Griese as the ideal quarterback.

To go along with Griese, the Dolphins had the ideal fullback in Larry Csonka, the ideal wide receiver in Paul Warfield, and the ideal offensive line, especially with Jim Langer at center and Larry Little and Bob Kuechenberg at the guards. Griese was like Bart Starr—neither one got as many headlines as some of their teammates. Big Zonk was the symbol of the Dolphin offense. When the Dolphins went to Super Bowl VII, Griese hadn't started since the fifth game of the season because of a broken bone in his right ankle. He had relieved Earl Morrall at halftime of the AFC championship game in Pittsburgh, but two weeks later, at the Super Bowl, Don Shula never hesitated.

"Griese is my quarterback," he announced.

Some skeptics wondered if Bob would be sharp after such a long layoff, if he was really ready for a Super Bowl game. But whenever people wondered about Bob, that's when he was at his best. Hey, maybe he wasn't ready, but the Dolphins beat the Redskins, 14–7—that's in the book. I learned the hard way that whenever you weren't sure Bob Griese could do something, that's when he did it. He wasn't supposed to have a gun for an arm, but just when you thought he didn't have a gun, he had a gun. He wasn't supposed to be able to scramble quickly, but just when you thought you had him sacked, he got away.

As ideal as Bob Griese was as the Dolphin quarterback, he also was blessed with the ideal coach for a quarterback: Don Shula.

In a quarter of a century as an NFL coach, Don has won in Baltimore with Johnny Unitas and Earl Morrall at quarterback, and in Miami with Bob Griese, Earl Morrall, David Woodley, and now Dan Marino at quarterback. Just as each quarterback was different, each time Don designed a different offense. I laughed when some people talked about how Don had changed his offense after Marino arrived. Suddenly the Dolphins were throwing all those passes after having ground it out when they had Big Zonk at fullback. Some people thought Don Shula had changed.

Wrong, only Don's personnel had changed. Those people didn't know, or had forgotten, that when Don Shula had Johnny Unitas in Baltimore, the Colts threw the ball.

Johnny was a daring passer, the NFL's best quarterback long before 1963, when Don succeeded Weeb Ewbank as the Colts' coach. Johnny had led the Colts to their 23–17 victory over the Giants for the 1958 NFL championship, the first sudden-death game, and the Colts had repeated as champions the next year. I had seen him only on game films and television until I took the Raiders to Baltimore for the 1970 AFC championship game. In today's era of situation substitution, a defense often uses five or six, sometimes seven, defensive backs in an obvious passing situation. But that 1970 game was the first time I ever used six defensive backs.

In that game, Nemiah Wilson was my sixth defensive back. His assignment was to cover Ray Perkins, the Colts' third wide receiver, who is now the Alabama coach. With all our other defensive backs, we were double-covering each of the Colts' other wide receivers. Not that Johnny Unitas knew that. But he did know that one of his wide receivers would be operating against single coverage. That's the trick for a quarterback against five or six or seven defensive backs—throw to the receiver who's operating against single coverage. Johnny spotted our single coverage on Perkins every time.

Of all the players who have been cut by NFL teams through the years, Johnny Unitas is the most famous.

As a Steeler rookie in 1955, he was cut in training camp. He hitchhiked home to Pittsburgh and played for the semi-pro Bloomfield Rams twice a week for $6 a game. But early the next year the Colts phoned him, brought him in for a tryout, and signed him. He threw 290 touchdown passes, including at least one in forty-seven consecutive games—pro football's version of Joe DiMaggio's fifty-six-game hitting streak.

Now that Johnny Unitas is in the Pro Football Hall of Fame, it's easy to ask how the Steelers could have cut him. But in those years, the scouting wasn't as thorough, and when a team drafted a player, the coach might not see him until training camp. Nowadays, a rookie will be seen at two or three minicamps long before training camp even starts.

No way Johnny would be cut today. No way Len Dawson would sit around for five years, as he did with the Steelers and the Browns before asking for his release in 1962 so he could join the Dallas Texans that year. After the team moved and was renamed the Chiefs in Kansas City the following year, Len would take it to Super Bowl I and to Super Bowl IV, which the Chiefs won. But as thorough as the scouting is now, mistakes are still made. In the 1983 draft, twenty-six teams ignored Dan Marino before Don Shula pounced on him.

"Our scouts had rated John Elway as the best quarterback prospect that year," Don says, "but they rated Marino next. And when it was our turn, he was available."

The Best I've Ever Seen

Quarterbacks   George Blanda
Terry Bradshaw
Dan Fouts
Bob Griese
Daryle Lamonica
Dan Marino
Joe Montana
Joe Namath
Jim Plunkett
Ken Stabler
Roger Staubach
Johnny Unitas
Norm Van Brocklin

At the time, five other quarterbacks had been taken: John Elway by the Colts (who later traded him to the Broncos), Todd Blackledge by the Chiefs, Jim Kelly by the Bills (who lost him to the Houston Gamblers of the United States Football League), Tony Eason by the Patriots, and Ken O'Brien by the Jets. As the losing team in the Super Bowl, the Dolphins had the twenty-seventh choice. No way Dan Marino should have been the twenty-seventh player in that draft. Some teams, it came out later, shied away because of rumors he had been involved in drugs, but Don Shula had the Dolphins check the University of Pittsburgh on that. He even had Dan undergo tests. All of which came up negative. Another factor was that scouts sometimes dissect a player too much. Paralysis by analysis. The longer anybody looks at a player, the easier it is to say, well, he's got this flaw and that flaw. Pretty soon a scout is looking at a few dead branches on a few trees instead of at the forest. Don Shula looked at the forest.

The way Dan Marino has performed, some people think Don Shula got lucky. Hey, if anybody got lucky, it was Marino in getting Shula as his coach. What Shula did wasn't lucky; what he did involved experience, preparation, and the checking out of the drug rumors. That's not luck, that's smarts. I know. I wasn't smart enough to draft Dan Fouts for the Raiders even after my best friend in coaching, John Robinson, had touted him to me. John is the Rams' coach now, but we grew up together in Daly City, just outside San Francisco. At the time of the 1973 draft, John was an assistant coach at the University of Oregon, where Dan Fouts had thrown thirty-seven touchdown passes over three seasons.

"This kid can play, he'll be a star," John Robinson told me. "And he'll play in the NFL for a long time."

After watching Oregon game films, I agreed that Dan Fouts would make it as an NFL quarterback. He had the arm, and at 6 foot 3 he had the size. But he looked a little slow to me. He didn't seem to have the quick feet I like in a quarterback.

"I know he's good," I told John Robinson, "but . . ."

"If you don't take him," he said, "you'll be sorry."

I was sorry. But hey, so were a lot of other NFL teams. Dan Fouts wasn't taken until the third round, by the Chargers, the sixty-fourth player chosen in that draft. And everything that John Robinson told me would happen has happened. Going into the 1986 season, Dan Fouts had thrown 228 touchdown passes. His total of 37,492 passing yards was third on the all-time NFL list, behind Fran Tarkenton (47,003) and Johnny Unitas (40,239).

So much for my judgment.

On those Oregon films and even with the Chargers all these years, Dan Fouts was slow. But what I didn't see was his ability to take a short drop and *zip*, get rid of the ball. Dan is a rhythm passer. He takes three quick steps, *boom, boom, boom,* then *zip.* Dan doesn't have quick feet, but he has quickness. George Blanda was like that, so were Bart Starr, Norm Van Brocklin, Y. A. Tittle, and Don Meredith—they weren't quick but they had quickness. That might not make sense, but believe me, it's true.

One test of quickness is being able to avoid being sacked. Dan Fouts has done that, just as John Brodie of the 49ers did.

Brodie was the best I've ever seen at not getting sacked. And when Dan Fouts was a teenager, he was a ball boy for the 49ers; his father, Bob, was one of the 49er broadcasters. Just by watching John Brodie avoid a sack, Dan was studying under the master. If none of his receivers were open, John didn't even try to run around until somebody got open, he just threw the ball away. No sack, no loss of yardage. He did it so often, the NFL tightened its rule on intentional grounding of a pass.

John Brodie could do something else better than any quarterback I've seen: throw a screen pass, that little floater out to a running back who then goes upfield behind a screen of blockers.

John would set up about 7 yards deep, draw the pass rush, retreat a few more yards, then flip that little floater out to Ken Willard or John David Crow and *whoom,* almost every time it was good for a first down, sometimes for 20 or 30 yards. What always annoyed me was that I was never a good screen-pass coach. I don't know why; if I did, I would've been able to coach it and my quarterbacks would've been able to get yardage with it.

I once asked John Brodie how he did it, but what he told me didn't seem to add up. That's how out of tune I was with the screen pass.

I should've asked Paul Brown about it, but I never did. As good as John Brodie was at throwing the screen pass, Paul Brown's teams at Cleveland and Cincinnati were the best at using the screen and also using the draw play, where the quarterback pretends he's dropping back to pass, then hands off to a running back who barrels up between the pass rushers. I studied films of how Paul's teams used the screen and the draw. I copied the blocking. But there was something about the timing. I could never copy the timing.

As thick as I was about the screen, I understood Paul Brown's legacy: how to protect a quarterback with a "pocket" of pass blockers. That pocket helped Otto Graham pass the Browns to ten consecutive divisional titles, from 1946 to 1955—six in the NFL (including three NFL titles) after four in the All-America Football Conference, where the Browns literally were too good. In winning four championships, the Browns were so much the best team, the AAFC folded. Not enough competition.

As important as the true pocket passer once was in the NFL, the world turns. Now the true pocket passer is almost outdated. Some still exist, like Marino and Fouts, but more and more teams are going with a quarterback who can run around to avoid the pass rush.

In a quarter of a century, the role of the quarterback has come full circle. Back when Fran Tarkenton broke in with the Vikings as the first scrambler, he was running out of necessity —he had no pass protection. But his coach, Norm Van Brocklin, still didn't like it.

"Francis," he would say, "a quarterback should only run from fear."

At that time, just about every coach thought that you couldn't win with a scrambling quarterback; you needed a pocket passer. Roger Staubach disproved that theory. So have Joe Montana and Jim McMahon. And now it's just the opposite. Except for Marino and Fouts—each a big, strong guy with a quick release—it seems you can't win with a pocket passer; you need a quarterback who can avoid the rush. One reason is that there's no pocket anymore. It used to be that, in a 4–3 defense, the four defensive linemen would rush the passer along with one linebacker, two at the most. If you got those guys blocked, your quarterback could stand inside that pocket of blockers and take a little time to look for a receiver. But with so much more blitzing nowadays, sometimes by a defensive back as well as several linebackers, a quarterback can have his pocket picked.

In other years, coaches always feared that the scrambling quarterback would get hurt because he ran out of the pocket. But now, the quarterback who tries to stay in the pocket is going to get hurt because, sooner or later, that pocket will be penetrated. And if he can't run, he can't escape.

Jim Plunkett couldn't escape early in the 1985 season. As big and as strong as he is, he went down with a damaged shoulder. He's thirty-eight now, but if anybody can come back at that age, he can. He's one of the finest competitors I've ever known.

In his life, Jim went from rags to riches, like a lot of people do. But then he went back to rags and then on to riches again as the Raiders' quarterback on their Super Bowl XV and XVIII championship teams. Jim was raised in San Jose by blind parents. His father, who owned a newsstand, had been legally blind from birth but could see a little through thick glasses. His mother had lost her sight at age twenty after an illness. His parents met at a school for the blind, where his mother was learning Braille.

"One of the things that always annoyed my parents," Jim once said, "was having others thinking they were handicapped. I remember them saying they weren't handicapped, that they could do just about anything except see."

With parents like that, no wonder Jim has been a competitor. He went to Stanford, where he won the Heisman Trophy; then the Patriots named him the first choice in the 1971 NFL draft. His opening game that season was against the Raiders—hey, a rookie quarterback on a team that had a 2–12 record the year before, no way the Patriots could beat us. But they did, 20–6. Jim was Rookie of the Year that season with nineteen touchdown passes, at the time a rookie record. But gradually the Patriots became disenchanted with him. After the 1975 season they traded him to the 49ers, who figured that returning to California might settle him down. As it turned out, that's exactly what happened, but it happened with the Raiders after the

49ers cut him. My last season as the Raiders' coach, in 1978, we signed Jim as a free agent. The day he joined us, I could tell he had lost his confidence.

"Relax, take your time, learn the system," I told him. "Kenny Stabler is our quarterback, and we've got David Humm and Mike Rae behind him. We don't need you now, but you're in our plans."

I meant it. David Humm and Mike Rae were pretty much the same quarterback. We didn't need both of them. We knew the Tampa Bay Bucs had asked about Mike, so we knew we could trade him for a draft choice, and we did. With Jim Plunkett around, I had what I always liked to have: an experienced quarterback as my backup, like George Blanda had been for Daryle Lamonica and then for Kenny Stabler all those years. When the Raiders traded Kenny to the Oilers before the 1980 season, Jim took over as the starting quarterback.

Plunkett was like Fouts, not too quick but with a quick arm. Neil Lomax of the Cardinals is that way, too. Good from the waist up.

That's a phrase Bill Russell, the center on all those Celtic championship teams, used to describe Chris Mullin after the Golden State Warriors drafted the St. John's forward. Bill acknowledged that Chris wasn't too fast, wasn't much of a leaper. "But he's good from the waist up," Bill said.

To be among the best, a quarterback needs to do everything that he does from the waist up—think, throw, inspire his teammates. If a quarterback also has good legs and good feet, like Joe Montana does, that's a bonus. It doesn't work the other way around. If you have good legs and good feet but you're not good from the waist up, forget it. You won't make it. But if you're good from the waist up, it doesn't make that much difference what you have from the waist down.

Even when Joe Namath could hardly move on his bad knees in his last few seasons, he terrified opposing coaches the way Marino, Fouts, and Lomax do now.

In his development as an NFL quarterback, the best thing to

happen to Neil Lomax was when the Cardinals hired Rod Dowhower as their quarterback coach. Rod was there two years,
then the Colts hired him in 1985 as their head coach. Rod had
been a quarterback himself at San Diego State, good from the
waist up. From the waist down, he was heavy-legged—his nickname was Bucket Butt—but he dedicated himself to learning
quarterback technique and then he taught young quarterbacks.

"The first day Rod joined the Cardinal staff," Neil once told
me, "he taught me things I'd never heard of before. Footwork
especially."

Rod was a stickler for the steps a quarterback uses in his drop
to set up to pass. The *distance* of each step. The *number* of
steps, depending on the depth of the pattern. On a short pass,
a quarterback has to get rid of the ball quickly, so he doesn't
have time to take many steps. Usually no more than three. On
a medium pass, he usually takes five steps. On a deep pass, he
usually takes seven.

Some quarterbacks do it differently. Fouts likes to throw
quickly, so he seldom takes more than three steps. Others throw
both their medium and deep passes after five steps.

Whatever the drop is, it requires an odd number of steps—
three, five, seven. When a right-handed quarterback takes the
snap, his first step back is with his right foot, his second is a
crossover step with his left foot. No way he can throw on that
crossover second step. In order to plant his right foot to throw,
he's got to take that third step. Or that fifth step. Or that seventh step. Translated into yards, a three-step drop would be
about 4 yards, a five-step drop would be about 7 yards, a seven-
step drop would be about 10 yards.

On a pass play, the number of steps in a quarterback's drop
usually is determined by the depth of the patterns being run by
his receivers.

It's all timing. If a quarterback is throwing a medium-range
pass with his wide receivers cutting at 15 yards downfield, it
doesn't make sense for him to be ready to throw the ball *before*
his receivers are ready to catch it. Conversely, a quarterback

can't be ready to throw *after* his receivers are ready to catch it. On that medium-range pass, a quarterback can take a five-step drop in about the same amount of time it takes his wide receivers to cut at 15 yards downfield.

On a quick pass to a receiver cutting at 5 yards downfield, a quarterback has time only for a three-step drop. On a long pass to a receiver running deep downfield, a quarterback might want to take a seven-step drop in order to give that receiver time to get deep. But some quarterbacks prefer to throw a deep pass from a five-step drop.

No matter how many steps the quarterback takes in his drop, he's got to be consistent. If he's not, his linemen who are pass-blocking for him don't know where he is. With their backs to him, if they don't know where he is, he's in trouble. Especially if he floats. If a quarterback scrambles or decides to take off upfield on a run, fine. Scramble or take off on a run, but don't float. Pass blockers hate a floater. If a quarterback starts to float forward, he might float up the back of his guard or center. If he floats to the side, he might float into his tackle. Either way, it's usually a sack.

I don't know a quarterback who hasn't floated occasionally. Hey, he's human. And he's got those pass rushers coming at him. Put the average guy back there to pass and he'd faint. But the better the quarterback, the less he floats.

Floating is the result of nervous feet. With most people in most situations, if they're nervous, their hands will shake. But if a quarterback is nervous, he shows it in his feet. If he's back there to pass and he realizes that the pass rush is closing in, his feet are jumping in place. Sometimes he throws the ball early. Sometimes he floats. It happens mostly with rookies and with old-timers. For a rookie, it's all too much for him. For an old-timer, he finally gets a little gun-shy. In between, the best quarterbacks seldom float; they think they can do anything. I never saw Joe Namath with nervous feet, but once in a while Terry Bradshaw had them. The average quarterback is always floating. That's one reason he's average. By floating, a quarterback will sack himself. He'll always blame one of his pass blockers, but he floated into the sack himself.

On the Raiders, we analyzed sacks. Our records showed who was responsible for a sack. Sometimes an offensive lineman got beat by a pass rusher. Sometimes our quarterback floated into a sack. And sometimes a sack was a pass receiver's fault.

If none of our pass receivers got open, our quarterback had nobody to throw to. In that situation, our quarterback might have run for a few yards, but chances are he either threw the ball away or got sacked. In watching game films, if nobody was open when Kenny Stabler was ready to throw, I would stop the projector.

"All right," I'd say, "this is all Kenny sees, what's there right now. But there's nothing there. Nobody's open."

In the next few frames after I restarted the projector, *boom*, Kenny would be sacked. And in the next few frames, our receivers would be waving their arms downfield. That's when I would stop the projector again.

"Too late," I'd say. "The hay's out of the barn."

Half the time the receivers were open then only because the defensive backs had seen the sack or had heard the crowd's reaction to the sack—hey, it's easy to be open then. But nobody was open when the quarterback needed him to be open. That's when a sack is a pass receiver's fault. So don't automatically blame a pass blocker for a sack. If the quarterback floated into a sack, it's his fault. And if a pass receiver isn't open, it's his fault.

On our Raiders' charts, sacks were split three ways: a third were the linemen's fault, a third were the quarterback's fault, a third were the receivers' fault. On some NFL teams, I'm told more than a third are the receivers' fault.

In looking to see which, if any, of his receivers is open, a quarterback has to read the defense correctly. Basically, reading a defense means finding the receiver who's open, period. But the way some football people talk, they make it sound as if reading a defense is as mysterious as reading somebody's palm. It's not that complicated. I've always believed that the better the quarterback, the more he sees generally but the less he sees specifically. The more average the quarterback, the less he sees generally but the more he sees specifically.

"I keyed the middle linebacker," I've heard average quarterbacks say, "then I keyed the strong safety, then the free safety."

So the middle linebacker went this way, and the strong safety went that way, and the free safety went this way. So what? If they all rotated to the right, does that mean the quarterback has to throw to his left? What if the receiver to his left is covered? Hey, if you're my quarterback, don't look to see what the defense is doing, look to see which receiver is open. To do that, you have to understand pass defense, but pass defense isn't nuclear physics.

When a quarterback is hunched over the center, he has what I call "presnap reads." When the ball is snapped, he has snap reads. Among his presnap reads, here are two.

If the strong safety is positioned outside and up near the linebackers while the cornerback on that side is well off the line of scrimmage, that's a strongside zone. If both cornerbacks are up closer to the line of scrimmage than the strong safety, that's a double zone.

When the ball is snapped, yes, a quarterback tries to watch the middle linebacker, the strong safety, and the free safety. But a quarterback doesn't have much time to see all that. And even if he had the time, how much can he see beyond those redwood trees in front of him?

The best quarterbacks just see the big picture; they see the receiver who is open. That's the basic thing for any passer. I can't say it often enough. Throw the ball to the guy who's open.

Sure, any quarterback has to know the pass patterns his receivers will be running. He has to know which pattern is supposed to open first. That determines his primary receiver. But it's even more important for a quarterback to *see* those receivers getting open. You'd be surprised how some quarterbacks, as they hurry back into their drop, see only half the field. As they take their drop, their shoulders are facing the right side of the field. No way they can see their receivers on the left side.

The next time you watch a quarterback take his drop, watch

his shoulders. As he back-pedals, his shoulders should be squared downfield. That way he can look to both sides. Joe Namath's shoulders were always squared, but Bob Griese's weren't. In Bob's drop, if he was going to throw to his right, his shoulders were always turned to the right. If he was going to throw to the left or over the middle, his shoulders were squared. That's one key the Raiders had on Griese when he was the Dolphin quarterback. I'm sure he didn't do it all the time, but he did it enough for us to use it as a key.

Once a quarterback sets, his hips also should be squared downfield. Some quarterbacks stand back there as if they were in a baseball batter's stance. But in that position they have to turn and step to the left. With their hips squared, they don't have to turn. They just step to the right and throw to the right or step to the left and throw to the left.

If a quarterback's hips aren't squared and he tries to throw to the left anyway, he's throwing the ball across his body. That's when the ball dies. And all too often that's when the ball is intercepted. But if his hips are squared and he steps to his left, he can gun it. To get leverage on a pass, a quarterback has to step with his front toe at the target.

For a quarterback, those passing mechanics are a must. His job is tough enough without being in the wrong position to gun the ball between all those redwood trees coming at him.

The job of a quarterback's pass blockers is to clear out lanes in that redwood forest. And with the popularity of the Bears' "46" defense, that job is getting tougher and tougher. During the 1985 season, most quarterback statistics were down from the year before. Dan Marino still led the NFL with 30 touchdown passes, but he'd had 48 the year before. Joe Montana's completion average of 61.3 still led the league, but he'd had a 64.6 average the year before. Midway through the season I was talking to Joe about it.

"Half the time when I throw the ball," Joe said, "there are so many people in front of me, I don't even see my receiver. I used to see the receiver all the time."

The more I thought about it, the more I realized what was happening—not just to Montana, but to every quarterback. With more and more teams using a "46" defense that has as many as eight defensive players up on the line of scrimmage, a quarterback no longer had lanes to throw through. Against a 4-3 defense or a 3-4 defense, his offensive tackles could ride the defensive ends out to the side, creating lanes on each side to throw through. But against a "46" defense, blitzing linebackers or blitzing defensive backs were filling those lanes. That's why Joe Montana wasn't seeing his receivers. Neither were the other quarterbacks.

Against the "46" defense, a quarterback has to hit quick, short passes, the way Marino did when the Dolphins handed the Bears their only loss, 38–24, of the 1985 season.

When a defense rushes eight men, that leaves only three defensive backs to cover pass receivers. In that case, the idea is for your wide receivers to work the corners quickly and for your quarterback to get rid of the ball quickly. But if the corner-backs can handle those wide receivers, then the quarterback is really in trouble—unless your offensive line can keep those pass rushers away from the quarterback to give him a little more time.

A pocket passer, like Marino and Fouts, wants to stay in his pocket. But a quarterback who is just as dangerous when he moves outside, like Montana or McMahon, is always looking to get outside.

From a defensive perspective, those pass rushers are always trying to get the quarterback to do what he doesn't want to do. Against a pocket passer who doesn't move too well, those pass rushers are trying to flush him outside. Craig Morton was like that. When he was with the Broncos, the Raiders wanted to get a big push up the middle into his face. That forced Craig to run, which he didn't do too well. But against somebody who liked to move, like Terry Bradshaw, we wanted to get a good pass rush from our defensive ends and maybe from our outside lineback-ers to prevent him from slipping outside.

"Just keep Bradshaw in there and we'll take our chances," I used to tell our defense. "Don't let him outside."

If a defense flushed Terry out of the pocket, he might run 50 yards. And if I were coaching now, I'd tell my defense to try to keep Joe Montana in the pocket. I think Joe is a better quarterback when he's moving around outside. Maybe he sees his receivers better out there. Maybe he prefers to throw on the run. Whatever it is, he seems to be more dangerous in those situations. Joe Thiesmann has also been more dangerous out there, just as Bob Griese and Len Dawson were.

In my early years with the Raiders, we had to play against Dawson when the Chiefs were the Super Bowl IV champions. Hank Stram used what he called the "moving pocket," which was just another term for rollout. If we got a big push in Dawson's face, we knew he would bring the ball down and run, then throw on the run—that's when he was at his best.

On the move or in the pocket, the best quarterbacks get the ball to the receiver, which is where a passer's timing is important. Since the receiver isn't standing still, the quarterback has got to lead his receiver with the ball. He's got to throw the ball to where his receiver is going, not where his receiver is.

On the Raiders, we had a timing play that most teams use. When we were on the opposing 20-yard line, we would throw a quick up to the wide receiver going straight up the field into the end zone. As the wide receiver ran across the 10-yard line, our quarterback would throw a pass at the orange pylon at the back corner of the end zone. Figuring the quarterback's drop to near the 27-yard line and the 10 yards of the end zone, that's nearly a 40-yard pass. But we knew that if the pass was thrown when the receiver was at the 10, the timing was such that it would get to the far corner of the end zone when the receiver did. When the timing was perfect, we had a touchdown. After a game in which we got a touchdown on that play, I heard somebody talk about Kenny Stabler's great "anticipation" in throwing that pass.

"No, no," I roared. "That's not anticipation, that's leading the passer."

As a coach, I always considered the word *anticipation* to have a negative context. I didn't want my quarterback anticipating anything. When you anticipate, you usually make a mistake. Somehow I always associated the word *anticipate* with interception. As a young coach, I heard quarterbacks say that too many times.

"I anticipated, Coach," they would say.

"And we got intercepted," I would say.

Just as a quarterback should never anticipate what his receiver will do, he should never anticipate what a defensive back will do. Neil Lomax of the Cardinals learned that in a Giant game. On the films the Cardinals had studied of the Giants' defense, whenever a quarterback sprinted out to the right, the Giants' free safety, Terry Kinard, would run that way, too. Knowing this, the Cardinals planned to get Kinard moving over and then have Lomax hit Roy Green in the area Kinard had vacated. But in the game, the Giants' strong safety, Bill Currier, got hurt and Kinard was moved to strong safety, with Ted Watts inserted at free safety.

When the Cardinals used the sprint-out, Lomax anticipated that Watts would react the same way Kinard always did. Lomax threw a pass into what he thought would be an open area, but Kinard swooped over to intercept it.

No matter what, a quarterback should never anticipate and a quarterback should never assume. He should *know* what his receiver will do and he should *know* what the defensive back will do. But above all, a quarterback should not worry. Let his coach worry. That's what his coach is paid to do.

Why Payton Is the Best

OF ALL THE RUNNING BACKS in NFL history, Walter Payton holds the two most revered rushing records: most yards in a career and most yards in a game. At the start of the 1986 season, the Bears' halfback had a regular-season total of 14,860 yards. Back on November 20, 1977, against the Vikings, he had 275 yards. But if you were to ask him, as I once did, what gives him his biggest thrill in football, you probably would be as surprised by his answer as I was.

"When a safety or a linebacker blitzes," he said, "you peel back and just as he's getting ready to get to the quarterback, you turn his lights out."

That's my kind of running back. Too many people judge a running back only by how many rushing yards he has. But running with the ball is only one of three factors I use in rating a running back. The other two are pass-receiving and -blocking. You seldom hear how many passes a running back caught for

66

how many yards. And you hardly ever hear how good a blocker he is, either as a pass blocker picking up a blitzing linebacker or as a run blocker for the other running back. But that's how coaches evaluate a running back. And that's why Walter Payton is the best back I've ever seen. He not only is a great runner, but he's a good pass receiver. In his career, he's caught 422 passes for 3,938 yards. He not only is a good blocker, but he blocks with the same enthusiasm he has for running and pass-receiving. Believe me, that's unusual.

Walter also has another dimension. He can pass. In a 1984 game against the Packers, he was actually the Bears' quarterback for four plays. But as a running back, he mostly throws the option pass. In his eleven seasons he has completed 11 of 29 passes, 8 for touchdowns.

But what separates Walter Payton from other great running backs is his blocking. If a running back can't pick up a blitzing linebacker, his coach has to bench him in certain passing situations. If a running back can't block on a sweep, it's like giving the opposing defense an extra tackler. Or if a running back can't get open as a pass receiver and catch the ball, it eliminates one of his quarterback's weapons. And the opposing defense is able to eliminate it. With a running back like Walter Payton, who can block and catch passes, you never have to think about trying to hide him on certain plays. And because he's in there all the time, the opposing defense has to key on him, which opens up other plays.

Walter Payton is the extreme example, but if you have a versatile back, you just let him play. Mostly, you just let him run.

You coach a running back on little things, like having his feet pointed straight ahead in his stance, or taking a handoff properly, with his arms and hands forming a basket, one arm at his waist, the other up near his chest. You coach a running back on how to cup the ball into his arm and body to avoid fumbling. Or you coach a running back on how to block a blitzing linebacker, or how to turn his head to catch passes.

Yes, you coach running backs, but *you don't coach a great runner*. You let a great runner run.

With defensive linemen and linebackers so much better and bigger these days, a running back isn't assigned to run through a certain hole much anymore. You just hope your offensive linemen get a push one way or the other against the defense, opening a hole somewhere. When the running back sees that hole, he tries to get through it before it closes. Because when that hole closes, it's like having a door slammed in your face.

In his eleven seasons, imagine how many doors Walter Payton has had slammed in his face. But through Super Bowl XX, he had started 147 consecutive games. In his Bears' career, he had missed only one game.

At a position that is one of the most vulnerable to injury, Walter's durability has been remarkable. Especially for a halfback who hates to go out of bounds. Near the sideline, Walter will stay in bounds and take the shot in trying to gain another yard or two, instead of scooting out of bounds to avoid the hit. That's a fullback mentality. Jim Taylor, who was Vince Lombardi's fullback on the great Packer teams, was like that.

"You got to sting 'em," Taylor once told Lombardi. "You got to hit 'em harder than they hit you."

Larry Csonka of the Dolphins was like that. So was Marv Hubbard, one of my Raider fullbacks. But halfbacks tend to slip out of bounds—except for Walter Payton.

"If that tackler is going to hit me," Walter once told me, "I'm going to deliver a harder blow to him than he does to me."

At 5 foot 10½ and 204, Walter isn't that big, but what's there is like cement. Long before weight lifting was popular, he developed his own conditioning program. Going into his senior year at Jackson State, he began running in a sandbank by the Pearl River near his Columbia, Mississippi, hometown. He set up a course about 65 yards long.

"Running sixty-five yards on sand," he once told me, "is like running a hundred and twenty on artificial turf. It helps you make your cuts at full speed."

He also worked out at a levee along the Pearl River, sprinting up a 45-degree slope. He usually ran up one side of the levee and down the other in sets of five. Once he ran up and down twenty times without stopping.

"The short, choppy steps," he said, "make your thighs burn."

When he settled in the Chicago area, he found a steep hill near his home where he could run up and down, up and down. That's his thing to strengthen his legs. Like most running backs, he has been a running back all his life. When he was a little kid in Mississippi, he sometimes played football by himself. He pretended he was the quarterback, handing off to himself. Then he pretended he was the running back, sprinting across the yard, jumping over a bush, feinting a fence post, and running through an open gate for a touchdown. As a kid being chased by invisible tacklers, he had the instincts of a running back.

"If you were a kid who loved to have people chase you," Larry Csonka once said, "you've got the beginnings of a running back."

By the time a rookie running back gets to the NFL, he's probably been a running back all his life—in his backyard, on the sandlots, on his high school team, on his college team. At other positions, a player often has to adjust as an NFL rookie. An offensive tackle usually has to learn how to pass-block, a defensive end has to learn how to pass-rush, a linebacker may have been a defensive lineman in college, a strong safety may have been a linebacker, a quarterback may have been on a team that ran the ball more than it passed. But being a running back in the NFL isn't really that much different. A running back has to learn new formations and new plays, but once he gets the ball and his blocking forms, he's doing what he's always done.

Not that every running back is a natural. With the same play and the same blocking, one running back will run into a teammate for no gain, but another running back will slice through for 20 yards. Same play, same blocking. But a different runner, a runner with vision.

All the great running backs are gifted with great vision. When a great runner sees the defense swarming toward him, he also sees his opening. It might be a matter of slipping through the hole before it closes. Or it might be cutting against the grain of tacklers. Whatever it is, a great running back seldom gets hit hard, especially a halfback who is usually quicker and faster than a fullback. I can't ever remember seeing O. J. Simpson take a hard hit. Sometimes he appeared about to be crushed between two linebackers, but he would dip his shoulder and those two helmets would fly by.

My first year as the Raiders' head coach was also O.J.'s rookie year. For our sixth game that season, the Bills came to Oakland with O.J. and their new coach, John Rauch, my predecessor with the Raiders.

The week before that game, I kept thinking, You can't lose this one, not to the guy you succeeded as coach, especially not at home. All the newspapers were building up the pupil-against-the-teacher theme. But more than anything else, I was worried about O.J. breaking loose. I had seen him on TV when he was at Southern Cal, where he won the Heisman Trophy, and I knew he had been a great high school runner in the San Francisco area. In their earlier games that season, the Bills had used him as a wingback in a double-wing offense. In that formation, he was mostly a decoy, more of a pass receiver than a runner. I figured the Bills had been bringing him along slowly, and that they were about due to turn him loose as a runner. But when the game started, O.J. was still a wingback.

Keep him there, I remember thinking on the sideline that day. Let him be a decoy.

They did and we won, 50–21, a big game in my career. The pupil had bettered the teacher, but I've always wondered what would've happened if O.J. had been the tailback instead of the wingback. Three years later, Lou Saban took over as the Bills' coach and let O.J. run. Whenever the Raiders played the Bills after that, we knew we had to stop O.J.—or try to stop him. Our idea was to gang-tackle him as much as possible, but he would always glide by. Watching him from the sideline was never fun, especially when that jersey with "Simpson" and "32" was running unmolested. You knew he was gone. The only time I truly appreciated him was watching him do that to other teams on game films. Then it was fun. But when you were watching O.J. from the sideline, you kept thinking, Get him, stop him, don't let him get away.

Like so many other running backs, O.J. eventually got stopped by a knee injury. No matter how great a running back is, a knee injury will turn him into an average runner. It's always sad to see that.

O.J.'s knee injury happened when he was with the Bills; then he got traded to the 49ers. He was still there in 1979 when I started out as a CBS analyst. On a sweep, O.J. tried to get around the corner but he couldn't cut. He still had his great vision. He saw the hole. But he couldn't plant his foot hard enough to cut sharply through the hole. When you plant a foot that hard, the shock doesn't go into the foot, it goes into the knee joint. And if a running back can't trust his knee to absorb that shock, he can't cut hard enough to avoid a tackler.

On his sweeps against the Rams that day, O.J. had to run out of bounds. One tackler nailed him late, which annoyed me.

You shouldn't be hitting him late, I remember thinking, because when O.J. was O.J., you couldn't have done it.

I never professed to be an orthopedist but I had my own test for a player coming off a knee injury, especially a running back. I simply asked him to run, then plant and cut. I didn't care how much weight he could lift with that knee, or how far he could extend that knee, or how normal his leg muscles were above and below that knee. The only thing that mattered to me was if a running back had hurt, say, his right knee, I wanted to see him plant his right foot and cut.

Some did. Most didn't. Their head was telling them to cut, their vision was telling them to cut, but that knee wouldn't let them do it.

When a running back doesn't trust his knee, his shoulders betray him. His shoulders continue to face the sideline instead of turning upfield. When a running back cuts properly, he squares his shoulders upfield in the same motion. When linebackers and defensive backs talk about Eric Dickerson, they talk about how they hope the Rams' tailback "doesn't get his shoulders squared." If he does, he's off and running.

When the Rams drafted Eric out of Southern Methodist, I had my doubts that he would adjust to running mostly on grass after having played mostly on artificial turf in college.

I knew John Robinson, the Rams' coach and my childhood pal, wanted to draft Eric with the second choice in the first round (after John Elway, now the Broncos' quarterback). I was concerned.

"You better check Dickerson out," I told John Robinson. "He's been a turf guy."

"Don't worry about him," John said. "He can play on anything. Grass or turf."

"But he's been playing mostly on turf," I said. "Sometimes those turf guys forget how to play on grass. Two of the other three teams in your division [the 49ers and the Falcons] play their home games on grass. You need a grass runner."

"He can run on grass," John said. "He can run on gravel if he has to. Or on a beach. Or in a wheat field."

John Robinson had him scouted properly, as I should've known. His rookie year, Eric Dickerson rushed for 1,808 yards, a rookie record. His second year, he rushed for 2,105 yards, breaking O. J. Simpson's previous NFL record of 2,003 yards. His third year he rushed for 1,234 yards after an early-season holdout. For a big guy, 6 foot 3 and 218, he can stop on a dime, take off, explode, all those things that smaller guys can do. And he's carrying an additional 9 pounds of protective equipment. Every pad that's ever been made, he wears it: a big lineman's face mask, goggles, a mouthpiece that pops out between plays, a neck brace, extra big shoulder pads, upper-arm pads, elbow pads, hip pads, thigh pads, knee pads, shin pads.

"If they make equipment," Eric once told me, "they make it to be used. I want to use it."

I don't blame him. In the NFL, or at any level of football, a running back takes a tremendous physical pounding. On grass, it's bad enough. But it's worse on artificial turf. On artificial turf, a running back takes a hit when he's tackled, then he takes another hit when he falls on the carpet. It's like falling in a parking lot. That's why all the players, not just running backs, wear elbow pads and other extra pads when they play on artificial turf—to protect themselves from skin burns when they're scraped along that plastic carpet.

Another reason Eric Dickerson uses so many pads is that he's usually the only running back in the Rams' offensive formation. In a two-back offense, the halfback and the fullback share the load. But as a tailback in a one-back offense, he shoulders the entire load. Sooner or later that's got to wear down a running back, no matter how good he is, as it did John Riggins of the Redskins.

John was my kind of fullback. Always there on Sunday, no matter how banged up he was during the week. In his last few seasons, John's back sometimes was so banged up, he not only couldn't practice, he couldn't sleep in his bed until Friday night. He slept on the floor. He looked like a plodder, a truck horse, but he had good quickness. He could run away from some linebackers. He also had interesting theories, like he thought he didn't need to practice.

"In practice," he once told me, "nothing looks like it does in the game. So why am I practicing?"

I reminded him that he can't think of just himself, that a football team has to practice as a team, not individually. But that's a coach's thinking. John Riggins thought differently— very differently. Still, when he got the football, he thought like every other great running back: Use your vision to gain yardage.

Tony Dorsett of the Cowboys is another running back with great vision: great peripheral vision, great staring eyes. Hawkeye, his teammates call him. Tony has proved that if you're a great running back, it doesn't make much difference how big you are. At 5 foot 11 and 185, he's shorter and smaller than most halfbacks. But it seems as if he never takes a square shot. While doing a Cowboy game on TV once, I mentioned that. Several days later, I got some letters from people who remembered a bowl game Tony had played for Pitt when he got racked by some tacklers. I'm sure he gets hit square by NFL tacklers once in a while, but not often. It seems like just before a tackler has him, he moves only enough to avoid a collision. The tackler still gets him, but not with the big shot.

Some running backs can plug themselves into a coach's system, as Tony Dorsett has in Tom Landry's system. Others need a system plugged into them, like Earl Campbell.

Earl is another one of those backs who are bigger than they look in the program or even in the game films. I knew Earl had been a great back at Texas in 1977, when he won the Heisman Trophy, but whenever I saw him on TV, he didn't look that big. Even when the Raiders were preparing to play him my last year as coach, he didn't look that big in the game films. But that Sunday I wandered out near midfield during the warmup, not far from where the Oiler offense was running plays. Suddenly Number 34 rumbled near me. I couldn't believe the size of Earl's legs, especially his thighs. They were tree trunks. In proportion to the rest of him, I think they were the biggest thighs I've ever seen. I hurried over to where my defensive players were working out.

"Hey, check out Number 34," I told them. "When you tie into that guy, you're not going to be tackling some fancy little halfback."

His first three years, Earl had great stats. His coach, Bum Phillips, built the Oilers' offensive system around him. His third season, Earl rushed for 1,934 yards—at the time the second-highest total in NFL history. But then Bum got fired, and his successors—Eddie Biles, Chuck Studley, and Hugh Campbell—put in different offensive systems that had Earl playing tailback and then fullback instead of using him the way Bum did. During the 1984 season, Bum, who had taken over as the Saints' coach, got Earl back in a trade. But late in the 1985 season Bum was out.

When the Dolphins reigned as Super Bowl VII and VIII champions, they had the best combination of backs I've ever seen: Larry Csonka at fullback and Mercury Morris at halfback. Zonk inside, Merc outside.

When the Raiders played the Dolphins in the 1973 AFC championship game at Miami, that's exactly how Don Shula used them. He'd send Big Zonk up the middle. As soon as we tightened our defense, Merc went outside. And as soon as we spread out to stop Merc, *boom,* Zonk went up the middle again. Either way, we were in trouble. If your defense is more vulnerable to a certain back, sometimes you can funnel him into your strength. It's almost an advantage. But if we geared our defense to stop Zonk inside and make Merc carry the ball, that was not a good deal. And if we spread out to stop Merc from sweeping and let Zonk carry the ball, that was definitely not a good deal.

In his big years, Zonk was the best first-and-ten running back I've ever seen, the primary reason for the Dolphins' success.

I don't mean to take anything away from Don Shula, or Bob Griese, or Mercury Morris, or Paul Warfield, or their No-Name defense, but Csonka was the Dolphins' best weapon—especially on first down. People usually talk about third down, about how often a quarterback keeps a drive moving by getting a first down with a third-down pass. But it's what an offense does on first down that puts it into a second-down situation that leads to the third-down situation. On those Dolphins, it usually was what Zonk did on first down.

You knew he was coming. Your tacklers would hit him as hard as they could and everywhere they could. In the helmet, the neck, the ribs. But when you finally got him down, he had gained 6 yards, sometimes 8. No matter how many yards his line got him, *he* would always get a couple more.

After everybody unpiled, the Dolphins had second-and-four, sometimes second-and-two. Hey, anybody can think of good plays in that situation. You can run up the middle or run outside. You can throw short or throw deep. Your defense has to play everything, which means it can't play anything hard. Try second-and-fifteen or second-and-nine—that's when coaches go to get a drink of water and try to think of something.

The Best I've Ever Seen

Running Backs	Marcus Allen
	William Andrews
	Larry Csonka
	Eric Dickerson
	Tony Dorsett
	Franco Harris
	Walter Payton
	John Riggins
	O. J. Simpson
Blocking Backs	Marcus Allen
	Clarence Davis
	Cookie Gilchrist
	Jerry Hill
	Marv Hubbard
	Walter Payton
	Matt Snell
Pass-Receiving Backs	Marcus Allen
	Roger Craig
	Tony Galbreath
	Walter Payton
	Preston Pearson
	Charley Smith

In those long-yardage situations, a defense knows a pass is coming. And if it gets to third-and-fifteen or third-and-nine, pass rushers really take off after the quarterback. But on second-and-two or second-and-four, if a defense spreads out against a pass, it's easy to run. And if a defense tightens up against a run, it's easy to pass. All you need is another 3 yards and the offense has a first down or third-and-one.

When the Dolphins had third-and-one, you knew Csonka was coming up the middle again. When he did, he put you right back where you started—first down.

Franco Harris was a different type of fullback. Just as great in his own way as Zonk, but different. He was as much halfback as fullback. With him, the Steelers ran a weakside trap better than any team I've ever seen. As good as his blocking was, Franco ran it better than any back I've ever seen. If you jammed him inside, he could bounce outside. If you played him wide, he could cut inside. He had that instinct to go where he should go. Especially on Three Rivers Stadium's artificial turf. On grass, Franco couldn't make the same cuts. When he ran that play in the Oakland Coliseum, he usually slipped on the wet grass. But in Three Rivers, he could plant one foot on that carpet and cut inside.

Playing against Franco was like playing Russian roulette. You knew he was going to get off a long run, but you didn't know when. You knew there was a bullet in the gun, but you didn't know when it would fire. And just when you thought you had him, *bang*, that's when the gun went off.

It's a shame that Franco's career ended the way it did—suddenly released by the Steelers in a contract dispute, joining the Seahawks, then being released before he could surpass Jim Brown's total of 12,132 yards. I don't want to remember Franco that way. Franco deserves to be remembered as one of the best running backs in NFL history. At the time his career ended, he had more rushing yards than Walter Payton or Jim Brown—that is, if you count Franco's yards in post-season games. I know I count them. To me, a yard is a yard. Actually, in playoff games, conference championship games, and Super Bowl games, a yard is even harder to come by.

I never saw Jim Brown enough to appreciate him. But his

numbers are enough to convince me he had to be great, especially one number, his average of 104.3 yards a game. Over nine
seasons, that was his average. Over three seasons, Eric Dickerson has a 111.9 average. But now Eric has to maintain that
average for another six seasons.

For all Jim's yards, the knock on him was that he didn't block,
especially on running plays. One reason for this was that when
the Browns ran the ball, Jim was carrying it. Another was that
if somebody like Ernie Green was carrying it, Jim went somewhere else as a decoy. On passing plays, he usually wasn't assigned to block because he flared out as a receiver. That was
Paul Brown's philosophy. And when Paul was criticized for
using Jim Brown too much, he had an answer.

"When you have a big gun," Paul once said, "you shoot it."

Jim was proud of his career rushing record, and rightfully so.
When it appeared that Franco Harris might be the first to break
it, Jim talked about how Franco sometimes stepped out of
bounds instead of slamming into a tackler. I don't think Jim was
criticizing Franco as much as he was defending himself and his
record—like Ty Cobb's family did when Pete Rose was closing
in on 4,192 hits, like Rocky Marciano's family did when Larry
Holmes was closing in on a 49–0 record. But when Walter
Payton broke the record, Jim didn't have much to criticize.
When the Bears give Walter the ball, he runs with it. When the
Bears throw the ball to Walter, he catches it and runs with it.
And when they don't, Walter blocks.

Marcus Allen of the Raiders is like that, too: a runner, a pass
catcher, a blocker. His rookie year, I visited the Raiders' training camp to get a look at this 1981 Heisman Trophy winner
from Southern Cal who had rushed for 2,342 yards, a major-
college record. Soon after I arrived, I was talking with Gene
Upshaw and Art Shell, two of my All-Pro offensive linemen
when I had been coaching.

"How does Marcus Allen look?" I asked.

"Wait until you see him block," Gene said.

"He blocks like Clarence did," Art said.

Clarence Davis had been the best blocking halfback I'd ever seen. He was only 5 foot 9 and 190, but he blocked like a guard —probably because he had been a guard briefly in high school. And instead of telling me about how Marcus Allen looked as a running back or as a pass receiver, all Gene Upshaw and Art Shell talked about was how good a blocker he was. Hey, they knew he could run. But now they knew that anytime Marcus Allen was in the game, they had a halfback who not only could block and would block, but, more important, *wanted* to block.

Blocking is mostly wanting to block. Wanting to stick your head in there, wanting to get the middle of your nose in the middle of the tackler's body. Then, wherever he goes, you go. Your shoulders move and you pick him up on your shoulders. But to do that, you have to want to stick your head and nose in him.

Position is also important. No matter how much you want to block, you have to do it correctly. You have to get into the proper position with your feet planted, your shoulders squared, your knees bent, your head up. Then you have to get into the tackler quick to pop him, to extend your power, to thrust. As long as a player wants to block, he can be taught to do it. Those who are willing to block but don't particularly enjoy it, they can be adequate blockers. Those who are willing to block and like it, they usually are good blockers. But watch out for those who are willing to do it and love it: They're the great ones.

The best blocking backs I ever saw were Cookie Gilchrist, a fullback with the Bills and the Broncos who had played in Canada earlier, and Jerry Hill, once a fullback with the Colts.

Back when I was the Raiders' linebacker coach, I put together a special film of Cookie's blocks. Now there was a man. At 6 foot 3 and 250, he really filled out a uniform. And he was tough. When he was responsible for picking up a blitzing linebacker, he literally picked that linebacker up on his shoulders and flipped him. Just pancaked him. We had one game film that showed Cookie flipping a linebacker so hard, the linebacker went into convulsions. The day I showed my linebackers the film of that play, some winced and turned away. Later on I spliced that play out of the film. I didn't want to scare anybody else.

Jerry Hill was the same way. The toughest block for a running back is what the Raiders called the "Bob block," the fullback blocking the strongside linebacker. Hill pancaked those line-backers, too.

As a pass blocker, Matt Snell, the Jets' fullback who rushed for 121 yards in Super Bowl III, was Joe Namath's best bodyguard. Matt flipped those blitzing linebackers the way William Andrews of the Falcons did before knee surgery interrupted his career. William had blocked at Auburn for Joe Cribbs and James Brooks, but the Falcons let William run and catch passes as well as block. Until his surgery just before the start of the 1984 season, if I had my pick of all the running backs in the NFL at that time, I would've taken him. The year before William had rushed for 1,567 yards and caught fifty-nine passes for 609 yards. He was on his way to the Hall of Fame as one of the NFL's most complete backs.

Roger Craig of the 49ers is the best pass receiver among the running backs now, the first NFL player to rush for 1,000 yards and to produce 1,000 yards on receptions in the same season.

His rookie year, Roger was open because defenses were concentrating on stopping Dwight Clark and Freddie Solomon, the 49ers' wide receivers. But when the defenses began to pay more attention to Roger, that left Dwight or Freddie open. During the 1985 season, when Roger led the NFL with ninety-two catches, he kept the heat off Dwight and the 49ers' rookie wide receiver, Jerry Rice.

"With a receiver like Roger coming out of the backfield," Joe Montana has told me, "somebody is usually open."

Preston Pearson of the Cowboys was once the best pass receiver among the running backs. Around that time, Charlie Smith was the best I ever had on the Raiders—he could catch the ball and then take off with it. Being a good pass receiver as a running back is different than it is as a wide receiver. When a team breaks its huddle, a wide receiver is exactly that—spread out wide toward one of the sidelines, away from all that grunting on the line of scrimmage. At the snap, a wide receiver works against a cornerback out there on the perimeter of the play. But a running back is coming from 5 yards behind the line of scrimmage. He has to get through linemen and linebackers, slide into openings, then turn and look for the ball.

At the start of the 1986 season, Tony Galbreath had caught 431 passes, the most of any running back in NFL history.

But even there Walter Payton was threatening to take over as the career pass-receiving leader among running backs. Walter was right behind Tony with 422, and counting. As a rusher, pass catcher, passer, as well as a kickoff returner and punt returner early in his career, Walter had gained more than 20,000 yards. That's more than 11 *miles.* Plus who knows how many thousand yards his Bear teammates have gained after being sprung or protected by his blocks.

Any way you look at him, Walter Payton is the best.

Moves,
Hands, and
Toughness

HE WAS THE FASTEST WIDE
receiver I'd ever seen. Hey, at one time, he was the fastest
human being *anybody* had ever seen. Jimmy Hines won the
Olympic 100-meter dash in a world-record 9.9 seconds at Mex-
ico City in 1968, then joined the Dolphins as a sixth-round draft
choice. He later played for the Chiefs before the Raiders signed
him. At our 1972 training camp, I thought he might have a
chance. At 6 feet and 175, he was strong and muscular. And
could he run! The trouble was, we discovered, he could only run
in a straight line, which is all a sprinter ever has to do. But for
a wide receiver, running is angles and cuts and moves. That's
how a wide receiver gets open. Jimmy didn't know how to get
open. And the few times he did, he dropped the ball too often.

"Ooops," he would say as the ball squirted away.

The more he said "Ooops," the more it became his nickname.
He would hop out of the huddle, line up at wide receiver, and
I'd hear the cornerback on that side saying, "All right, I got
'Ooops.'" After a few weeks, we cut him. Jimmy Hines could

run, but he couldn't play football. No matter how fast a wide receiver is, it doesn't help if he can't play football.

To play in the NFL, a wide receiver needs some speed. Not necessarily world-class speed, but enough speed. Enough to shake that defensive back. Enough to be a threat to go deep.

But he needs more than speed. He needs the moves to get open. And when he's open, he needs to catch the ball. Plus one more thing: He needs the toughness to go inside for a pass. It's easy to go outside and it's easy to go deep, but inside, those linebackers and safeties are waiting to sledgehammer him. If a wide receiver wouldn't go inside, I didn't want him.

When a wide receiver has speed, moves, hands, and toughness, he's got it all, like Roy Green of the Cardinals.

Not counting quarterbacks—because you can't compare quarterback to any other position—I think Roy Green is the NFL's most explosive offensive player when he's healthy. Lower leg injuries limited him to 50 receptions for 693 yards and 5 touchdowns during the 1985 season. But when he's healthy, as he was in 1984 when he caught 78 passes for 1,555 yards and 12 touchdowns, I'd take him over any of the running backs as an offensive weapon. When he's healthy, Roy is a touchdown player, a home-run hitter. Not many wide receivers can get open on a deep post pattern—take off down the field, then angle deep toward the goalposts. In a zone, the free safety's job is to sit back there in the middle as deep as the deepest man with everything in front of him. But somehow Roy would get behind that free safety.

Roy Green is the only wide receiver I know who can outrun an entire defense on a post pattern. As a coach, I'd have my quarterback throw five of those post patterns to Roy in every game. Out of five, he'd catch at least two for touchdowns. Another great thing about him, he runs at the same speed the whole game. Some wide receivers get tired or slow down in the fourth quarter. Not him. He's still running deep in the fourth quarter. And he's still running as fast as he was in the first quarter.

Roy Green reminds me of one of my Raider wide receivers,

Warren Wells, who never played long enough to establish himself as one of the great ones. But those who were around Warren knew how good he was, like Emmitt Thomas, then a cornerback for the Chiefs and later the Cardinals' pass-receiver coach.

Emmitt had to cover Warren, who in his three big years caught a total of 130 passes for 3,332 yards and 36 touchdowns. At a Cardinals' workout once, I was talking to Emmitt about how Roy Green had joined the Cardinals in 1979 as a defensive back but had been switched to wide receiver during the 1981 season. As a defensive back, Roy's uniform number had been 25, but when the Cardinals decided to use him mostly as a wide receiver, he needed a different number. As we talked, Emmitt stared at me.

"Who does Roy remind you of?" he asked.

"Warren Wells," I said. "As soon as I saw him, the first guy I thought of was Warren Wells."

"Why do you think he's wearing 81?"

Emmitt had suggested that Roy wear the same number Warren had, his ultimate tribute. Roy Green not only runs the best post pattern today, he also runs the best corner pattern—to the far corner of either side of the end zone. But on short and medium passes, a receiver cuts at a certain distance.

On short passes, I wanted my wide receivers to cut at 5 yards. On medium passes, I wanted them to cut at 17 yards, though some coaches prefer 15. Deep passes were any distance beyond that.

Pass patterns are named for where the receiver goes in the short, medium, or deep areas. On short passes, a receiver can run a square-out to the sideline, a slant angled up across the middle, or a drag pattern where he comes in across the middle. On medium passes, he can run a square-out, a square-in, a hook on which he buttonhooks back in toward the passer, and a comeback, where he cuts toward the sideline but then angles back slightly (if he cuts, say, at 17 yards upfield, he might catch the ball at 12 yards). On deep passes, he can run a post, a corner, an up—straight up the field (also known as a streak)—or a cross, meaning across the field.

Of all those patterns, only one is run in a straight line—the up, or the streak. Straight up the field. All the other patterns are run off angles. Think about it. You can't cut off a straight line, at least not at full speed. The pattern that's known as a square-out, you can draw it that way—straight up the field for 5 yards, then straight to the sideline. But you can't run it that way, at least not at full speed. If you did, the foot you cut off would snap at the ankle. To run it that way, you've got to slow up and gather your feet, and as soon as the defensive back sees you doing that, he knows where you're going.

That's why you cut off angles. And that's why a wide receiver can't just run in a straight line, as sprinters and hurdlers do. Still, that doesn't mean you can't have been a sprinter or a hurdler.

O. J. Simpson once ran the 100-yard dash in 9.6 seconds at Southern Cal; he also ran on a world-record 4×100-meter relay team. Bob Hayes won Olympic gold medals in the 100-meter dash and the 4×100-meter relay at Tokyo in 1964. Several other running backs and wide receivers have been world-class sprinters or hurdlers: Herschel Walker, Cliff Branch, Willie Gault, and Ron Brown. The difference is that they were college football players who also ran track, not track stars who decided to try out for the NFL just because they were fast.

Renaldo Nehemiah joined the 49ers in 1982 as the world-record-holder in the 110-meter high hurdles. He had played football at Scotch Plains–Fanwood (N.J.) High School, but not at the University of Maryland. He's scored a few touchdowns for the 49ers, but he's basically a straight-line runner. He's still a track star who's trying to learn how to be a wide receiver. He's a luxury that a good team like the 49ers can afford. But he's nowhere near being the football player that Bob Hayes was—the only guy in history with both an Olympic gold medal and a Super Bowl ring.

Bob Hayes was fast, a blur, a bullet. But when he had to run off angles, he wasn't any faster than Roy Green is now. And not that much faster than Dwight Clark of the 49ers, or Fred Biletnikoff of my Raider teams.

Fred really wasn't fast enough to do what he did: 589 receptions for 8,974 yards and 76 touchdowns over fourteen seasons. Fred was 6 foot 1 and 190, but more important, he was a worker, a perfectionist. If he dropped a pass in practice, he would not only cuss himself out, but after practice he would get one of our quarterbacks to throw him that pass. Sometimes as many as a hundred times. But he didn't drop many passes. He not only had what football people call "good hands," but he once was able to explain to me what good hands are.

"Good hands means both hands work together," he said. "If your right hand reaches out for the ball, your left hand reaches out on the same plane. They move together. Guys with bad hands, when they reach out for a ball, only one hand moves. The other hand stays where it is."

Until he was open, Fred kept those good hands close to his body, the way all good receivers do. When a receiver is running downfield, he should keep his elbows in. You can't run fast with your elbows turned out. But when the ball is coming, you raise your hands to catch the ball. Fred had good feet, too. He liked to plant his feet as he ran a pattern. That's why he was better on grass than he was on artificial turf.

Cliff Branch was more of a light-footed receiver. He was more likely to slip on grass than he was on artificial turf. But even in his sure-footed way, Fred Biletnikoff was faster than he appeared.

Dwight Clark is like Fred was: faster than the defensive backs *think* he is. Dwight can catch the ball inside, outside, coming back, and deep. The minute the defense doesn't think he can go deep, he goes deep for a touchdown. Just as fast guys try to tell everybody how fast they are, slower guys try to tell everybody how slow they are. Ken Margerum of the Bears wore black high-top shoes in Super Bowl XX so the Patriots would think he was even slower. Lull those cornerbacks to sleep.

Cornerbacks mostly worry about the wide receivers who can burn them deep. That's a touchdown. If a cornerback plays several yards off a dangerous wide receiver, he'll probably get stung with completions in front of him. But if the cornerback tightens his coverage, he's taking a chance on the wide receiver running by him. Either way, the cornerback is in trouble for the same reason: speed. If the wide receiver has it, the cornerback has to worry about it. Just the threat of speed is sometimes enough. In Super Bowl III, the threat of Don Maynard's speed helped the Jets stun the Colts.

During the week, Maynard had been bothered by a pulled hamstring muscle. But on the Jets' second series in the first quarter, Maynard ran all-out down the sideline. Joe Namath's long pass sailed inches beyond him. Despite the incompletion, Maynard had shown the Colts that he could go deep. For the rest of the game, the Colts respected that threat by rotating their zone defense toward Maynard, using two defensive backs to cover him while the Jets' other wide receiver, George Sauer, operated against single coverage. Maynard never caught a pass, but Sauer caught eight as the Jets won, 16–7.

In the locker room, Maynard thought he had let the Jets down. Namath had to cheer him up, reminding him that just by forcing the Colts to double-cover him, he had made it easier for Sauer to catch eight passes.

Maynard was my idea of a *dangerous* wide receiver. Somebody you really worried about. And with Namath throwing to him, you really worried. My second season as the Raiders' linebacker coach, we rallied in the last minute to beat the Jets, 43–32, at Oakland in what is known as the "Heidi" game. The last few minutes never appeared on TV in some parts of the country because the NBC network preferred to start the children's movie *Heidi* on time. But early in the fourth quarter, we had the Jets backed up on their 3-yard line. On first down, Namath hit Maynard at the 50-yard line. On the next play, he hit Maynard in the end zone. Touchdown—97 yards in two plays in twenty-four seconds.

That's how dangerous Don Maynard was. With his long strides, he just ate up yardage. At the start of the 1986 season, he still held the career record for pass-reception yardage with 11,834 yards, and his 633 receptions ranked third. Even when

Charlie Joiner of the Chargers went by Maynard's total of receptions, he was still more than 1,000 short of Maynard's yardage total.

Joiner and Cliff Branch kept their speed longer than any wide receivers I've ever known. Sooner or later, every wide receiver slows down. But those two postponed the inevitable. Every year I kept thinking, Joiner is too old this year. But then I'd watch him play. He didn't look old. He didn't seem to have lost a step. He was still spry and lively. He also was playing for a coach, Don Coryell, and with a quarterback, Dan Fouts, who believed in the pass. And he's out there with other feared pass catchers: Wes Chandler at the other wide receiver, Lionel "Little Train" James at running back, and Kellen Winslow at tight end after recuperating from knee surgery. Now that's a package.

Against five, six, or sometimes seven defensive backs, a team's passing package is more important than ever. One of the best packages these days has Dan Marino throwing to Mark Clayton and Mark Duper, the Dolphins' two wide receivers. Each is only 5 foot 7—until he jumps. Clayton's vertical jump has been measured at 38½ inches, which means he plays at a height of 8 feet 9½ inches. Duper can jump nearly as high. During the 1984 season, when Marino threw his record 48 touchdown passes, Clayton caught 18 to set the NFL record. Together, the two Dolphins were the first pass receivers on the same team to go over 1,300 yards in the same season.

"You don't play football on height," Clayton says. "You play it on heart."

And on ability. Just because Clayton and Duper have been so successful doesn't mean that the ideal wide receiver now is a little guy. What makes Clayton and Duper good is not their size, but their ability to run and get open and catch the ball. Clayton and Duper know how to play football, period.

"You don't let defensive backs dictate to you," Duper says. "You dictate to them."

When the Dolphins had Paul Warfield, he not only dictated to defensive backs, he dictated to opposing coaches. I know. As important as Larry Csonka was to those Dolphin teams that swept through Super Bowl VII and VIII, Warfield was almost as important. Bob Griese wasn't really a deep passer, but he was very accurate. If you tightened your defense to control Zonk and Mercury Morris on the run and Griese on the short pass, then you were leaving yourself open to Warfield getting clear on a wide pass. *Boom,* that's when Griese would hit you deep and ring the bell. So you had to be aware of Warfield every play.

Warfield might catch only two or three passes, but they would be the difference in the game.

The Best I've Ever Seen

Wide Receivers	Lance Alworth
	Fred Biletnikoff
	Cliff Branch
	Roy Green
	Don Maynard
	Lynn Swann
	Otis Taylor
	Paul Warfield
	Warren Wells
Tight Ends	Dave Casper
	Raymond Chester
	Kellen Winslow

One of the best packages any team ever had was Lynn Swann and John Stallworth, the wide receivers who were rookies together when the Steelers started their reign of four Super Bowl championships in six seasons. Swann was the best I've ever seen at throwing his body, diving, jumping, and still catching the ball. He was so good, most people seemed to ignore how good

Stallworth was. When the Steelers won their fourth Super Bowl, I thought Stallworth was maybe the best wide receiver in the NFL that season. But everybody still talked about Swann, who was still good. I never understood why more teams didn't decide to double-cover Stallworth and take their chances with Swann, instead of the other way around. Stallworth did everything that Roy Green does now. He ran the post. He went deep. He also got lost in the shuffle of all the great players the Steelers had: Terry Bradshaw, Franco Harris, Joe Greene, Jack Lambert, Swann.

By the time people got around to talking about Stallworth, somebody would say, "Oh, let's go eat."

In those years, Swann and Stallworth were so good, the Steelers didn't throw to their tight end that much. Larry Brown and then Bennie Cunningham—each was more of an offensive lineman than a pass receiver. Brown was shifted to right tackle when Cunningham took over. But a tight end who can go deep is a rarity. Ideally, a tight end should be as good a blocker as an offensive lineman and as good a receiver as a wide receiver. But that's asking too much. Nobody has ever blended both those skills into the position. I think the player closest to it was my Raider tight end, Dave Casper, who had been an offensive tackle at Notre Dame.

The position has changed in recent years. The way the game is played today, with situation substitution, many teams alternate their tight ends. The tight end who's a good blocker is used in a run situation, and the tight end who's a good receiver is used in a pass situation. With so much passing, if a team primarily uses one tight end, he's usually a better receiver than a blocker.

Until knee surgery stopped Kellen Winslow of the Chargers during the 1984 season, he was the prototype tight end of today's passing game. He hardly ever had to block. Instead of lining up close to a tackle, he would be split out in a slot, not far from the wide receiver on that side. Sometimes he would go in motion.

To call Winslow a tight end was really a misnomer as the position is defined. Strategically, the tight end, by lining up close to either the right tackle or the left tackle, creates the strong side of the offensive formation. But because of his skill as a pass receiver, Winslow lined up everywhere and anywhere. Maybe the position should be renamed. Inside receiver, say. As it is now, the tight end is part receiver and part blocker. Which means that no matter how good he is at one, he's usually deficient at the other. That might be the reason a tight end has yet to be elected to the Hall of Fame; nobody is quite sure what a guy is supposed to have done to have the credentials.

Since the tight end developed in the early sixties, a few have achieved recognition: Ron Kramer of the Packers and Mike Ditka of the Bears, later John Mackey of the Colts, then Raymond Chester and Dave Casper of the Raiders, Ozzie Newsome of the Browns, Kellen Winslow of the Chargers, and Todd Christensen of the Raiders.

Years ago you could never run to the strong side without a good tight end who could block down on the defensive end. Some coaches still believe in that philosophy. Every team uses two tight ends in short-yardage and goal-line situations, but some use them in every situation. Then there's Kellen Winslow lining up everywhere and anywhere without having to worry about blocking somebody. But back when Sid Gillman coached the Chargers, they were using goofy formations. In our first game against the Chargers one season, Sid even used Lance Alworth, the Hall of Fame wide receiver known as Bambi, as a tight end on their left side, with Dave Kocourek lined up as usual as a tight end on their right side. As soon as I saw Alworth at tight end, I yelled out to Dan Conners, our middle linebacker.

"Dan, Dan, work toward Alworth," I shouted.

Dan moved over toward Alworth, then Kocourek slid into the middle that Dan had vacated to catch John Hadl's pass for a first down. The rest of that game, the Chargers didn't show us that double tight-end formation, but we knew we'd see it the next time we played. So we devised a different defense. One of our defensive tackles, Dan Birdwell, ol' Birdie, a tough Texan who smoked thin black cigars, was assigned to slide over to line up over Alworth, with Conners staying in his usual area as middle linebacker. All week in practice we worked on that defense. The night before the game I was standing outside the Stardust Hotel coffee shop in San Diego when one of our wide receivers, Bill Miller, strolled by. Bill called everybody "Stud," even his coach.

"Stud," he said to me, "when you put Birdie on Lance tomorrow, Birdie won't touch him. Lance is gonna eat us up."

I thought, Hey, he's a wide receiver, he knows how good Lance Alworth is, maybe he's right. But it was too late now. We had practiced the defense. We had to go with it, at least once. Sure enough, in the first quarter, Alworth spun out of the huddle, lined up at tight end on the left side, and ol' Birdie slid out to line up over him. This, remember, was at the time when Deacon Jones was popularizing the head slap, which was then within the rules. And ol' Birdie had fingers as big as some people's wrists.

At the snap, Alworth came off the line. *Whaaaaap.*

Ol' Birdie had hand-slapped him across the helmet, and ol' Birdie might as well have hit him with a table. Alworth took a step or two, then he started to stagger. He looked like somebody in an old-time cowboy movie who got shot in the dusty street outside the saloon. He just staggered along for a few steps, then he fell forward. Unconscious. When he came to, Lance wobbled to the sideline. I don't remember if he came back in that game, but I do know he never lined up at tight end against us after that. Sid Gillman didn't want his Bambi going against ol' Birdie ever again.

With that memory of ol' Birdie *whaaaping* Bambi, it's time to go on to defense.

Getting Sacks and Respect

HE'S A TERRIFIC PASS RUSH-er, but he's not so good against the run. That's a label Richard Dent of the Bears doesn't want slapped on him. He's an All-Pro defensive end now, the Most Valuable Player in Super Bowl XX, where he shared in three quarterback sacks and forced two fumbles. He led the NFL in sacks in the 1984 season and again in the 1985 season—17½ one year, 17 the next. He all but tore Phil Simms limb from limb in a divisional playoff, sacking the Giants' quarterback three times and sharing in another. But what I like best about Richard is that he doesn't want to be known just as a pass rusher.

"I want to be All-Pro against the run, too," he told me.

At any position, there's a certain shame surrounding a player who can't do it all. The running back who can run but won't block. The defensive back who can cover but won't tackle. That running back will get his yardage and that defensive back will get his interceptions, but neither will get much respect. That's what Richard Dent wants now: respect as a defensive end who can stop the run as well as he can sack the passer. Richard doesn't want to be another Mark Gastineau, the Jets' defensive end who is known primarily as a pass rusher. Richard wants to be like Howie Long, a blue-collar guy who plays the run, who rushes the passer, who does whatever needs to be done.

As good as Richard Dent is, in my travels around the NFL these days, whenever I ask offensive linemen who's the best pass rusher, the answer is usually Howie Long.

When most players are asked a question like that, they will name the guy they want to be like. That guy is Long, who's listed as a defensive end but who also lines up for the Raiders at nose tackle in a 3-4 defense and at defensive tackle in a 4-3 defense. Sooner or later, just about everybody on the offensive line has to block him. And at 6 foot 5 and 270, strong and quick, that's a day's work, because Howie always puts in a day's work. He's the most respected defensive lineman around. He's a football player's football player.

Most defensive ends are like most football players. They don't like to be moved around. Just let them line up in the same position and rush the passer. Don't ask them to adjust to anything different.

That's why Howie Long and Dwaine Board are two of my favorite defensive linemen. Dwaine is usually the 49ers' right defensive end, but when Fred Dean comes in as their designated pass rusher, Dwaine moves to the left side. When the 49ers won Super Bowl XIX, Dwaine sacked Dan Marino twice, the only defensive lineman to do that to the Dolphin quarterback in nineteen games that season. But at his best, Fred Dean was the best pass rusher I've ever seen. Only a few days after Fred joined the 49ers in a 1981 midseason trade with the Chargers, I was in San Francisco for the 49ers-Cowboy game. After the 49er practice on Saturday, I asked Bill Walsh what his plans were for his new defensive end.

"Fred just got here," Bill said. "If he plays, I don't think he'll play much."

Fair enough. As good as Fred had been with the Chargers, as I knew only too well from my years as the Raiders' coach, new players just don't jump into your lineup, especially against the Cowboys in a big game for a 49er team that was struggling with a 3–2 start. When the game started, Fred Dean stood on the sideline, but when the Cowboys got backed up in their first passing situation, Fred hurried onto the field.

At the snap, *whooosh,* Fred flew by Pat Donovan, the Cowboys' left tackle, and sacked Danny White.

His first play in a 49er uniform—*whooosh,* a sack. Exactly what the 49ers got him to do, and Fred Dean did it on his first play. He got two more sacks that day and the 49ers won, 45–14. The 49ers didn't know it at the time, but they would lose only one more game that season, to the Browns, and they would roar through the playoffs to the Super Bowl XVI championship. To me, Fred Dean made the difference in that 49er team. He was the "one more" player they had needed. They were a good team without him, a team ready to be a Super Bowl contender, but he gave them the great pass rusher they needed to be the best team that season.

At first glance, Dean doesn't look like a defensive lineman. He's not that big. He's 6 foot 2, but he usually plays at less than 230 pounds. Good size for a linebacker, but not for a defensive end who has to get by those huge offensive tackles.

Except that Fred Dean gets by them. He's just too quick and too strong. If he gets his hands on the tackle, he's in charge. Hand strength is so important. Dan Hampton, the defensive end the Bears nicknamed Danimal, is a terrific pass rusher, but he might be even better if he could close the ring finger on his right hand. He needed surgery after he caught the finger on a helmet.

"As a defensive lineman," Dan told me, "I'd rather have a knee go than my fingers. Without good fingers, I can't grab a guy's jersey."

I'd never heard that before, but Dan's right. Without hand strength, a defensive lineman can't move an offensive lineman so easily. I still think I'd rather have bad fingers than a bad knee, but Dan disagrees.

"I've had 'em both," he said, "and I'll take the good fingers."

I never asked Fred Dean about his fingers, but they must be strong. As a kid in Louisiana, he baled hay on a farm, developing what he calls "natural" strength. He jokes about lifting weights.

"Whenever I get the urge to lift weights," he likes to say, "I go lie down until it goes away."

When Dean was at his best, offensive linemen wished he would go lie down on the sideline. So did quarterbacks and coaches. In every passing situation he was the 49ers' defensive player the offense had to worry about. Where was he? Which way was he coming? Did we have an extra blocker on him? Not many defensive linemen create that much of a problem.

Howie Long does. Richard Dent does. Mark Gastineau does. Jack Youngblood did.

Jack Youngblood has been described as the John Wayne of football. Talk about true grit: In 1979, when the Rams went to Super Bowl XIV against the Steelers, he suffered a broken left leg in the second quarter of a playoff game. But he played in the NFC title game in Tampa the next week and in the Super Bowl two weeks later.

"Ain't no time to lag back," he said before the Tampa game. "Ain't no heroics involved."

The doctors called it a hairline fracture of the fibula. But with Jack's 240 pounds on it, his ankle area was swollen in every shade of purple. To me, Jack not only typified what a defensive end is, he also typified what a football player is. If a Martian landed in my backyard, knocked on my door, and asked me, "What's a football player?" I'd go get Jack Youngblood. But looking back, when Jack was coming out of the University of Florida in 1971, I didn't think much of him. At the time, he had been one of the first football players to get into weight lifting. He was ahead of his time, but I snickered.

"He's just a Muscle Beach guy, he can't play," I remember saying. "Muscle Beach, that's all he is."

But whenever Jack came up for discussion in the Raider meetings before the draft, Al Davis touted him.

"Jack Youngblood," Al would say, "can play."

"Al, you lift weights," I would say, "so you like the kid because he does, too."

"That's not it," Al would say. "He can play."

Al was right. But not only could Jack Youngblood play, he proved to old-fashioned football people like me how important weight lifting was. His first few years he got up to 275, but then he got down to 240 on a diet of poultry and fish. He stayed at 240 the rest of his career. For him, 240 pounds were more than enough. As a pass rusher, he had a way of getting underneath the offensive tackle, forcing him to stand up almost straight. That way Jack had all the leverage. Watching him on films, I was fascinated by how he did it.

"Watch this," I would tell my defensive ends, "watch how Youngblood gets under that tackle."

They would watch it, and they would try it, but they couldn't do it. Of all our defensive ends, Tony Cline came the closest to doing it, but he couldn't quite lean into that tackle the way Jack did, getting underneath the tackle's shoulder pads and taking away his strength. Other good pass rushers used quick moves, or got an arm on the tackle's shoulder and spun him, or *whaaped* the tackle with a head slap (before it was ruled illegal). But nobody else literally got underneath a tackle.

Jack also made the adjustment that Mark Gastineau has had to make with the Jets: being a defensive end in a three-man line after several seasons in a four-man line.

Mark also had to make another adjustment. Jack stayed on the left side, but Mark sometimes switched to the right side, which reversed his moves. That might not sound important, but it is. As a left end, Mark had been accustomed to lining up outside the offensive tackle's right shoulder. As a right end, he had to line up outside the offensive tackle's left shoulder. When he broke his right thumb in training camp, it affected the strength in his right hand, which now had to be his outside hand, his power hand. And for sheer power, Mark is the best big athlete I've ever seen. He's 6 foot 5, 270, and not only quick but fast.

He's a showman, too. He invented the Sack Dance, jumping around and pumping his arms whenever he sacked a quarterback. To some extent, the Sack Dance hurt him. People knew him more for the Sack Dance than as a great pass rusher. Before the 1984 season, the NFL outlawed the Sack Dance, but his hot-dog image had been formed. It's no secret that some of his Jet teammates resented him. Some even sniped at him, saying that he wasn't anywhere near as good against the run as he was against the pass. But hey, until Howie Long arrived, I didn't know any defensive end who was a great pass rusher and anywhere near as good against the run.

For a defensive end, it's nearly impossible to be as effective against the run as against the pass. The reason is, if he's in the proper position for a good pass rush, he's out of position to stop the run.

In lining up to rush the passer, a defensive end lines up wide outside the offensive tackle's outside shoulder. At the snap, that tackle now has to turn to block, but he can't turn in time to square himself at the defensive end. By lining up outside, the defensive end already has the tackle out of square. And when the tackle has to turn to block, the defensive end can grab him and turn him some more. But by doing all that, a defensive end takes a chance that he's lined up too far outside. That's when the tackle can turn him out as the running back shoots up inside where the defensive end was.

It's not a sin to be better against the pass than the run. All the great defensive ends were that way: Deacon Jones, Bubba Smith before he hurt his knee, Cedrick Hardman, Gino Marchetti.

Not enough football people talk about Gino Marchetti anymore. As a kid growing up in Daly City, I knew about Gino when he played at the University of San Francisco, along with ten other guys who went on to the NFL, including Ollie Matson, the Hall of Fame running back who had been a 1952 Olympic gold medalist in the 4×400-meter relay. When the Colts won the NFL championship in both 1958 and 1959, Gino was their defensive left end, one of the first great pass rushers. Before that, most defensive linemen were geared to the run, but Gino was geared to getting to the passer. Years later, after Bubba Smith joined the Colts as the NFL's first draft choice in 1968, he met Gino.

"You know what Gino told me?" Bubba said to me once. "Gino told me that the best game I'll ever play will be the day I have the cleanest jersey. He told me, 'If you have a dirty jersey, it means you were on your back. But if you have a clean jersey, the tackle didn't touch you.' "

The tackle didn't always touch Cedrick Hardman, another quick defensive end. In his big years with the 49ers, he made me do something as the Raiders' coach that I never did in preparing for any other pass rusher. Instead of having Art Shell just work against our defensive ends that week, I lined up Art against Cliff Branch, our fastest wide receiver. They'd go at it for ten snaps each day after practice. At the snap, Cliff would dart up the field and Art would try to stay with him as best he could. I wanted Art to see that speed, to adjust to getting back quickly against somebody with that speed.

Not that Cedrick was as fast as Cliff, who was once a world-class sprinter. But this way, Art wouldn't be so shocked by Cedrick's speed. Offensive linemen are used to being down in that pit with defensive linemen, wrestling and grappling around. They're not used to somebody like Cedrick who could just *whoom,* go right by.

Cedrick's speed forced the tackle to make a move to try to block him. Cedrick's next move countered the tackle's move, especially if he got the tackle's feet crossed. The difference between good pass rushers and ordinary pass rushers is the ability to move the hands and feet at the same time. Good pass rushers do that. Average pass rushers move their hands, but their feet never move. So they never get anywhere. One of the best at moving his hands and feet was Richard Jackson, who thrived with the Broncos after the Raiders traded him.

The Best I've Ever Seen

Defensive Ends	Fred Dean
	Richard Jackson
	Deacon Jones
	Howie Long
	Gino Marchetti
	Bubba Smith
	Jack Youngblood
Defensive Tackles	Buck Buchanan
	Joe Greene
	Tom Keating
	Bob Lilly
	Merlin Olsen
	Alan Page
	Randy White
Nose Tackle	Curley Culp

"Big bodies," Lou Saban, then the Broncos' coach, had said to Al Davis. "I need some big bodies."

Lou had taken over the Broncos in 1967, around the same time I joined the Raiders' staff as an assistant coach. The previous season Richard Jackson had been a Raider rookie without a position. He was used at linebacker on the defensive line and on the special teams, but he hadn't been really aggressive. Looking back, maybe that was because he didn't know what he was. Whatever the reason, the Raiders shipped Richard, along with guard Dick Tyson and linebacker Ray Schmautz, to the

Broncos for wide receiver Lionel Taylor and center Jerry Sturm.

Not many good players ever got away from the Raiders, but we had to live with that deal for a few years. Richard Jackson turned into an All-Pro defensive end, and to make matters worse, he was right there haunting us in our own division. We had to worry about him twice a year.

The day Richard arrived at the Broncos' training camp, he learned he would play left end. Sometimes that's all a player wants to know. He'll take it from there, and Richard did. As a pass rusher, Richard was a bear. He'd head-butt the tackle, or arm-drag the tackle, anything to get the tackle out of square. He was a big barreling guy who depended on his strength. And for a great pass rusher, he was better than most against the run. In those years, the 4-3 defense was standard. But you could always depend on Hank Stram, the Chiefs' coach, to do something different. That's how Hank came up with the forerunner of today's nose tackle. Hank lined up one of his defensive tackles, Curley Culp, at what is known now as a nose tackle, playing opposite the center instead of a guard.

In the NFL today, most teams use a 3-4 defense with a nose tackle (also known as a middle guard) between two offensive ends. But no matter how much the position has evolved in recent years, Curley Culp, who later played for the Oilers, is still the best nose tackle I've seen.

Nose tackle is not a glamorous position. Never was. Never will be. He's down there across from the ball, about to be blocked by the center, maybe by both the center and one of the guards, maybe even by the center and both guards. The offense knows that if it's going to run the ball for any substantial yardage, it has to move that nose tackle. If the nose tackle holds his ground, the linebackers flow in behind him and there's nowhere for the ballcarrier to go. If you can get a push on the nose tackle, push him back a yard or two, then there's a hole. That's why the nose tackle is usually double-teamed, sometimes triple-teamed.

And that's why Curley Culp was the best I ever saw. Hey, I

know all about Joe Klecko of the Jets and Jim Burt of the Giants—they're terrific. But believe me, Curley Culp was the best to play the position.

Built like a sumo wrestler, Curley was 6 foot 1 and 270, as strong as any player I've ever known, and as physically suited to a position as any player I've ever known. For a defensive lineman, the worst possible stance is straight up. If he's straight up, he has no power, no leverage. If he's straight up, it's easy for an offensive lineman to push him back. The idea, especially for a nose tackle, is to be bent over. He has maximum power that way, maximum leverage, and that was Curley's natural stance. He even walked leaning forward, as if he was about to stare at the center, eyeball to eyeball.

David Logan of the Bucs reminds me of Curley—somebody who ate a lot of Pablum as a baby. He seems to crawl more than run. But that's what makes a good nose tackle. His butt is behind his head.

Curley Culp played every down, not just against the run. No matter what, he was there. Passing downs. Short yardage. Goal line. But with the 3-4 defense now, the nose tackle takes an awful beating. On almost every play, he gets hit by two or three blockers. Sometimes he gets clipped, legally, meaning he gets hit across the back of the legs from behind. Anywhere else, clipping is illegal, but in what the rule book calls "close line play," the area between the two offensive tackles extending 3 yards on each side of the line of scrimmage, clipping is permitted. That area of "close line play" is where the nose tackle gets his mail.

To protect the nose tackle, the NFL should change that rule and disallow clipping anywhere on the field. But even if the rule is changed, the nose tackle would still take a beating. Some teams have started to platoon that position with two players. One in the first and third quarters, another in the second and fourth quarters.

But anybody who's born to be a nose tackle, like Jim Burt, would resist being platooned. Jim was an All-American at the

University of Miami (Florida), but he was ignored in the NFL draft. He had to talk the Giants into signing him. At training camp, he heard that when a rookie got cut, an equipment boy would knock on the door of his room and tell him to go see the coach.

"You know what Jim did?" Bill Parcells, the Giants' coach, told me. "Jim slept on the floor under his bed. He figured if somebody came to his room but couldn't find him, he wouldn't get cut. I found out when I asked him why he looked like he wasn't getting any sleep. He told me he had been sleeping on the floor the last five nights."

Jim made the Giants, but three years later, when he was recuperating from surgery for a herniated disk, he didn't consider himself a member of the team. He moved everything in his locker to another room. He wouldn't even eat the pizza that Phil Simms buys every Friday for all his teammates. He brought a sandwich in a brown bag. When he started playing again, he moved back to his locker and he ate the pizza like everybody else. He also started taping his jersey to his shoulder pads so the offensive lineman couldn't yank his jersey. Jim's not the only one. I think Mike Webster, the Steelers' center, started it, then other offensive linemen did it, then the defensive linemen. Before a game, most players need only ten or fifteen minutes to get dressed. But somebody like Jim Burt who tapes his jersey to his shoulder pads will need as much as two hours.

Tape with stickum on both sides is used. The tape is put on the shoulder pads first, then the player puts the jersey over the shoulder pads; the jersey sticks to the outside layer of tape. The player then puts his shoulder pads and his jersey on at the same time.

The front of Jim Burt's jersey gets so bunched up, his "64" is hard to see. But he doesn't need a number. Just looking at him out there, you know he's the nose tackle in a 3-4 defense, taking care of the middle on the line of scrimmage all by himself with two inside linebackers behind him. In a 4-3 defense, which the Bears and a few other teams still use, the two defensive tackles have the middle linebacker behind them. The two tackles work in tandem. Ideally, each is a different type. One chases everything that moves; the other stays at home, protecting the line of scrimmage.

For some defensive tackles, staying at home is an excuse to be lazy. Against a sweep, there's a fine line between staying at home and dogging it. But the good stay-at-home defensive tackle knows that once the opposing offense is committed to a sweep, he goes all out after it.

When the Vikings had their Purple People Eaters, their left tackle was Gary Larsen and later Doug Sutherland, each a stay-at-home. The right tackle was Alan Page, who could raise hell with your offense. You just hoped Alan would take off in the wrong direction, away from where the play was going. As good as Carl Eller and Jim Marshall were as the Vikings' defensive ends, Alan Page was the best player of the four. One of the best defensive tackles who ever played.

When people asked me about Alan Page, my answer was always very simple. You couldn't block him.

Even at 6 foot 3 and 240, Alan Page was too quick. Henry Jordan on Vince Lombardi's championship Packer teams had that same quickness. So did Tom Keating on my early Raider teams. But most defensive tackles are too big to be quick, too big like Dave Butz of the Redskins is now, like Louie Kelcher of the Chargers was in his All-Pro years. You couldn't run at Louie, but you couldn't make a living running around him either. At 6 foot 5 and 282, he had arms as big as some people's legs, and he had legs as big as some trees.

Other defensive tackles have the gift of being both big and quick: Joe Greene, Merlin Olsen, Bob Lilly.

Randy White of the Cowboys is one of today's best defensive tackles. He's not only quick, but he has great upper-body strength. If he gets his hands on the defensive guard trying to block him, he can turn that guard around. Most defensive tackles can't do that, but Randy just picks up guys and tosses them around like sacks of potatoes. Of all the guards, Russ Grimm of the Redskins probably does as good a job as anybody on Randy, not that it's easy.

"Randy White," Russ once told me, "is an all-day sucker. You got him all day."

Back when I was coaching, the toughest teams to run against were the Chiefs with Buck Buchanan and Curley Culp at tackle and Willie Lanier at middle linebacker, and later the Steelers with Joe Greene and Ernie Holmes at tackle and Jack Lambert at middle linebacker. If you ask me which was tougher, I couldn't choose between them. I know the Chiefs' combination was so tough that when we were putting together a game plan on Wednesday night, I hardly got more than two hours' sleep. I'd be in the Raiders' office with my assistant coaches, studying films of the Chiefs' defense and chalking plays on a blackboard.

"I think I got it," I'd say.

One of the coaches would put up the play I mentioned, then we'd stare at it for a few seconds.

"No, that won't work," I'd say.

We would check the films again and try another play. Same thing. That went on for hours. And we always came up with the same answer—no answer. We knew we couldn't move Buchanan and Culp and Lanier, at least not enough for any substantial yardage. And by four o'clock that morning, I would finally send everybody home. I'd drive home, get two hours' sleep, get up, drive back to our practice complex, and try to think of something else.

At 6 foot 7 and 287 before dinner, Buck Buchanan was one of the first tall defensive tackles. Before him, most tackles were squatty, which meant the guards blocking them could be squatty.

Every pass rusher is coached to try to get to the passer. But if he doesn't get the sack, he's told to get his hands up into the quarterback's vision. With his height, Buck's hands were up higher than the passer's eyes. The more Al Davis watched Buck harass the Raiders' quarterbacks, the more he knew he needed a guard who was almost as big as Buck was. That's why the

Raiders' first choice in 1967 was Gene Upshaw, who was 6 foot 5 and 255.

As good as Buck was, Joe Greene was better, especially against the run. Joe played a different style. In the Steelers' defense, Joe was the left tackle. But instead of lining up over the right guard as left tackles usually did, Joe lined up at an angle in the gap between the right guard and the center. If you were trying to run to your right, you had to block your right guard on him because the center couldn't get him. If you were running to your left, you had to block the center on him.

That may sound simple enough, but it didn't really work. And the reason was that Jack Lambert lined up at middle linebacker behind Joe Greene.

If you tried to block Greene, you couldn't block Lambert, and if you tried to block Lambert, you couldn't block Greene. So you couldn't run to the right or to the left. And if you were passing, you had to use your right guard and your center to block Greene. Whatever you did, it might work occasionally. But not often.

"Let's try this," I once said. "Let's try to push Greene back into Lambert."

That sounded good, except that you couldn't push Joe Greene back. I used to call that a Gap Stack, with Greene in the gap and Lambert stacked behind him. But as effective as it was for the Steelers, no other NFL team ever used it. Probably because no other team had Joe Greene to make it work, or had Jack Lambert behind him.

All the talk about the Steel Curtain in those years, *that* was the Steel Curtain to me—Joe Greene in the gap, with Jack Lambert behind him.

Of the defensive tackles around now, my favorite is Steve McMichael of the Bears, known to his teammates as Mongo, or Ming the Merciless. In the off-season back home in Texas, he hunts rattlesnakes. During the season he hunts quarterbacks. Buddy Ryan called him a "throwback to the black high-top shoe guys." That would be enough for me to love him, but Steve told me something I've never heard another player say.

"I want to play the best I can in every game," he said. "You never know what game is going to be your last. And you have to live the rest of your life with your last game."

As big and tough as NFL players are, every one fears the injury that will end his career. They don't talk about it. They try not to think about it. They hope it's not going to happen. But they know it might. Maybe a knee injury, maybe a back injury, maybe a head injury. Or maybe an auto accident. And when it happens, it's too late to say, hey, I wish I had played better in my last game.

But the way Steve McMichael plays, he'll always be proud of his last game, whenever that is. That's my kind of defensive tackle, my kind of football player.

Linebacker Instincts

I NEVER LIKED TO HEAR A young player say, "Hey, Coach, my legs are tired, I need a rest." That always pissed me off. Older players, sometimes they shouldn't have to work as hard. But a young player, don't tell me you're tired. If you're a young player, you should be ready to play, ready to do whatever you have to do. That's what I always liked about Lawrence Taylor, the Giants' outside line-backer who has been All-Pro in each of his five NFL seasons.

After practice one Saturday during the 1984 season, L.T.'s teammates strolled off the field at Giants Stadium to their locker room. But he stayed out there to have some fun by himself.

As a linebacker, L.T. hardly ever touches the ball in practice. But now he emptied a bag of balls on the far 20-yard line. One by one, he began to throw the balls toward the other goalposts —90 yards away. I didn't realize it at first, but he was having a contest with himself. He was trying to hit one of the uprights —from 90 yards away. One after another, the balls sailed by an upright, only a few feet to either side. Then one of his throws careened off the goalpost. He yelled and jumped up and down like a little kid.

Lawrence Taylor was just out there playing with a football. He wasn't thinking about saving himself for tomorrow's game. And he had only just begun to play. He scooped all the balls into the bag, went back to around midfield and started punting— again to see if he could hit an upright. He didn't, but he came close. Again he scooped up all the balls, went back to midfield, put down a tee, and started placekicking. Some of his kicks floated between the uprights. This time, after he scooped all the balls into the bag, he carried it through the exit toward the Giants' locker room.

Watching him go, I thought, hey, sooner or later even Lawrence Taylor gets tired.

As I followed him underneath the stadium, he suddenly stopped. One of his teammates was shooting a basketball at the hoop and backboard attached to the wall near the Giants' locker room. As the ball bounced off the rim, Lawrence grabbed it, then dribbled away from the other player.

"One on one," I heard him say. "Let's go."

Lawrence obviously wasn't tired—but just watching him, I was. I went into the CBS truck parked underneath the stadium, stayed in there for maybe twenty minutes. When I came out, L.T. was still playing basketball. When people asked me that year what made Lawrence Taylor such a great linebacker, I thought of him sacking a quarterback, making a tackle on the other side of the field, intercepting a pass, but I also thought of him just having fun that Saturday after practice.

But whenever I was at a Giants' practice during the 1985 season, Lawrence seldom stayed out afterward to have some fun. And his play on Sunday usually showed it.

Not that Lawrence played poorly. Sometimes he was the same force he had been in his first four seasons. But sometimes just a good linebacker, sometimes just an average linebacker. His reputation put him on the All-Pro teams, but he didn't make the All-Madden team I do for CBS every year. And two months after the playoffs, he acknowledged that he had sought "professional assistance" to help him with "substance-abuse problems."

At his best, I don't think Lawrence Taylor knows why he's a great linebacker, and that's precisely why he's capable of being a great linebacker. More than most positions, linebacker demands football instincts.

As a coach, I learned that the better the player, the less he knows why he does what he does. Especially a linebacker. Willie Lanier of the Chiefs and Mike Curtis of the Colts taught me that at the Pro Bowl after the 1974 season. I was never thrilled being the AFC coach in the Pro Bowl because it meant the Raiders had lost the AFC championship game. My first year at the Pro Bowl, after the 1970 season, I moped around. I was still disappointed about having lost the AFC championship game to the Colts, who went on to win Super Bowl V two weeks later. But when I got back to Oakland after the Pro Bowl game, I realized I had wasted an opportunity to learn from all the great players on the AFC squad. After that, whenever I was the AFC coach, I always talked to the best players, hoping to take something home. At the Pro Bowl after the 1974 season, I got Willie Lanier and Mike Curtis aside.

"At the snap," I asked them, "what do you guys think about?"

They looked at each other, then they looked at me. They didn't seem to know what I was talking about.

"You get to the play so quickly," I said. "How do you do that?"

Awaiting a play, a middle linebacker has what football people call a "read" and a "key" in trying to decipher what's going to happen. When he lines up over the center, he reads the formation by checking one of the running backs, sometimes both. Then he keys on, say, the two guards. In coaching, that's about all you can do. You line him up, then tell him what to read and who to key. But as soon as the ball is snapped, he's on his own. That's when Willie Lanier and Mike Curtis were at their best. If you ran at Willie or Mike, he was always there. If you ran away from Willie or Mike, he was always there.

"What gets you to the play all the time?" I asked them.

"I just watch what happens," Willie said, "then I just go to where the ball is."

"Yeah," Mike said, shrugging, "that's all I do."

"But don't you take the same first step on every play? Don't you have it figured out where you're going?"

"I just see the ballcarrier and I go," Mike said.

"And if it's a pass, you see that," Willie said.

"That's all you do?" I said. "You just wait to see what happens and you react?"

"That's all I ever do," Willie said.

"That's all you can do," Mike said.

By not telling me anything, they told me everything. After that, the more I watched the great linebackers, the more I realized they don't analyze what they do, they just do it. I once asked Lawrence Taylor to analyze what he does, but he didn't know either. When he comes out of the defensive huddle knowing that he's going to be blitzing the quarterback, he's not thinking about how he's going to blitz. He's not figuring out a scientific formula. He just takes off and does what he has to do.

On a blitz during the 1985 season, L.T. pounced on Joe Theismann so hard, the Redskin quarterback suffered a compound fracture of his lower right leg.

"I heard the snap," L.T. said later, "and at first I thought two helmets had hit. Then I heard the yell and saw the bone sticking through the leg."

So did millions of TV viewers that Monday night. Then they saw L.T. waving for the Redskins' doctor and trainer. Then he put his hands up to his helmet, then he walked around in circles, returning every so often to see how Joe was.

"The idea of this game is to hit a guy hard and make him feel it," L.T. said later. "But you don't want to see any kind of major injury or a broken bone. You hate to see anything like that."

In his own way, L.T. *felt* that hit just as much as Joe Theismann did. And by L.T.'s reaction, millions of TV viewers *felt* that he was genuinely sorry for having caused Joe's injury. You can't fake what L.T. did. Watching that scene, I suddenly had more respect for L.T. as a man than I had for him as a line-backer.

The way L.T. flies across the field on a sweep to the other side, you should be able to get him out of position on a reverse or a bootleg. But he doesn't keep flying across the field if that sweep doesn't develop.

Everyone is going to get fooled for a split second, but how long they stay fooled is the difference between an All-Pro, a good player, an average player, and a bad player. If you're lucky, you'll fool an All-Pro for no more than a split second. You might fool a good linebacker for another step, an average line-backer for two steps, which is like an eternity.

Through the years, I asked some average linebackers to ana-lyze what they did. "My feet and shoulders are lined up to-gether," one told me. "My first step is short, only six inches, then my next step is . . ."

The more he talked, the more I realized he was a robot. He was trying to play linebacker the way some dance students try to learn the tango. By the numbers. One, two, three, four. You don't play linebacker by the numbers. You play it by instinct. You play it like the tough guy Frank Howard, the legendary Clemson coach, once talked about at a clinic I attended.

"I know a guy who's so tough," Frank said with a straight face, "when he goes to the can, he takes a baseball bat with him. He never knows when he's going to shit a wildcat and he'll have to beat it to death."

Every time I watched Mike Curtis play middle linebacker, I thought about Frank Howard's story. The way Mike ran around, his eyes blazing, I thought, He just might shit a wildcat.

At a 1971 game in Baltimore, the Colts' defensive unit was waiting for the Dolphins to come out of their huddle when a thirty-year-old fan suddenly ran onto the field and grabbed the ball. All the other Colt players stood there stunned, but Mike reacted with a linebacker's instincts. Mike sent the man sprawl-ing with what was described as a "crunching arm block from the rear." *Wham*, the guy had to be scraped off the field. He was arrested and fined $100 for disorderly conduct, spent a couple of hours in jail, then spent a couple of hours in a hospital being treated for dizziness and a hip injury.

"You shouldn't have hit him so hard, Mike," somebody said.

"He shouldn't have been out on the field," Mike replied.

As the Raiders' coach, I saw much more of Mike Curtis and Willie Lanier in those years than I did of Dick Butkus, the Bears' middle linebacker. We played against Dick only once, in 1972, when he was hobbling on bad knees. But once was enough to convince me that Dick was as great as everybody said he was. Dick didn't think about where to go, he just went. And when he got to the ballcarrier, he just pancaked him. Flattened him. Dick's reputation made running backs think. The first time O. J. Simpson played against the Bears, he kept looking around.

"Every time I carried the ball," O.J. has said, "I was wondering, 'Where is he? Where is he?'"

Sooner or later, O.J. knew where Dick was—all over him. Dick also distracted quarterbacks. The first time Bob Griese played against Dick, he walked up to the line of scrimmage and looked across to see where Dick was. Then he started calling signals and put his hands down to take the snap from the center.

"Except that I was behind my right guard, Larry Little, instead of my center," Bob says. "Larry jumped, then turned to me and yelled, 'What are you doing here?'"

Coaching against Dick, you wanted to get him to step up to stop the run. So you would run the ball to bring him up, then bring him up even more. Then you'd fake a run and hit a pass in behind him to the tight end. But you couldn't make a living doing that. If you tried it too often, he'd be all over your tight end.

"One thing I used to love," Dick Butkus has told me, "was hitting those tight ends."

That was Dick Butkus the middle linebacker, not Dick Butkus the actor I've gotten to know when we do Miller Lite commercials. At a taping, we sit around between takes more than we're in front of the camera. That's when Dick has his fun.

Especially at our group commercials, when everybody works for the same money. During a break once, Dick strolled over to Bubba Smith.

"Bubba," he said in a stage whisper, "did you get your one-hundred-thousand-dollar bonus check yet for this commercial?"

There was no $100,000 bonus check, but Dick made it sound as if he had already spent his. Of all the other guys in the commercial, Steve Mizerak, the pool player, usually bites the hardest at Dick's practical jokes. Even before Bubba could answer, Steve bit.

"What check?" Steve asked. "I didn't get any bonus check."

"Oh, you didn't get it?" Dick said. "It must be in the mail."

Marv Throneberry is another guy Dick gets to. As a Christmas present one year, Miller Lite sent each of us a Tiffany lamp, the kind that hangs over a pool table. At our group commercial about a month later, Dick was talking to me between takes when Marv sat down nearby.

"John," he said, winking, "did you get your pool table first and then the lamp?"

Hey, nobody got a pool table, just the lamp, but Marv's head spun around.

"I got mine the same day," I said with a straight face. "Same delivery."

"That's strange," Dick said. "I got my lamp first and then the pool table came the next week. But the other guys say they got the pool table first, then the lamp came later."

By now, Marv was staring at both of us. "What pool table?" he asked. "Ah didn't get mah pool table."

"You didn't get your pool table?" Dick said. "That's strange, everybody else got a pool table."

Marv stood up and hurried over to one of the Backer and Spielvogel advertising people who were at the taping. "Hey," we could hear Marv saying, "how come Ah didn't get mah pool table?" Dick loved it. That's the Dick Butkus that I know. Nothing physical. Nothing violent. As a coach, I've learned that there's nothing gentler than true toughness, and there's nothing tougher than true gentleness. Guys who are truly tough are usually that way. I've seldom seen a player who's truly tough on the field act tough off the field. But maybe nobody was ever as truly tough on the field as Dick Butkus was. Before his bad knees slowed him down, Dick was the symbol of the middle linebacker, the position that Sam Huff of the Giants had popularized.

As good as Sam was, I've always thought that Jim Brown was primarily responsible for bringing Sam into focus, as well as for bringing the position of middle linebacker into focus.

As the Browns' fullback, Jim Brown was such a big story, he made Sam Huff a big story. In those years, the Browns and the Giants were fierce rivals. Throughout the fifties, only two teams won the NFL Eastern Division title: the Browns seven times, the Giants three times. From 1957 on, whenever the Browns played the Giants, the sportswriters boiled the rivalry down to Jim Brown the fullback against Sam Huff the middle linebacker.

By the early sixties, Sam Huff was as famous as Jim Brown, maybe more so. I don't remember Jim being the subject of a prime-time TV special, but Sam was—"The Violent World of Sam Huff."

That TV show made middle linebacker a glamour position. Sam Huff suddenly was a star, and so were the best of the other NFL middle linebackers of that era: Ray Nitschke of the Packers, Joe Schmidt of the Lions, Bill George of the Bears. After that TV special, it was easy for fans to identify with the middle linebacker. The man in the middle. The man the fullback couldn't run away from. The man who was your team's best linebacker—that's why he was the man in the middle.

If you put your best linebacker on either side in those days, the other team would run to the opposite side, away from him. But the other team couldn't run away from the man in the middle.

In a 4-3 defense, the two outside linebackers have more responsibilities than the middle linebacker. On the outside, a linebacker has to worry about different blocking combinations. If the tight end blocks down on the defensive end, he may have to fill that gap. He may have to take on the pulling guard or a blocking back. Or in a passing situation, he may have to slow up the tight end.

The middle linebacker has more freedom. He just goes where the wild goose goes, like Nick Buoniconti did.

Nick is a lawyer today, the president of the United States Tobacco Company. He was always a bright guy. But as the middle linebacker in the Dolphins' No-Name defense, he didn't play like a bright guy. Not that he was dumb, but he was reckless, the most reckless player I've ever seen. When he saw a play developing, he just ran and dived. Just threw his body, *whoom*. I never saw a guy play with that much disregard for his body. At 5 foot 11 and 220, he wasn't that big, he wasn't that strong. His back pockets didn't fill that much, he didn't have much butt on him. But he just bounced up. On the next play, he threw his body again.

Jack Lambert was almost as reckless, and at 6 foot 4 and 220 he was bigger. When he lined up behind Joe Greene, you seldom could block him on a running play. He was a great tackler, but he was so aggressive, sometimes you could fool him by faking a run up the middle. He'd step up, then you could bring your tight end in behind him for a pass.

Bill Bergey was another aggressive middle linebacker. His rookie year with the Bengals, I was standing on the sideline at Riverfront Stadium as the Raiders tried to run a sweep around the right end. Jim Otto was supposed to block Bergey, but *boom*, Bergey blasted by him and made the tackle right in front of me. Bergey could do that. He was a wild man, he made tackles all over the field.

"Damn it," I yelled at Jim Otto, "you got to block Bergey, we can't run the ball if you don't block Bergey."

Jim didn't say anything. He didn't have to, and I didn't expect him to. But then Bergey stood up, and looked over at me, his eyes burning through his facemask.

"Coach," he said, "Otto can't block me. He's too old. I'm too fast for him. He can't touch me."

Jim didn't say anything then either. Jim just turned and hurried back to the huddle, but I knew what he was thinking and I knew Bill Bergey had made a big mistake, a rookie mistake. He had insulted an old pro. The rest of the game, Bergey didn't make a tackle. Several years later, when Bergey was the Eagles' middle linebacker, I told that story on television. The next time I did an Eagles' game, Bergey called me aside at practice the day before.

"Coach," he said, "that story about me and Jim Otto you told on television, you didn't tell the rest of the story."

"What was that?" I said.

"The next quarter, I was downfield about to dive into the pile when Otto launched himself like a missile at me. He hit me square in the helmet with his helmet. After that, I didn't remember anything about the rest of the game. At home that night, I kept getting up to puke. I hardly slept a wink. It took me about five days to recover. I learned my lesson."

"Now that you mention it," I said, "I do remember that hit, I just never realized how it affected you."

Helmet to helmet, that hit sounded like two trucks colliding. Bill Bergey learned not to mess with an old pro, to let a sleeping dog lie. When he woke up Jim Otto, he woke up an attack dog.

Not all the good middle linebackers depended on aggressiveness. Some were smart thinkers, like Lee Roy Jordan of the Cowboys.

Looking back now, Jordan was maybe the last of the real thinking middle linebackers. In those years, the middle linebacker was the defensive quarterback. He called all the defensive fronts and the defensive coverages. Nowadays the coaches wigwag the defenses, but in Jordan's time, he called the defense there just before the snap. It wasn't always that easy, not with the Flex defense Tom Landry used. But the Flex wasn't nuclear physics. Basically, it was a variation of the Gap defense, a short-yardage defense that Amos Alonzo Stagg probably used nearly a century ago. In the Gap 8, eight defensive players were assigned to fill the eight gaps across from the offensive line. In their Flex defense, the Cowboys did the same thing. No matter what a player did, he filled his gap first.

"What we do," Harvey Martin, one of the Cowboys' defensive ends, once said, "is fill all the gaps."

No matter what a Cowboy player did, he filled the gap first, then he went from there. To deceive the offense, the Cowboys put one guy on the line, the next guy off the line. Basically, those on the line were penetrators, those off the line were readers. The penetrators and the readers might alternate depending on the offensive formation. That's what Lee Roy Jordan had to call, depending on the other team's offensive formation.

Not many real middle linebackers exist anymore. Mike Singletary of the Bears is one of the last—solid, smart, and serious. Another was Jack "Hacksaw" Reynolds in his years with the Rams before he finished up with the 49ers.

Hack was in there to coordinate the defense, to concentrate on stopping the run, and to help out on pass defense. He had great instincts, great vision, and he was happy as hell to hit the ballcarrier. He also had one of football's great nicknames. When the Rams were in Super Bowl XIV, some of the writers wanted to know the story of how he got his nickname. He told that story all week. But when the 49ers went to Super Bowl XVI the year he joined them, he again had to tell the story all week. When the 49ers went to Super Bowl XIX, three years later, he handed out a press release:

THE HACKSAW STORY
(or How I Got My Nickname)
by Jack Reynolds

In 1969, when I was a senior at the University of Tennessee, we had already clinched the Southeastern Conference title but still had to play Ole Miss (where Archie Manning was the quarterback). If Tennessee won the game, we would have gone to the Sugar Bowl. The previous year, Tennessee had beaten Ole Miss, 31–0.

Things went badly that day and Mississippi beat us, 38–0. I played a good game, but I was really upset at the outcome.

We had an old car (a '53 Chevrolet with no motor) on top of a bluff above the school. We used to push it around with a guy's jeep and practice driving into things . . . like demolition derby. When I got back to school, I decided to cut that old Chevy in half to make a trailer for a new jeep I had just purchased. It was a good outlet for my frustrations. I went to K-Mart and bought the cheapest hacksaw they had . . . along with 13 replacement blades. I cut through the entire frame and drive shaft, all the way through the car. I started on Sunday and finished Monday afternoon. It took me eight total hours. I broke all 13 blades. When I finished, I got one guy from the dorm, Ray Nettles, to witness it.

The next day we took the rest of our friends from the dorm up the hill to see it. When we got there, both halves of the car were gone, with just the 13 blades lying on the ground. To this day, I don't know what happened to that car!

Sawing that car in half was the theme for Hacksaw's first Miller Lite commercial. But like that car, the middle linebacker has pretty much disappeared. Twenty years ago Lawrence Taylor would have been a middle linebacker in a 4-3 defense. But in a 3-4 defense he's the right outside linebacker, the new glamour position for a linebacker. The right outside linebacker usually is out there free to roam, without a tight end or an offensive lineman to block him—except for L.T., who forced opposing coaches to design a blocker just for him.

"On offense," Bill Walsh of the 49ers once told me, "you can't let Lawrence Taylor play against air."

That's one of the new coaching phrases, playing against air.

It means without somebody lined up on him. When the 49ers eliminated the Giants in the 1981 playoffs at the end of L.T.'s rookie season, Bill Walsh assigned a guard, John Ayers, to block him on pass plays. After that, some teams copied that strategy, while other teams lined up their tight end on L.T.'s side— anything to keep him from playing against air. When he saw the tight end lining up on his side, L.T. sometimes shifted to the left side so he could play against air. Then some teams used two tight ends, one on each side, to prevent him from shifting over.

More than any other player, Lawrence Taylor has been responsible for NFL teams using two tight ends.

The original "outside" linebacker in a 3-4 defense was Bob Matheson of the Dolphins' No-Name defense, who is now Don Shula's linebackers' coach. Bob was inserted on passing downs, replacing a defensive lineman. Bob's number was 53, which prompted Bill Arnsparger, then the Dolphins' defensive coordinator, to call it the "53" defense. Bob usually lined up as an outside linebacker.

"I was the primary rusher, outside away from the tight end," Bob recalls. "I had the option to freelance, so I was an inside linebacker maybe twenty percent of the time. I mixed it up."

In the 3-4 defense, the two inside linebackers usually don't have much identity. Of the current inside linebackers, Harry Carson of the Giants and Matt Millen of the Raiders are two of the best known. In a 4-3 defense, the two outside linebackers sometimes are forgotten because of all the attention on the middle linebacker. But when I was coaching, there were five outside linebackers in a 4-3 who could not be ignored: Ted Hendricks, Jack Ham, Andy Russell, Tommy Jackson, and Bobby Bell.

I had Ted on the Raiders my last four seasons as coach. When he blitzed from the weak side, a running back couldn't block him. And even against a tight end, he was a great blitzer.

Ted dominated a tight end. If he wanted to get by the tight end, he got by him. If he didn't want the tight end to get off the line of scrimmage, the tight end didn't get off. I'm convinced that Ted once so completely dominated Ken MacAfee that the 49er tight end never recovered. In our 1978 preseason game, Ted was playing the way he always plays in the preseason. He wouldn't let the tight end beat him, but if the tight end didn't embarrass Ted or do anything extra to him, Ted wouldn't do anything extra either. Our players knew from practice scrimmages not to get Ted mad, but MacAfee didn't know. MacAfee was the 49ers' first-round choice that year, an All-American at Notre Dame, 6 foot 4 and 250. But after a play ended, he made the mistake of hitting Ted from behind.

Ted played the rest of that game like the Super Bowl was at stake. MacAfee couldn't get off the line to catch a pass. And when Ted blitzed, MacAfee couldn't block him. I know MacAfee had knee problems, but I've always thought that his career turned downward after he hit Ted from behind. MacAfee hit the wrong guy.

I don't know if Jack Ham of the Steelers will make the Pro Football Hall of Fame, but he deserves to. Of all the outside linebackers I coached against, he was the best. He had the best feet, the best footwork. He was never out of position. If you tried to run inside, he could close down on the ballcarrier. If you tried to run outside, he could string it out and stop it. If you tried to pass against a zone, he could get back into his zone. If you tried to pass against man-to-man coverage, he could cover his man. If you tried to fool him with a play-action pass, he might take a quick step in the wrong direction but he always recovered in time.

Jack Ham was the Steelers' left linebacker, Andy Russell was their right linebacker. No team ever had two outside linebackers that good in a 4-3 defense, plus Jack Lambert in the middle. Andy was a very smart linebacker. You could never fool him.

Ham and Russell were good tacklers. But the best linebackers usually are—Lawrence Taylor, Willie Lanier, Mike Curtis, Phil Villapiano, Jack Reynolds, and Bobby Bell to name a few. To me, tackling means open-field tackling. Stopping that running back or that wide receiver before he busts a big gain. It's not necessarily hitting hard. It's staying with the ballcarrier's move. Those running backs and wide receivers aren't coming at you in a straight line, they're weaving and sliding and dipping. The old theory was to watch the ballcarrier's belly button. No matter how much he faked, his belly button wasn't going to move. And that's true. But a good tackler knows he can react as quickly as the ballcarrier can move.

The Best I've Ever Seen

Middle Linebackers	Dick Butkus
	Mike Curtis
	Willie Lanier
	Ray Nitschke
Outside Linebackers	Bobby Bell
	Jack Ham
	Ted Hendricks
	Andy Russell
	Lawrence Taylor

In the open field, a good tackler never loses his feet. Coaches have a phrase for that now: clean feet. It means a tackler who knows how to stay on his feet. He doesn't get tangled up. He doesn't trip or fall. He's always balanced. Clean feet usually means a clean tackle.

Tommy Jackson of the Broncos wasn't very big, but he was a quick linebacker before there were quick linebackers. And he was the wildest linebacker I've ever seen. You never knew where he was going to turn up. He was tough, but not disciplined, which made him that much harder to figure out. Against a disciplined linebacker, you knew that if you did this, he would do that. But with Jackson, you had no idea. One time he might run in here, the next time he'd run out there. And for some reason he didn't like me.

"Take that, fat man," he would yell.

He was the only player who ever yelled at me like that. Of course, he usually yelled when the Broncos were winning, especially when they were winning in Denver.

In Oakland, he never yelled much.

Bobby Bell you could fool every once in a while, but never twice with the same play. When he was the Chiefs' left linebacker, you might fool him, but you might also see the ball coming back at you after he intercepted it. Sometimes for a touchdown. In his career, Bobby Bell ran back six interceptions for touchdowns, more than any other linebacker in NFL history. If you could fool him, it was only that one time. I remember fooling him once with a play-action pass. We faked the run, then the tight end sneaked in behind him for the pass.

"Hey, let's try that again," I told my quarterback.

The next time, Bobby Bell stayed with the tight end and knocked down the pass. At 6 foot 4 and 225, he was one of the first big outside linebackers—and one of the smartest. If you were looking to put something into your game plan to get him on, it had to be a play that you not only had never used before, but also one that nobody else had used before. Once he saw a play, he never forgot it. The great linebackers never do.

One-Steppers

JUST AS A CORNERBACK MEA-
sures a pass receiver, he is always being measured himself. His
height: usually the taller the better. His speed: the faster the
better. But as a coach, I measured a cornerback differently.

Watching game films, I stopped the projector as the receiver
made his cut. At that frozen moment, the cornerback was usually back-pedaling. As the receiver moved away from him, the
cornerback's momentum kept him back-pedaling. But how
many more steps back did he take before he reacted and moved
up on the receiver? That's how I measured the cornerback.

The best cornerbacks usually take only one more backward
step before reacting. Other cornerbacks take two or three backward steps, some take four.

Mike Haynes of the Raiders is a one-stepper. Years ago, Mel
Blount of the Steelers, Willie Brown of the Raiders, Emmitt
Thomas of the Chiefs, and Roger Wehrli of the Cardinals were
all one-steppers. Anybody who's a two-stepper is usually a good
cornerback. But a three-stepper or a four-stepper has trouble

staying with a good receiver. You would be surprised how many three-steppers and four-steppers somehow stay in the NFL for several seasons, and they make the one-stepper that much rarer, that much more valuable.

Of all the different positions in football, I consider cornerback the third toughest to learn to play as a NFL rookie. To me, quarterback is the toughest, then offensive tackle, and then cornerback.

Out there near the sideline, a cornerback is all alone. One of my Raider cornerbacks, Skip Thomas, used to tell me, "Coach, I'm naked out here, naked on an island." Especially in man-to-man coverage. In a zone defense, it's not so bad. In a zone, a cornerback is responsible for an area. But in man-to-man coverage, his job is to go wherever that wide receiver goes. In our defensive huddle, middle linebacker Dan Conners would call the pass coverages. One was known as "Cover Three," a strongside zone. Whenever one of our cornerbacks, Kent McCloughan, got tired, he would always go into the huddle with three fingers out hoping Dan would call that strongside zone instead of man-to-man.

In those years, Kent developed what was known as the bump-and-run in covering a wide receiver. At the snap, bump him hard. If possible, knock him down with a forearm shiver. But if the receiver got away, run with him forever, and bump him as many times as you could—until the pass was in the air.

Kent joined the Raiders in 1965, two years before I got there. To find out how good he was, he had to pass the test given every rookie Raider cornerback. The test was: Move up against a wide receiver on the line of scrimmage. Not a yard back, but right there on the line. Our thinking was, if you could cover a wide receiver from there, then it would be a little easier from 3 yards back of the line of scrimmage, even easier from 5 yards, and much easier from 7 yards. And for most cornerbacks, it was—but not for Kent McCloughan. When he was up on the line of scrimmage, a wide receiver couldn't get away from him. But the farther back he moved, the worse he covered.

"Is it all right," he finally asked, "if I line up tight every time?"

From then on, that's what he did. Most cornerbacks were always more comfortable lining up 5 or 10 yards back, sometimes 15 yards. If they got beat on a short pass, they weren't embarrassed because they could make the tackle. But if they got beat deep for a touchdown or a big gain, that was embarrassing. So they all felt that the farther back they lined up, the least chance they had of getting beat deep. All except Kent McCloughan. He always felt that when he was up close to a receiver, he could run with him every step. And react to him every step.

In those years, a defensive back could keep his hands on a pass receiver until the ball was in the air. But when Kent covered a receiver, he used his hands the way basketball players use a hand-check on defense: to feel which way the other player is going. When he lined up a few yards back, he never knew which way the receiver was going. Like every defensive back, he had to guess. But when he stayed with a receiver from the line of scrimmage, Kent could feel where that receiver was going. In a way, that receiver took Kent with him.

As good as Kent was, Willie Brown was even better, the master of the bump-and-run. Willie was elected to the Pro Football Hall of Fame in his first year of eligibility.

Willie is now coaching the Raiders' defensive backs. If he's the same way he was as a player, Willie doesn't want his cornerbacks to let anybody catch a pass. Not ever. Not even in practice. Not even in training camp. In our 1967 training camp, we had acquired Lionel Taylor, a wide receiver who caught a hundred passes for the Broncos in the 1961 season. In his career with the Broncos and the Oilers he caught 567 passes for 7,195 yards, but in our 1967 training-camp scrimmages, as I remember, Lionel never caught a pass when Willie was covering him.

Despite all those passes Lionel had caught for the Broncos, we cut him.

Willie was so good in practice and in training camp, he sometimes let a receiver get a stride or two away. But that was to get some action. Just when the receiver thought he was in the clear,

Willie would swoop in from behind and bat the ball away or intercept it. He did that in games, too. In Cincinnati in 1969 he did it once too often. He lined up loosely on Chip Myers, a rookie wide receiver. The next thing Willie knew, he was watching Myers go into the end zone with a 35-yard touchdown pass. On the sideline I exploded.

"You didn't respect that kid," I yelled. "You gave him too much room and he burned you."

I yelled at Willie at halftime. I yelled at him after the game. I yelled at him on Tuesday when we watched the game films. And I was yelling at him on Wednesday in practice when he turned to me.

"Coach," he said, "I got your point."

Willie was right. I had overdone it. But he had gotten my point, that a cornerback has to respect every wide receiver. No matter who the wide receiver is, if he's in the NFL, he's capable of burning a cornerback. Especially a cornerback who doesn't respect him. Now that Willie is a Raiders' assistant coach, I'm sure he tells his cornerbacks the same thing. And while most NFL teams are using zone-pass defense now, Willie prefers the man-to-man coverage he used.

"The only way to stop the passing game," Willie says, "is to put more pressure on the quarterback. If you play man-to-man, you can send more people at the quarterback. You can blitz a couple of linebackers because you don't need them for zones."

The Raiders, of course, have two of the NFL's best cornerbacks in Mike Haynes and Lester Hayes, each with All-Pro credentials. It's not a coincidence. In building a football team, Al Davis has always believed that your two cornerstones are your two cornerbacks. In my years as the Raiders' coach, I always disagreed with him. I believed you needed offensive linemen first, then cornerbacks. Al went for cornerbacks, then offensive linemen. After a while, it developed into a running gag, especially when we were preparing for the draft.

"Let's not forget," Al would say, "to get some offensive linemen for John."

"Yeah, yeah," I would say, "after you get some cornerbacks for yourself."

Al loves his cornerbacks. During the last few minutes of the Super Bowl XVIII warmup, Al was standing at midfield with Mike Haynes and Lester Hayes, each staring at the Redskins' offensive unit that was running plays coming out from around the 10-yard line. They watched half a dozen plays, maybe more. When the Raiders lost to the Redskins, 37–35, early that season, Mike wasn't with them. He hadn't played against the Redskins since the 1981 season. He wasn't sure how some of these Redskins came off the line of scrimmage. That might sound silly, but every team looks a little different for the simple reason that every player looks a little different.

"I check out the other team in the warmup before every game," Mike says. "I want to know how guys are running, especially if they've been hurt."

Al got Mike six weeks into that 1983 season. Mike had been a holdout with the Patriots, and the price was high. Not only for the dollars Mike wanted in his contract but also for what the Patriots wanted for him: the Raiders' first-round 1984 draft choice and their second-round 1985 choice. But to get a cornerback of Mike's ability, Al considered it a bargain. Back in 1978, my last year as the Raiders' coach, we got another bargain. We drafted Lester Hayes in the fifth round. He had been a safety at Texas A & M, but when he joined us as a rookie, we put him at cornerback.

"No, no," Lester said, "I'm a safety."

"Not here," I told him. "You're a cornerback now."

"No, no," he kept saying.

"If we say you're a cornerback," I told him, "you're a cornerback."

"I guess so," he finally said.

No matter how quick a cornerback was, I never wanted him to line up more than 7 yards off a wide receiver. In training camp, in fact, I never let them line up more than 5 yards off. That way, they had to cover tight and short. When a cornerback was more than 7 yards off, I always felt he tended to sit back and wait for something to happen rather than reacting to what was happening. I also had passing drills with no receivers so that our defensive backs could practice *catching* the ball. You'd be surprised how many teams never let their defensive backs catch a ball in practice, except by accident. In our man-to-man coverage, we wanted our defensive backs to be as proficient in intercepting a pass as they were at knocking it down.

To me, man-to-man was true pass coverage. But in 1978 the NFL, to open up the passing game, ruled that a defensive back could bump a receiver only once within a 5-yard area beyond the line of scrimmage, and not at all after that. Contact with the receiver within that 5-yard area could be maintained "as long as it is continuous and unbroken." In other words, if the cornerback got his hands on a receiver, he could keep his hands on that receiver in that 5-yard zone as long as his hands remained on the receiver. That's why Lester Hayes used so much stickum on his hands before stickum was outlawed. Most people thought the stickum was to help Lester intercept a pass. Wrong! He used it to stick his hands to the receiver to maintain that "continuous and unbroken" contact through that 5-yard area.

After the 1984 season, after Dan Marino threw 48 touchdown passes that year, the NFL decided that maybe the passing game was too wide open. The pass-interference rule was changed to allow a defensive back to look back at the ball without worrying about colliding with the pass receiver.

Of all the penalties in football, pass interference has always been the harshest. If there's interference on a 50-yard pass, that's a 50-yard penalty. And if there's interference in the end zone, the ball is spotted on the 1-yard line—an automatic first down and an almost sure touchdown. Even so, if a pass receiver is wide open, a defensive back is better off fouling him, thereby preventing a touchdown. As harsh as the penalty might be, at least the other team didn't get a touchdown. Who knows, on the next play the other team might fumble.

The way the rule was until the 1985 season, if any contact occurred when the ball was in the air, interference had occurred. That yellow flag had to be dropped. Then the official ruled whether the interference had been caused by the defensive player or the offensive player.

Under the new rule, the defensive player can look back at the ball while he's covering the receiver. That's the key—looking at the ball. If he's looking at the receiver and interferes with him, that's a penalty. But if he's looking back at the ball, it's not a penalty. That way, the defensive back has as much right to look for the ball and go for it as the receiver does. If both are looking for the ball, there can be contact without a penalty, unless the defensive back pushes him away or grabs his arms.

I like that rule. It gives the defensive player an even chance. Under the old rule, a receiver could slow up and cause a defensive player to run into him. Penalty.

But the new rule needs officials with subjectivity. Especially regarding the "uncatchable" pass. Every so often an official will drop a flag for pass interference, but then he will pick up the flag. No penalty. He considers the pass to be uncatchable. Sometimes that's true, but not every time. Back when I was coaching, my argument was that you never knew how much closer to the ball the receiver would have been if he hadn't been fouled. I don't know if every official appreciates the speed of some pass receivers.

Remember that pass play I talked about? The one we used to run when the Raiders were on the 20-yard line going in—what we called a Quick Up, a pass to the orange pylon in either far corner of the end zone?

In timing that pass, when Cliff Branch crossed the 10-yard line, Kenny Stabler would throw for the corner pylon. In the time it took for the ball to go 37 yards (from the 27-yard line where Kenny set up to the back of the end zone that's 10 yards deep), Cliff could run 20 yards. With that in mind, if a pass receiver is fouled and the ball winds up even 10 yards beyond him, I defy an official to prove that the ball was uncatchable.

No matter what the rules, the better the cornerback, the better he will cover a receiver. But the better the pass rush, the better any cornerback will cover.

Put a quarterback out there throwing passes in a drill in his underwear, with no pads and no linemen blocking for him. If he waits long enough, a receiver eventually will get open. But in a game, with that pass rush in his face, if a quarterback has to hurry or has his vision disrupted, it's different. In a game, a quarterback has only a few seconds to find an open receiver and get the ball to him.

In those few seconds, a cornerback's heart stops and starts again. Of the current cornerbacks, Everson Walls of the Cowboys seems to get the most headlines. He's an All-Pro, the only player ever to lead the NFL in interceptions his first two years. As a rookie free agent out of Grambling, he had 11 interceptions.

No question Everson Walls is good, but I've got a theory as to why he's had so many interceptions. My theory stands 6 foot 9 and weighs 275 pounds. My theory's name is Ed "Too Tall" Jones, the Cowboys' defensive end who plays on the same side Everson does. Too Tall is not the NFL's best pass rusher, but he is the best pass rusher I've ever seen at batting down passes and forcing a quarterback to alter the trajectory of his pass. Other pass rushers get their hands up, but the ball zips past them. Too Tall has a knack for getting a hand on the ball. He's so good at it, quarterbacks alter their passes to make sure he doesn't bat it down.

When Too Tall jumps, his hands are up there close to ten feet high, maybe higher. When a quarterback sees that, he usually tries to throw the ball higher than he should. On a short pass, he might even try to throw it lower and harder than he should, hoping to zip it underneath Too Tall's arms.

Whatever the quarterback does, anytime he tries to throw it over, under, or around Too Tall Jones, that pass is not where it normally is, not where the wide receiver is expecting it to be. And back there Everson Walls is waiting to pounce on that pass. No other pass rusher affects the passing lanes the way Too Tall does, and no other cornerback benefits the way Everson Walls does.

With the rules now permitting only one bump in the 5-yard area beyond the line of scrimmage, a cornerback needs all the help he can get. Before that rule change, a cornerback could be more physical. In a game at Oakland once, Mel Blount of the Steelers threw Cliff Branch on his back. No flag.

"Hey, what was that?" I yelled at the officials. "What's Blount doing?"

The officials hadn't seen it. The play had been on the other side of the field from where Cliff went down. Not that Mel intimidated Cliff by throwing him down. I don't think a real pro is ever intimidated. If he were, he wouldn't last. But yes, Cliff was surprised and pissed off. And determined to catch a few passes against Mel. But that was never easy. Mel was 6 foot 3 and 200, taller and stronger than most cornerbacks. He also had what all good defensive players have, no matter what the position: long arms.

Defensive linemen use their arms to push and pull blockers, to turn and jerk them. If a defensive lineman has short arms, he has to get too close to that blocker. He needs long arms to keep from blocking himself. And a defensive back needs long arms to reach over or around that receiver and knock the pass away.

Emmitt Thomas had long arms. He also had a long memory. In his thirteen seasons with the Chiefs, we fooled him once. And that was by accident. One day before we were to play the Chiefs in Oakland, we were practicing our goal-line offense. On one play, Cliff Branch lined up as our wide receiver to the left, then he went in motion behind our offensive line. Just as he got behind where the quarterback was, I noticed two of our linemen were spaced too far apart for a goal-line play.

"Hold it, hold it," I yelled.

As soon as Cliff heard me, he stopped, turned, and trotted back toward where he had lined up originally. But the cornerback covering him—I think it was Willie Brown—kept trying to weave his way through the defense. In covering a wide receiver in motion, a cornerback has to take his eyes off the wide receiver in order to get past the linebackers. That's what Willie was doing. As soon as I saw Willie keep going, I forgot about the spacing of the linemen.

"Hey, let's put that in," I said. "Cliff, you come in motion as far as the quarterback, then go back. Maybe you'll be open."

Sure enough, in a goal-line situation against the Chiefs, we used that play. Cliff came in motion as far as the quarterback, then turned while Emmitt Thomas did exactly what Willie Brown had done. Emmitt took his eyes off Cliff to get past the linebackers. Emmitt never saw Cliff run into the end zone all alone. Touchdown. Not long ago I was talking to Emmitt, now on the Redskins' staff, about coverages. Suddenly he laughed.

"You got me on a motion play once," he said. "On the goal line in Oakland, you sent Cliff Branch in motion. I remember that."

The Best I've Ever Seen

Cornerbacks	Mel Blount
	Willie Brown
	Mike Haynes
	Jim Johnson
	Emmitt Thomas
	Roger Wehrli
Free Safeties	Johnny Robinson
	Jake Scott
	Donnie Shell
	Jack Tatum
Strong Safeties	Dick Anderson
	Ken Houston

I remember Emmitt Thomas, too. Like all the best cornerbacks, Emmitt had the footwork of a tap dancer. In lining up against a wide receiver, a cornerback should have one foot up ahead of the other. His up foot should be on the side where he doesn't want the receiver to go. In other words, if a cornerback has help to the inside from a linebacker, his outside foot is up, hoping to force the receiver inside. If he has no help, his inside foot is up, hoping to force the receiver outside where he can use the sideline as help. No matter what, a cornerback never lines up with his feet square to the receiver. That way, the receiver can go either way on him.

It's not legal anymore, but Pat Fischer, who played for the Redskins and earlier for the Cardinals, stopped wide receivers by moving up and "axing" them—chopping them at the knees with a rolling body block. *Whap,* the receiver would go down like a tree. When the quarterback looked over, nobody was there. Pat was smart. When he axed a receiver, he usually had some help behind him in case he missed.

In man-to-man coverage, maybe 95 percent of all cornerbacks have a weakness, something you can get them on. Some are good on the outside, not so good on the inside. Some are good on the inside, not so good on the outside. Some are good short, not so good deep. Some are good deep, not so good short. Some are good on the post, not so good on the deep corner. In his time, Lem Barney of the Lions was All-Pro, but he was so aggressive in covering a post, if your wide receiver could really sell him on a post, you'd get him. At least the Raiders did. Twice.

During the 1970 season we were playing the Lions in Detroit on Thanksgiving Day in Tiger Stadium. Early in the game Fred Biletnikoff faked a post and Lem went for it, then Fred cut to the corner for a 23-yard touchdown. We did it again, *boom,* a 21-yard touchdown.

Maybe that was just an accident. When we tried it again, Lem didn't bite as hard. We never got another touchdown and we lost, 28–14. After that, we didn't play the Lions enough to know if Lem always bit on the post. Probably not. He had a reputation as one of the best cornerbacks, and you could never get anything on the best ones like Mike Haynes now, like Willie Brown, Mel Blount, Emmitt Thomas, and Roger Wehrli then. Al Davis was always trying to make a deal with the Cardinals to get Roger, but the NFL isn't like baseball. Very few trades are made in the NFL, especially for a player of Roger's caliber. As much as Al wanted him, Al never got him.

No matter how good a cornerback is, he's going to get beat once in a while. But when he does, he can still create an incompletion if he knows how to do what Ken Riley of the Bengals did as well as anybody else: hit the receiver just as he catches the ball, usually in the back, which is legal.

Ken's nickname was Rattlesnake, and he could put the bite on your pass offense. In his fifteen seasons, he had 65 interceptions, the fourth-highest total in NFL history and the second highest to Dick "Night Train" Lane's 68 among cornerbacks. Night Train was so good, Vince Lombardi ordered Bart Starr not to throw in his area. When the Raiders played the 49ers, we never threw in Jim Johnson's area. And when we played the Bengals, we never threw in Ken Riley's area. In that quick body, Ken also had a quick brain. As soon as Forrest Gregg took over the Packers after four seasons as the Bengals' coach, he hired Ken as his defensive backfield coach. Ken now is head coach at Florida A & M.

During Ken's first season with the Packers, his defensive backs had 22 interceptions, almost double the 12 they'd had the year before. No telling how many completions they spoiled if they learned how to hit that receiver the way Ken did.

I don't know where the 49ers' two All-Pro cornerbacks got that knack of timing a hit—maybe from Bill Walsh, who was the Bengals' quarterback and receivers coach when Ken Riley was there—but Ronnie Lott and Eric Wright know how to break up a pass that way. Ronnie Lott is an unusual corner. He likes the action, the contact. On a sweep to his side, he'll try to bust up the blocking and nail the ballcarrier. On a sweep, some cornerbacks just flutter their fingers, like they're playing an invisible piano, but Ronnie moves up like he means it, like a tough free safety does. Sometimes that toughness can get a free safety out of position. His toughness takes him exactly where the opposing team wants him to go: up near the line of scrimmage for what he thinks will be a run instead of staying back in his pass coverage.

On defense, a free safety is just that: free to roam within the confines of the pass coverage. I've always thought that a free safety should be a free spirit.

Jake Scott of the Dolphins was one of the best free safeties and one of the best free spirits. I've known players who like to think they're free spirits, but they're all talk. Jake was a true free spirit. I got to know Jake at the Pro Bowl when he was on my AFC teams. He was always the first one up. If breakfast was at eight, he was there at seven, helping the waitress make coffee or reading the newspapers. One morning he told me how in the off-season he lived up on a mountain in Colorado, just him and his dog and his snowmobile.

"What do you do up there," I asked.

"I ski," he said. "I go fishing."

"Don't you ever come down?"

"Just once in a while to get some food," he said, "then I go back up there."

"So you just stay up there?"

"Yeah, I just stay up there."

I could never understand that, but hey, Jake probably never understood me. Jake was what a free safety has to be: a little reckless. But he was never *too* reckless. As much as Jake liked to come up and make the tackle on a run, he wouldn't bite at a fake run. Even the best free safeties usually bite, especially during their first few seasons. Jack Tatum, my free safety on the Raiders, went for everything. Jack also liked to use the safety blitz, the play Larry Wilson of the Cardinals invented.

In the early sixties, only the linebackers blitzed a quarterback. Nobody ever thought of using a free safety. That would subtract a defensive back from the pass coverage.

But then Larry Wilson developed the safety blitz. He lined up in his usual position, a few yards off the line of scrimmage. He timed his blitz so that a split second after the snap, he would be shooting the gap between, say, the left guard and the left tackle. If he timed it just right, he was on top of that quarterback within a step or two. But if he timed it wrong, a blocking back might toss him up like a piece of popcorn. More often than not, he timed it right. At 6 feet and 190, he wasn't that big, but he had the soul of a linebacker.

"And," he once joked, "the mentality of a mule."

Not really; a free safety has to be a smart player, like Larry Wilson was, like Johnny Robinson of the Chiefs was. As the Raiders' coach, I was always looking for the home run, the long touchdown pass. Preferably on a post pattern behind football's center fielder, the free safety. But on a post, you've got to do something to draw the free safety out of position. If he blitzes, great, as long as one of your blocking backs picks up the blitz. But a free safety doesn't blitz that much. So you try to fool him into moving toward either sideline. Some free safeties will fall for that, but Johnny Robinson never did. He always stayed back there in the middle of the field, as deep as the deepest receiver.

With a good free safety, deep pass coverage is very simple. From sideline to sideline, a football field is 160 feet across, just a little more than 53 yards. If a free safety is in the middle of the field, he has about 26 yards to either side.

All pass defenses are based on the free safety being in the middle of the field—that's why he's known as football's center fielder. In the time it takes a deep pass to get there, he should be able to get to either sideline. But once the opposing team gets down to his 30-yard line or inside it, he no longer has enough time on a pass to get from the middle of the field to either sideline.

On the Raiders we never used a zone defense inside the 30 because the safety couldn't react in time. But that never stopped Don Shula from keeping the Dolphins in a zone down there. Several other teams also keep their zone at all times.

The strong safety has a different responsibility from the free safety. He's called the strong safety because he lines up across from the offensive team's strong side, the side with the tight end. His responsibility in pass coverage is usually covering the tight end. More and more, the strong safety should be almost as fast as a cornerback. Not that the tight ends are getting faster. But the strong safety often has to cover a third wide receiver. If your strong safety can't run, that's a mismatch a coach worries about—a fast wide receiver getting away from your slower strong safety. When the Raiders' strong safety was George Atkinson, I never worried. George wasn't that sturdy at 165 pounds on a 6-foot frame, but he more than made up for it with his speed, quickness, and toughness. Especially his speed. George could run with any wide receiver. Another strong safety who could really run was Ken Houston, the Hall of Famer who started out with the Oilers and was traded to the Redskins for five players.

Ken holds the NFL record for touchdowns on interception returns—nine, including four in 1971 with the Oilers. Not only could he run, but he could run away from everybody else on the field.

Kenny Easley of the Seahawks is supposed to be the best strong safety now, All-Pro four consecutive seasons. But in my CBS travels, I hardly ever see him. One safety I do see is Gary Fencik of the Bears, a real hitter. He's now their free safety but for years he was their strong safety alongside Doug Plank, another real hitter who once had me wild. In a game at Soldier Field in Chicago, one of my Raider running backs, Mark van Eeghen, was out of bounds when Plank speared him, dove at him helmet first. Van Eeghen wobbled to his feet but never said a word. He didn't want to give Plank the satisfaction. But it had happened right in front of me, and I almost hyperventilated.

I yelled at Plank, he yelled back. So did Fencik, sticking up for his teammate.

I didn't particularly like either one then. I never got to know Doug Plank, but in recent years I've gotten to know Fencik, a bright guy from Yale with the face of an altar boy. He's been with the Bears ten years now, and when I asked him during the

1985 season how long he planned to continue playing, he laughed.

"I'll play," he said, "until Buddy Ryan tells me I can't play anymore and that will be the end of it."

When the Bears were rolling to an 11–0 start in the 1985 season, Gary asked his defensive coordinator for a midterm grade.

"Buddy gave me a pretty good grade," Gary said, "so I knew I'd be around for the rest of the season."

Until the Eagles hired Buddy Ryan in 1986 as their head coach, Gary wasn't joking about Buddy telling him how long he would be playing. Not long after Terry Schmidt completed his eleventh season as a Bear cornerback, he was walking by Buddy's office.

"Hey, Schmidtty," yelled Buddy, "what are you going to do now that you've retired?"

That's how Terry found out that the 1984 season had been his last.

When Gary Fencik isn't playing football anymore, he'll still be a success. He has his Yale degree, plus a master's in management from Northwestern, which he earned between seasons. Donnie Shell of the Steelers is also like that. Donnie has a master's degree in guidance and counseling. As a young strong safety, he already had a master's in toughness. When the Steelers played the Raiders early in his career, he always ran by George Blanda in the pregame warmup.

"You can't kick anymore, old man," he would snap at George. "You shouldn't be playing."

At the time, George, who kicked until he was 49 years old, was the grand old man of the NFL, even older than his coach. Everybody loved George. More important, everybody respected George, everybody but Donnie. He developed into an All-Pro strong safety, a successor to Dick Anderson of the Dolphins, who was maybe the smartest strong safety of all. In a game plan, you're always trying to create a mismatch, to exploit a strong safety's lack of speed by forcing him to cover a fast wide receiver. But no matter how fast our wide receiver was, Dick Anderson made up for his lack of speed with knowledge and experience. He was never out of position.

Dick not only knew where his help was, but he knew how to force a receiver into the area where his help was waiting.

As a pass receiver comes out, the strong safety never wants to play him straight up or square. The strong safety should stay to one side, angling the receiver toward the area where the free safety will be able to help in the coverage. If the receiver goes the other way, into the strong safety's area, then he's not open. Dick Anderson could always make the receiver go where he wanted the receiver to go.

If there's a first commandment for defensive backs, that would be it: Make the receiver go where you want him to go.

Controlled Fanatics

WHEN I TOOK OVER AS THE Raiders' head coach, I wanted to make our special teams as important as everybody in football was saying they were. Our special teams had meetings every day, they practiced every day. But in my enthusiasm, I got a little carried away.

"Special teams," I told my players, "breed fanaticism. You've got to be a fanatic. Don't worry about the horse being blind, just load the wagon."

I liked the word *fanaticism*. So did the players, especially those with that wild look in their eye, the kind you need running around out there on kickoffs, punts, and placekicks. The trouble was, they took me at my word, especially on kickoffs. In trying to prove their fanaticism, some guys were flinging their bodies into the wedge with reckless abandon. But they were forgetting to tackle the other team's kickoff returner, who was running by all those fanatics out to the 35 or the 40, sometimes to midfield. To make it worse, we were getting too many penalties for clipping—throwing your body across the back of an opponent's leg or hitting him below the waist from behind.

We got so many clipping penalties, I told my players, "If you can read the guy's name on the back of his jersey, don't hit him." But in their frenzy, I wondered if they could *read* those names. "If you can *see* the guy's name," I said later, "don't hit him."

That didn't help much either. I finally had to tell my players, "Special teams breed *controlled* fanaticism." I still wanted them to run down under that kickoff as hard as ever, but then they had to get themselves under control and try to make the tackle. After that they kept their fanaticism in perspective. They created an award among themselves, the Fanatic of the Week, that was presented each Tuesday after we watched films of our previous game. It wasn't much of an award, sometimes an old piece of wood with tape wrapped around it. On the tape was written "Fanatic of the Week" with the date. But the players cherished it. The week George Buehler won it, he hurried to the phone in the locker room and called his father, a doctor.

"Hey, Dad," he announced, "I'm the Fanatic of the Week."

I doubt if his father was as thrilled as George was. But that award helped my players appreciate how important the special teams are. If we tackled a kickoff returner inside the 20-yard line, that was like our defense throwing the other team for a loss. If our kickoff returner ran the ball out near midfield, that was like our offense getting two first downs. The same philosophy applied to punting situations. Even more important were field goals and extra points. By making them, they were points on the scoreboard for us. And if we could block a field goal or an extra point, those were points we were taking off the scoreboard for the other team.

That's why I always had all our offensive and defensive players who weren't on the special teams watching the films of the special teams—to remind them that the special teams were just as much a part of our offense and defense as they were.

You need a few controlled fanatics on special teams, but you also need some solid citizens. Warren Bankston was a solid citizen. One of my most treasured Raider pictures shows me after Super Bowl XI with our three captains: Gene Upshaw, our offensive captain; Willie Brown, our defensive captain; and Warren Bankston, our special-teams captain. On our kickoff-coverage team, Warren lined up third from the left. On both our punt-coverage team and our punt-return team, he lined up at tackle. On our kickoff-return team, he lined up on the outside of our first wave of blockers. On placekicks, he lined up as wing blocker.

"I don't know who our first forty-three guys will be," I used to say at training camp in those years, "but Warren is our forty-fourth."

Then there are the placekickers themselves, definitely a different breed, especially those who don't do anything but kick. I was lucky. For most of my Raider years, my kicker was George Blanda, who was also my backup quarterback. George was a football player, not just a kicker who stands around during practice while all the other players bust their butts. It takes a special type of guy to be just a kicker, someone the other players still like and respect even when he's standing around, tossing a football in the air, waiting for the full workout to be over so he can practice his kicking.

The easiest way to be liked and respected, of course, is to win games with last-minute field goals, as all the good ones do. But even the good ones are a little goofy. When it gets cold in the northern cities late in the season, I've seen kickers wearing gloves. Hey, wide receivers, defensive backs, linemen, even running backs and quarterbacks I can understand. But kickers wearing gloves, that's goofy. Maybe that's why they're kickers.

Ray Wersching, the 49ers' kicker, doesn't even look at the goalposts when he lines up for a field goal. Kickers are supposed to keep their head down, just like golfers are. Ray *really* keeps his head down. When he trots in from the sideline, he has his head down. In the huddle, he has his head down. When the huddle breaks, he has his head down, looking at where his holder, Joe Montana, will spot the ball. Then he keeps his head down to line himself up with the hash marks. After the snap and the hold, he keeps his head down on his follow-through. And he keeps his head down until Joe tells him he's made it. Or missed it.

"But how do you aim," I once asked him, "if you don't look at the goalposts?"

"I just look at the hash marks," he said. "They tell me all I have to know."

I'd never thought of it that way, but Ray's right. If you check the hash marks, those chalked lines about 23 yards inside each sideline, you'll notice that they are 18½ feet apart, the same width as the goalposts. In a sense, the goalposts come up out of the hash marks.

"The farther away you are, the narrower the goalposts look," Ray told me. "But the hash marks always look wide."

I wish I had thought of that when I was coaching. But with George Blanda around, I didn't have to. I just let George do it. Over his career with the Raiders, Oilers, and Bears, he did it better than anybody. He holds the NFL career scoring record with 2,002 points that include 335 field goals and 943 extra points. He kicked until he was 49; then we signed Errol Mann, the kicker on our Super Bowl XI championship team. The next year we thought we had drafted a great young kicker, and we had, but we outsmarted ourselves. We thought we could get him through waivers on the last cut in 1978, but the Chargers claimed him. Rolf Benirschke is still their kicker.

Not only that, Rolf still thinks I hate kickers. We laughed about that when I attended a "roast" in San Diego for him.

Rolf remembered how I put him in "pressure" situations at training camp. That was the only way I could find out if a rookie kicker could stand up to pressure. Lots of guys can kick in their underwear in practice, but the only way you can learn how they'll respond under pressure is how they kick when people are watching them with something at stake. So you have to create the pressure of having something at stake. After practice,

I had all my players run what we called "strides," the length of the football field and back. Up and back, sometimes a dozen times or more. All the players hated those strides, especially in the summer heat.

When the kickers were practicing, I kept all the other players around to create pressure—and then I added to the pressure.

"All right," I'd say, as the field-goal unit lined up, "fifty-two yards, no time left, we're down by two points, we need this kick to win." I'd look around and say, "Benirschke, you kick." And then I would add my own kicker.

"If he makes it," I'd say, "no strides today."

Now all the other players were involved, which really put pressure on the rookie. Rolf is 6 foot 1; he's 180 now, but I remember him as a skinny little kid peering out of his facemask at all the big, burly Raiders staring at him with the strides at stake.

"I was scared to death," he told me at the roast. "I could hear those big guys growling, 'You better make it.' "

Rolf made most of them. The players loved him. Thanks to him, they didn't have to run strides every day. We thought we had found a jewel of a twelfth-round draft choice. But then we made the mistake of thinking we could slip that jewel through waivers. If the Chargers hadn't claimed Rolf, he probably would've been our kicker that season. After all those years of having old-fashioned straight-ahead kickers like George Blanda and Errol Mann, I was ready to accept a sidewinder, a soccer-style kicker.

As a traditionalist, I still prefer the straight-ahead kicker, just as I prefer grass to artificial turf, and the elements to a dome. On grass, especially in rain or snow, a straight-ahead kicker will always be better. When he plants his left foot, his cleats dig firmly into grass as his right foot comes straight ahead. But a sidewinder plants his left foot at an angle as he approaches the ball. He's much more likely to slip, especially on artificial turf. Even more so on wet or loose grass. One year in Oakland against the Steelers, our baseball infield had just been sodded.

Roy Gerela went out to kick a field goal. When he took a few practice steps, chunks of sod flew up like golf divots. He kept replacing those chunks of sod, but when he lined up to kick, he had to be worrying about slipping on his plant foot.

"No way he'll make it," I said on the sideline.

Sure enough, he missed. Another thing about sidewinders is that they usually don't get the ball up high as quickly as the straight-ahead kickers do. That's what impressed me about Ali Haji-Sheikh of the Giants in 1983, when he was All-Pro as rookie. He not only kicked the ball up and through, but he got it up high quickly, above the reaching arms of the opposing linemen who were hoping to deflect it. You've got to say this for the sidewinders: They can boom the ball. I realized that the first time I saw a sidewinder. Back in 1966, I was an assistant coach at San Diego State. We were about to play Montana State in the Camellia Bowl at Sacramento and I was out on the field for the warmup. I kept hearing this strange new sound—*thoom*. Half thud, half boom. I looked over at a slim blond kicker.

"Who is that guy?" I asked.

"Jan Stenerud," I was told.

I couldn't believe the power he had in his leg. He had come to Montana State as a skier from Norway, and his right leg was a cannon. That was the first time I was ever aware of a kicker as a weapon. He joined the Chiefs in 1967, the same year I joined the Raiders as an assistant coach, so I saw a lot more of Jan Stenerud after that, sometimes more than I wanted to. Over his nineteen seasons with the Chiefs, the Packers, and the Vikings, he kicked 373 field goals, the most in NFL history. As much as anybody else, Jan has helped set the standard for kickers.

"When I came in," he once told me at a Packer workout, "there weren't many good kickers. But now *every* team has a good kicker."

At the time, Jan was worried about being cut. Not long after that the Packers did cut him, but he joined the Vikings and kicked for two more seasons. In the beginning, all the sidewinders had a foreign soccer background. Peter Gogolak joined the Bills in 1964 out of Cornell, but he had learned to kick a soccer ball in Hungary as a youngster. His family immigrated to Ogdensburg, New York, up near the St. Lawrence River, where he began kicking soccer-style as a high school junior. After two seasons with the Bills, he signed with the Giants in 1966, the same year his younger brother Charley joined the Redskins as their kicker.

One of the best was Garo Yepremian, a left-footed sidewinder from Cyprus who was originally signed by the Lions before he turned into an All-Pro with the Dolphins.

At the Pro Bowl one year, Garo taught my son Mike how to placekick. I always felt I neglected my two boys during the season when I was coaching the Raiders, so whenever I coached the AFC team in the Pro Bowl, I took Mike and Joe along. They loved going to practice, shagging balls. Mike does everything right-handed, but Garo showed him how to kick left-footed, so Mike learned to kick with his left foot.

No matter how good a kicker is, he's no better than his holder and his snapper. It takes all three.

The holder needs sure, quick hands. He's got to be able to catch the snap without bobbling it, then get the ball down quickly, spotting it with the index finger of his rear hand while getting his front hand out of the kicker's way. Some coaches like to use their starting quarterbacks as the holder, but I never did. I always figured that if we had to kick a field goal, my quarterback would be upset at not getting a touchdown or a first down. I wanted my holder to be concentrating completely on being a holder, not to be thinking about a pass that misfired on third down.

I preferred to use my backup quarterbacks as holders. Ken Stabler when he was young, David Humm later on. One reason was that a kicker likes to be around his holder on the sideline. If his holder is in the game, as the starting quarterback is, the kicker can't stand around with him. To a kicker, his holder is a security blanket. So is his snapper.

The snapper, the center who snaps the ball back, is even more important than the holder. With a good snapper, the ball will come into the holder's hands with the laces facing the goalposts. That way it's easier for the holder to spot the ball with the laces away from the side struck by the kicker's foot. You never want the kicker to kick the laces. When that happens, it's easier for the ball to skid off line or to go low. Every good snapper knows where to position the laces in his grip so that the rotation will bring the ball into the holder's hands with the laces away from the kicker.

With a good snapper, it's simply a matter of spiraling the ball at the same speed to create the same number of revolutions over the same distance—7 yards for a placekicker, 15 yards for a punter.

As a coach, I'd ask my holder or my punter every so often where the laces were on the snap. If he told me the laces were down, I'd yell, "Hey, get those laces up." Sure enough, the next snap the laces would be up. The snap is mostly wrist. It's like throwing a pass between your legs. Some snappers look back between their legs just before they snap, others look the whole time. It's an art that coaches appreciate.

In the NFL, some snappers hang around for two or three extra seasons just because they are dependable snappers.

I've heard coaches talking at training camp about which players should be cut from the roster. One will say, "We ought to cut Smith," but another will say, "Hey, we can't cut Smith, he's our snapper." Until that team gets another dependable snapper, Smith stays. In my ten seasons as the Raiders' coach, I was lucky. I had two snappers, Jim Otto and Dave Dalby, two of the best. Even before Dave succeeded Jim as our center, he was the best snapper I'd ever seen. If he had never played a down on offense, he was worth a fourth-round draft choice.

Some people don't seem to understand how important a good snapper is. That's because most snappers are so good, they get taken for granted. But as a coach, I'll guarantee you, when it's fourth down and you need a good snap on a field goal or a punt, it's important to know that the snap isn't going to sail over the head of the kicker or the punter.

Waiting for the snap, the biggest prerequisite for a punter is his hands, not his leg. When he's standing back there, the first thing a punter has to do is catch the ball. To do that consistently, he needs good hands. The hands of a good baseball or basketball player. That's the difference between placekickers and punters. Guys who never really played football or guys from other countries can be placekickers. But you'll never see a punter who isn't an American athlete. He has to catch that snap. If he gets a bad snap, he has to make a quick move to avoid a tackler and still get the punt off. And if the punt returner gets by everybody else, he has to make the tackle.

It all starts with his hands. With the Raiders one year, Jerry DePoyster drove me crazy. He seldom caught the snap cleanly. He would bobble it, or it would bounce off his chest. Every punt got to be an adventure. The next year we used our first-round choice to draft Ray Guy, the best punter I've ever seen. He had a great leg. He punted the ball high and far—great hang time, as coaches say. But just as important to me, he had great hands.

Ray always wanted to be our placekicker for field goals and extra points. I used him on kickoffs because that was all power. But to me, your punter shouldn't be your placekicker. When you punt, your toes are down, which means you shorten your Achilles tendon. When you placekick, it's the opposite. Your toes are up, which means you lengthen your Achilles tendon. If Ray had done both, sooner or later he had to mess up his leg. I think he would've been an average punter and an average placekicker. To me, Ray was more valuable as the NFL's best punter. Maybe the best in NFL history.

When the Pro Football Hall of Fame selectors chose an All-Pro team of those who played from 1960 to 1984, Ray got the most first-team votes, twenty-three—one more than Jim Brown and Dick Butkus, seven more than Johnny Unitas and Gino Marchetti.

As good as Ray was, I always got letters from fans on why I

didn't order him to punt to the coffin corner, meaning down inside the 5-yard line near the sideline where the ball might bounce out of bounds. To do that, a punter has to aim the ball at that coffin corner. When a punter shanks the ball 10 or 15 yards off the side of his foot, it's usually because he's aiming the ball. When you have to do something that takes a full range of motion, you can't aim, no matter what it is—a baseball pitcher throwing a fastball, a golfer hitting his tee shot.

Believe me, if a punter tries for the coffin corner, he may bounce it out of bounds inside the 5 every once in a while. But more often than not, he's going to shank it. And when he shanks it, your team is really in trouble.

My theory was: Just punt the ball as high and as far as possible. Ray was good at dropping the ball in around the 5-yard line between the hash marks, then letting our coverage guys run in to down it. They loved that. But no coffin-corner punts. I didn't want the coverage guys saying, "Hey, Ray, kick it out of bounds." I put the onus on them to get down there and make the tackle on the 2.

If you've really got a fast coverage guy, he can catch his own team's punt. It doesn't happen very often, but it's a legal play.

On punt coverage, the only two guys who can run down at the snap are those on the outside, one on the right, the other on the left. Everybody else has to wait until they hear the thud of the punt itself. On a punt that figures to land near the other goal line, the opposing team will usually put its punt returner on the 10-yard line. If the ball comes down in front of him, he's supposed to catch it and try to run it. If the ball is over his head, he's supposed to let it go.

When the punt returner lets it go, he usually runs away from where the ball is going to land. When that happens, if your outside coverage guy is down there in time, he's permitted to down the ball by catching it.

We practiced this play on the Raiders hoping we could make it work in a game. In my early years as coach, Warren Wells was our best outside guy on the punt-coverage team. Later on, we used Morris Bradshaw, a wide receiver from Ohio State, and Charley Phillips, a defensive back from Southern Cal, as outside guys. Each could run as far as Ray Guy could punt. All that practice finally paid off. Morris and Charley each caught a couple of Ray's punts inside the 10-yard line, to the surprise of everybody but their teammates.

Not many people are aware of another rule: If you fair-catch a punt, you're entitled on your first play to a free kick, meaning a placekick or a punt.

Normally, if you fair-catch a punt, you would try to move down the field and score. But in the final seconds of the first half, if you were to fair-catch a punt within the range of your field-goal kicker, a free kick would be good strategy. In my ten years as the Raiders' coach, I tried to set up a free kick maybe fifty times. But after the fair-catch by my punt returner, we were never close enough to try for a field goal.

Punt returners are like punters. They've got to catch the ball before they do anything else. The worst thing for a coach is to have a punt returner back there who has trouble catching the ball. If he doesn't catch it cleanly, it doesn't make much difference how darting a runner he is.

Unless our punt returner was standing on our 10-yard line and let a punt sail over his head, I always wanted every punt to be caught. The worst thing a punt returner can do is let a punt bounce in front of him, then watch that ball bounce behind him. Or have that ball hit his leg or a teammate's leg, and have the opposing team recover it.

George Atkinson was the best punt returner I ever had. George had good hands and he was fearless. Neil Colzie and Rod Sherman also had good hands.

When a punt is up there in the sky, a good punt returner can tell from the height of the ball how soon the opposing team's punt-coverage tacklers will be all over him. If the ball is up there a long time, say a 4.4-second hang time on a 42-yard punt, he knows he's got to fair-catch it. And a good punt returner will know that almost as soon as the ball comes off the punter's foot.

Just like a good outfielder in baseball will see a fly ball when it comes off the bat, a good punt returner will see a punt come off the punter's foot. But if he sees that it's not too high or isn't taking off, he knows it's a returnable ball.

As a rule of thumb, any punt that has a hang time under 4.4 seconds is a returnable ball, which means a good punt returner has to have a stopwatch in his head.

On a punt return, you don't expect much yardage. If your punt returner gets anywhere from 5 to 10 yards, he's doing his job. Anything more than that is gravy. When the other team is punting, your defense has done its job—it has stopped the other team's offense. Now your team is getting the ball. When that punt spins down out of the sky, you want your punt returner to catch the ball cleanly out in front of him with his hands and then bring it into his body. You don't want him to catch the ball against his body. If he does that, the ball might bounce off his shoulder pads.

Another no-no for a punt returner is running sideways. When the Raiders drafted Cliff Branch, he was projected as a punt returner, but he had two faults: He didn't catch the ball cleanly, and he ran sideways too often.

With his speed, Cliff had run sideways in college and high school, then scooted past tacklers. But in the NFL, those guys thundering down to tackle the punt returner are as good at tackling him as he is at getting away from them. I just wanted my punt returner to catch the ball, go straight up the field, and get behind his blockers.

Billy "White Shoes" Johnson of the Oilers and the Falcons had everything a good punt returner needs: good hands and real quick moves. Any time he was back there waiting for your punt, he was a threat to go all the way. So was Rick Upchurch of the Broncos.

Your kickoff returner is usually bigger and stronger than a punt returner. He's usually more reckless, too, because it's a more reckless job. Billy Johnson also has been one of the best at that, but there aren't many who can do both. If a guy is a good player on offense or defense, most coaches won't risk him on special teams. With two kickoff returners waiting back there, the one who isn't going to catch the ball has the responsibility to tell the one who is catching it what to do. He should yell, "Stay, stay, stay," meaning stay in the end zone, or "Go, go, go." But he should never yell, "No, no, no," which could sound like "Go, go, go." The one who's yelling should be watching the ball and the other team's kickoff-coverage team. If the ball is high and the coverage is within 20 yards when your returner catches the kickoff, he definitely should stay in the end zone. But if it's a line-drive kickoff, you run it out.

I always preferred to use one of my older Raiders to yell, like Charley Smith or Pete Banaszak, especially if our best returner was a little flighty. I wanted a solid guy back there with him.

According to our film breakdown, if a kickoff returner brought the ball out from the front half of the end zone, he would get to the 20-yard line. But if he tried to run it back from beyond halfway into the end zone, he usually never got it past the 12-yard line. Wherever he starts, the returner runs up behind the wedge—meaning the four players who line up on the 20-yard line, drift back while the ball is in the air, form a wedge in front of the returner, then start running upfield as he starts running. The good kickoff returner shoots up the middle into his wedge of blockers in his first 10 or 15 yards, then he goes right or left or straight. You don't want your returner to go right or left before he gets to his wedge. If he does, there's no wedge for him to run behind.

On the Raiders' wedge, I had three big linemen types along with my "captain of the wedge." The captain was usually a fullback who could run with a short kickoff—Pete Banaszak at first, Mark van Eeghen later on. Of the four, the captain was the only guy on the wedge who was allowed to handle the ball. I didn't want those linemen types handling the ball. Chances are they would fumble. That might seem a little harsh, but the Cowboys might have won Super Bowl XIII if they hadn't had Randy White in the wedge with a cast on one hand. At the time, the Steelers had gone ahead, 28–17, midway in the fourth quarter. On the short kickoff, Randy couldn't hold the ball properly.

Dirt Winston, a Steeler linebacker, pounced on it at the 18, then Terry Bradshaw hit Lynn Swann for a touchdown.

The Steelers won, 35–31, holding off a Cowboy rally. Jackie Smith, a tight end the Cowboys had picked up from the Cardinals, got the blame for the loss. He dropped a touchdown pass in the end zone that would have moved the Cowboys into a 21–21 tie in the third quarter. To this day, Jackie Smith has had to live with the blame for that Super Bowl loss, but I've always thought Randy White shouldn't have been out there in a ball-handling position.

Don't confuse a short kickoff with what is known as an onside kickoff. Usually a short kickoff doesn't go as far as it's intended to, but it still gets down around the 20-yard line. But an onside kickoff is squibbed deliberately, usually late in the game, so that the ball can be recovered by the kicking team after it has traveled 10 yards or been touched by the receiving team. Your onside-kickoff-return team is different from your regular kickoff-return team. Usually you put several wide receivers and defensive backs out there, the "good hands people." You keep your two kickoff returners back near the goal line as a precaution, but you put nine guys up near midfield. When the kick is squibbed, the guy nearest the ball tries to catch it and the others try to surround him, to protect him.

Since the ball might be squibbed to any of those nine guys, you must remember not to use anybody with an injured hand. And you must have your team set.

My first year as the Raiders' coach, I got stung. I had to assemble an onside-kickoff-return team on the spur of the moment. As it turned out, we recovered the onside kickoff and held on to win the game. But walking off the field, I vowed that mix-up would never happen again. It never did. After that, we lined up our onside team and our onside-return team every week in practice. The players always enjoyed that. Just as the onside-return players are trying to pounce on that squibbed, squirming ball, the onside-kickoff players are trying to recover it.

Your onside-kickoff team is usually the same as your regular kickoff team. Your kicker is in the middle with five coverage guys on each side.

On the Raiders, the coverage guy immediately to the right of the kicker was the R1 man, out to the R5 man on the outside; the coverage guy immediately to the left of the kicker was the L1 man, out to the L5 man on the outside. At the Pro Bowl, it was sometimes hard to fill out some of your special teams. Some players hadn't played at all on special teams, but a few always volunteered. Larry Csonka of the Dolphins and Willie Lanier of the Chiefs always did.

"Just put me on any team," Zonk would tell me.

Now that's a real football player. But most Pro Bowl players are. At one Pro Bowl my special-teams coach, Joe Scanella, needed to fill out the kickoff team, especially at the inside R1 and L1 positions, the guys who were expected to run down and bust the wedge of the NFC's kickoff-return team. Joe finally came up to me.

"I got an R1," he said.

"Who is it?" I asked.

"Greg Pruitt," he said.

"You're kidding me."

"No, he told me he does it on the Browns. He likes it."

"That's a surprise."

Greg Pruitt was a swift but small running back for the Browns, not the type you would expect to enjoy hurling his body in trying to bust a wedge. But at the special-teams meeting, when I called "kickoff team" and then said, "R1," Greg raised his hand. When we got out on the practice field, Joe Scanella called for "R1" and Greg hurried over.

"Right here," Joe said. "Next to the kicker."

"Oh, no," Greg said. "On the Browns, the R1 is the outside man on the right, not the inside man."

"Too late," Joe said.

To his credit, Greg didn't renege. On our first kickoff in that Pro Bowl, as I remember, he hustled down and made the tackle —that's a football player. Maybe that's one reason the Raiders later got him in a trade, using him primarily as a punt returner and kickoff returner. For a coach, when you select your team at the end of training camp, you must have the special teams in mind. Not the kicker and the punter, they're obvious. I'm thinking more of the guys who are going to cover kickoffs and punts, the guys who can run in the open field and not get blocked, also the guys who can block in the open field for your kickoff returner and punt returner.

On defense, remember, the toughest thing to do is tackle in the open field. In covering kickoffs and punts, all the tackling is done in the open field.

To cover, you need tough players who are accustomed to working in the open field, guys who are agile, quick—linebackers, running backs, defensive backs, sometimes even a wide receiver. In my years with the Raiders, our best kickoff coverage guy was Warren Wells, a wide receiver who lined up as our R4 man. In covering a kick, the most important thing is being able to avoid being blocked while staying in your coverage lane. Since a football field is roughly 53 yards wide, the coverage lane for each of the ten guys is roughly 5 yards wide. You can always avoid a block by going out of your lane. But if you do, the other team's returner has a lane to run in.

On a kickoff, the inside R1 and L1 men are responsible for busting the returning team's wedge. But if all a guy is trying to do is bust the wedge, the kickoff returner sometimes can shoot up the middle for a big gain, sometimes for a touchdown.

Ideally, a good inside R1 or L1 comes straight down the middle, stays in his lane, avoids the blocker, gets through the wedge with his hands free, and makes the tackle. Sometimes you send your R2 and L2 down to try and make the tackle. But sometimes you want them to peel off around the 40-yard line and join the kicker in a triangle of safeties—one on the left, the kicker in the middle, the other on the right.

If you have good coverage guys, you can afford that safety triangle, which is the best way to go. But when Ray Guy was my kickoff man, I knew I had a good tackler back there. I could take a chance with one safety more than some teams could.

Before the Bears played the Rams in the 1985 National Conference championship game, they put Willie Gault on the kickoff team as their safety in case Ron Brown of the Rams got loose. During the season, Brown, who was on the United States' gold medal–winning 4×100-meter relay team at the Los Angeles Olympics, had scored three touchdowns on kickoff returns. He was considered the NFL's fastest player. But when Willie Gault was at Tennessee in 1980, he qualified as a sprinter for the U.S. Olympic team that never went to Moscow because of the boycott. He also was a world-class hurdler.

"I hope Willie catches him—after seventy or eighty yards," John Robinson joked. "But the biggest question is, will Willie tackle him? He might race him and beat him across the goal line."

As it turned out, Ron Brown appeared about to break loose along the sideline when Kevin Butler, the Bears' rookie placekicker, nailed him with a cross-body block. No wonder the Bears loved that rookie kicker. But if you use your R2 and L2 man on each side as safeties, the guys who should make most of your tackles are your 1, 3, and 4 men on each side. Your 3 men are just outside the other team's wedge, your 4 men are just outside the 3 men. Meanwhile, the two outside guys, the 5 man on each side, try to make sure the ballcarrier never gets past them along the sideline.

In my years with the Raiders, my special-teams coach, Joe Scanella, always alerted our kickoff-return and punt-return blockers to watch for two coverage guys in particular—Hank Bauer of the Chargers and Jimbo Elrod of the Chiefs.

"I don't think but one thing," Bauer once said. "That I'm going to make the tackle."

When the Chargers went to the 1981 AFC championship game, Bauer had already made more than fifty tackles that season. Elrod was a good tackler, but his specialty was wiping out your wedge of blockers in front of your kickoff returner. He would slide into the wedge and take all four guys down with him.

One day Joe Scanella called me over to watch a film of a Chiefs-Chargers game.

"Look at this," Joe said.

As soon as Elrod slid, the four guys in the Chargers' wedge jumped up in the air like they were in a ballet. Elrod never touched a one. Of all the cover guys in the NFL now, Bill Bates of the Cowboys is the best. He's just a hell-raiser. When he tackles, he sometimes forces a fumble. That's what you want to see, that ball flying out and one of your guys jumping on it. When the Pro Bowl ballots handed out to coaches and players late in the 1984 season finally included a coverage player, Bill made it, along with Fredd Young of the Seahawks.

During the Super Bowl XX playoffs, two forced fumbles on kickoff coverage were the big plays that put the Patriots into the AFC championship game—a 15-yard touchdown run by Johnny Rembert after he stripped the ball from Johnny Hector of the Jets, a recovery in the end zone by Jim Bowman after Sam Seale of the Raiders had fumbled the kickoff.

In studying the films of a kickoff return, I always stopped the projector the moment the kickoff returner got the ball. You could usually determine how many yards he was going to get by how many yards our coverage was away from him. If we were within 5 yards, he wasn't going to get much. If we were within 10 yards, he might get 20 or 25 yards. But if we didn't have somebody within 10 yards, we were in trouble. That's when we needed a great play to stop him from getting out past the 30, maybe from going all the way. To avoid even the slightest runback, coverage men want no runback at all. When you see those coverage guys talking to the kicker in the moments before the kickoff, they're all giving him the same pep talk.

"Kick it out of the end zone," they're saying.

The next best kickoff is a high one. The longer the ball stays in the air, the closer the coverage men can get to the kickoff returner. The worst kickoff is a low one that doesn't give the coverage men much time to get down there. If that kickoff returner can break through that first wave of coverage, you're talking about stopping him with one of your three safeties—sometimes with your only safety, your kicker. That's why I had my kickers work more on tackling than they did on kicking. I didn't expect them to make a devastating tackle, the way a linebacker or defensive back would. I just wanted them to work on their position—angling the kickoff returner toward the side-line, pushing him out of bounds, sometimes just holding on until they got some help. Anything to keep him from going all the way.

Another thing to remember about special teams is your opportunity to block a field goal, an extra point, or a punt. I always had Ted Hendricks on those teams. Just as Too Tall Jones has a knack for blocking passes, Ted had a knack for blocking place-kicks and punts.

The Best I've Ever Seen

Placekickers	George Blanda
	Rafael Septien
	Jan Stenerud
	Garo Yepremian
Punters	Ray Guy
Returners	Billy "White Shoes" Johnson
	Rick Upchurch
Coveragers	Bill Bates
	Hank Bauer
	Jimbo Elrod

There's no NFL record for the most blocks of placekicks and punts, but Ted would probably hold it. He had twenty-five blocks, including two blocked punts that he turned into touch-downs. If anybody knows of a player with more than twenty-five blocks, please tell me.

In rushing a placekicker or a punter, some guys can get their hands up high, but they never touch the ball. Yet wherever Ted came from, if he got close to the ball, *boom,* he would deflect it. Because he was 6 foot 7 with long arms, I usually put Ted in the middle where his height could be used to maximum advantage. Out on the end of the line you're better off with a rusher who's not only fast but also quick off the mark. Of my Raider players, Lester Hayes was the best outside rusher. I always put Lester and another fast rusher on the outside left of our defensive line. I wanted them there so that they would be barreling into the face of a right-footed placekicker, especially a sidewinder. No matter how hard even Ray Wersching refuses to look at the goalposts, he has to be aware of the outside rushers coming at him. Especially the first one in.

"Dive at him," I always told those rushers. "And when you get up, tell the kicker you almost had that one and you'll get the next one."

Keep those kickers and punters thinking. Most of them will turn away like nobody had been even close to blocking the placekick or punt. But believe me, the next time that kicker or punter is out there he's thinking about how close he had come to being blocked. Sooner or later a good outside rusher will block a kick or a punt. It's harder to block a punt, unless the snap is high or low or the punter bobbles the ball. But on a placekick, the outside rusher has a good chance if what is known as the wing blocker misses him.

On your placekick team, there's a wing blocker on each side of the line, usually a fullback. His job is to block two rushers: Stop the inside man and bump the outside man.

If the wing does his job, and if the snapper, holder, and kicker do their jobs, it's impossible for either of the outside rushers to block the kick. With the ball spotted 7 yards behind the line of scrimmage, there just isn't enough time for one of those outside rushers to get to the kick in time. All the wing blocker has to do is slow up each of those outside rushers for a split second. Meanwhile you're hoping that your blockers up on the line are holding their ground. Shoulder to shoulder, foot to foot, they form a wall that shouldn't be penetrated. But if one of those blockers turns a shoulder or drops a foot, he can create a gap that might allow a rusher to penetrate just enough to reach up and block the kick.

When you see a penalty on a placekick, it's usually on the wing blocker. He's reached out to hook or grab one of those outside rushers.

As a coach, I always studied films of the other team's wing blockers. I wanted to learn if he had a tendency to hook or grab in a close game. If our game got to where the other team needed a field goal in the closing minutes, I would tell my special-teams captain to alert the official on that side.

"Watch the wing," my captain would say. "Keep your eye on the wing."

But sometimes the wing has to be watched by your own team because on a fake kick, he's an eligible receiver. The holder is usually somebody who can throw a pass to any of his eligible pass receivers: the two wings and the two tight ends as well as the kicker himself. In 1977, the Broncos lined up for a 35-yard field goal late in the first half at the Oakland Coliseum, with Jim Turner kicking. But at the snap, his holder, Norris Weese, stood up to throw.

"Fake, fake," all our guys were yelling. "Fake, fake."

Jim Turner was a great kicker, but a little thick through the middle, not the type you would expect to run out for a pass on a fake field goal. None of our guys covered him. Jim swung out to the left, took the pass, and scored a 25-yard touchdown that put the Broncos ahead, 21–7. They won, 30–7. I can still see Jim chugging down the field. All by himself. Nobody near him. When we showed films of that play on Tuesday to the special teams, I deserved to be the Fanatic of the Week.

Not too controlled either.

Time-outs
and
Types

I COULDN'T BELIEVE IT. MY middle linebacker, Monte Johnson, had formed a T with his hands. Time-out.

Through all my years as the Raiders' coach, my first commandment to my offensive players had been: Thou shalt not take a time-out. No matter what the situation, the only Raider allowed to take a time-out was me. Over and over I had preached that commandment to my offensive players, especially my quarterback. But here was my middle linebacker running toward me on the sideline, so proud of himself for having called a time-out.

"We were out of position," Monte explained. "We didn't adjust to their formation."

"No, no, don't ever do that again," I said. "I'm the only one who calls a time-out."

It was more my fault than his. In all my preaching to the offense about never calling a time-out, it never occurred to me

162

to preach to the defense. About the only time the defense takes a time-out is to stop the clock near the end of the game or near the end of the first half. But now Monte Johnson had done it early in the second half, which meant we had only two time-outs left. We won that game, but that's not the point. The point is that the use of time-outs, especially late in a close game, is a big factor in what separates good coaches from bad coaches. I can never understand coaches who let somebody else on the sideline keep track of how many time-outs his team has left. That's like letting somebody else carry your driver's license. Hey, it's your responsibility to carry your driver's license. And if you're a coach, it's your responsibility to keep track of your time-outs. It's also your responsibility to make sure a time-out isn't wasted.

Every so often from the TV booth I see a quarterback step away from the center and call a time-out. He's confused. Or he knows one of his running backs or one of his wide receivers is confused.

Hey, take a 5-yard penalty for delay of the game but don't call a time-out. On the next play you might get the 5 yards back and more. But you'll never get the time-out back. Each team has only six time-outs in a game—three in the first half, three in the second half. Obviously, the three in the second half are more important. If we were behind in the last minute of a close game, I always wanted to be able to use all three of my time-outs. With all three, my quarterback could complete three passes down the middle and stop the clock instead of being limited to throwing deep or to the sideline.

In the last minute, most teams are going to stack their defense in those areas. If you don't have any time-outs left, you've got to throw deep for a quick touchdown or you've got to throw to the sideline where your pass receiver can get out of bounds to stop the clock.

If you have all three of your time-outs, you can throw over the middle. If you complete it, you can call your first time-out. Then you can throw over the middle again. If you complete it, you can call your second time-out. Then you can throw over the middle again. And if you complete that one, you still have your third time-out. If you've made any substantial yardage with those three completions, you should be close enough to go for what you need to win the game—either a field goal or a touch-down.

You also can use the officials' time-out at the two-minute warning as a fourth time-out. And on a change of possession, you get what amounts to a fifth time-out.

On defense, if you've been able to keep all three of your time-outs until the last two minutes, you can get the ball back —as long as your defense can prevent the other team from getting a first down. After each play, simply take a time-out— *boom, boom, boom.* Now the other team has to punt. But if you've kept only one or two time-outs, the other team can run out the clock.

Whatever the situation, never trust the scoreboard to know how many time-outs you have left. Sometimes the scoreboard is wrong. And sometimes the official in charge of time-outs, the field judge, is wrong. When the other team took a time-out, he could conceivably have marked it against your team by mistake. When that happens, luckily, one of the other officials usually has it right.

In the NFL, a coach's responsibility begins long before he has to think about how to use time-outs late in a close game. It begins several months earlier with his decisions on how to use his team's draft choices in the grab bag of college talent. For any coach, it's important that his type of player be selected; *his type* means a player who will fit into *his* system, whether it be offense, defense, or special teams. If a coach doesn't like a cer-tain type of player, it's silly to draft that type. Whenever our Raider scouts got together, Al Davis reminded them of that.

"If we draft a player who doesn't fit into what John likes to do," Al would say, "that player isn't going to play anyway. So why draft him?"

My type of player varied according to his position, but I had one constant. He had to be a grass player, not an artificial turf player. Beyond that, I wanted wide-butted offensive linemen who could block man-to-man in a fullback-oriented offense. On defense, I wanted linemen who were tough guys, linebackers who were very active and were hitters, and defensive backs who could run with any wide receiver.

I also knew what type I didn't want: fancy guys with a reputation for producing a big play once in a while. I didn't want a big play once in a while, I wanted a solid play every time.

Most coaches prefer a certain type of player. Don Shula looks for the cerebral type—intelligent players who can do whatever he asks. Shula has deep football roots developed under Paul Brown as a Browns' defensive back three decades ago. He is a very disciplined person himself. He wants his Dolphin players to be that way, in a mold. Not that *every* player can be that way. But the more players who fit a mold, the better Shula likes it. He's like Vince Lombardi, who believed there was only one way to do things. His way. So he goes out and gets the type of player who will do things his way.

But strategically, Don Shula is a very flexible coach. He has always adjusted his offense to his personnel, especially his quarterback.

People saw Dan Marino throwing all those passes for the Dolphins and they were shocked that Shula would let a young quarterback do that. They forgot, or maybe they never even knew, that when Shula took over the Colts in 1963, he had Johnny Unitas at quarterback. Unitas threw the ball like Marino does—hard and often. When Shula went to the Dolphins, he had Bob Griese, who didn't have that gun, so Shula had to build a running game. Whenever Unitas and Griese got hurt, Shula had Earl Morrall or Don Strock as a backup. Then when Griese stopped playing, Shula went with David Woodley, who liked to run around, and the Dolphins took Woodley to Super Bowl XVI with them. But no matter who the Dolphin quarterback is, he does it Don Shula's way. In that sense, all Don's quarterbacks have been in that mold.

I never felt players had to fit a mold. To me, coaching was being creative, giving your players a little freedom. I just wanted the best players, no matter how cerebral they were.

I don't mean to say that Shula's right and I'm wrong, or that I'm right and he's wrong. I'm just saying that every coach is attracted to a different type. Tom Landry wants players who are good athletes. He looks at players—and I say this out of respect—as pawns. He wants this player to do this, that player to do that. In developing the Cowboys into a finesse team, especially on offense, he prefers the slim-hipped player who can run and jump. He would enjoy taking a bunch of basketball players and turning them into football players.

Two of Landry's former assistants, Mike Ditka and Dan Reeves, are now two of the NFL's best head coaches. Each has done it his way, along with some of Tom's way.

As an All-Pro tight end for the Bears on their 1963 championship team, Ditka was a tough player. As the Bears' coach, he still has that toughness, plus the coaching toughness he learned from George Halas, the Papa Bear himself. He also has the coaching organization he learned from Landry. When he was hired by Halas as the Bears' coach in 1982, some people chuckled at the memory of how Ditka had left the Bears in a salary dispute after the 1966 season.

"George Halas," Mike said at the time, "throws nickels around like manhole covers."

But that didn't stop the Papa Bear from hiring Mike Ditka, and it didn't stop Mike from taking the job. As a head coach, he considers himself to be a combination of what he was like as a player and what he learned from his two famous coaches. I'd say he's 90 percent himself and Halas, and 10 percent Landry.

Ditka is a throwback to the old days when just about every NFL coach had been an NFL player. At heart, he's still a player. He'd like to line up with twelve guys, with him out there against the other coach.

As a coach who was a player not that long ago, Mike knows how players think, how they live. With some of the characters he's got on the Bears, that knowledge helps him understand his players. "These guys can't get away with anything with me," he says. "I don't care what they do, I've done it." When he hears Jim McMahon complaining about having a cold on Friday morning after his weekly Thursday night out with his offensive linemen, Mike just nods.

"How come McMahon only has that cold on Friday mornings?" Mike once told me. "I've had that cold. Only it's not a cold, it's a hangover."

McMahon bugs Ditka a little. When McMahon couldn't play for several weeks during the 1984 season because of tendinitis in his throwing shoulder, Mike hardly talked to him. But when Ditka was asked if he wasn't talking to his quarterback, he bristled.

"That's not true," he said. "On the sideline in Dallas, I told him to shut up. That's talking to him, isn't it?"

The Bears won that game in Dallas, 44–0, with McMahon standing on the sideline in boots, a pair of faded jeans, a scruffy shirt, and a baseball cap with a real-estate logo. Before the Bears played the Falcons the following week, Ditka told me that McMahon would be in uniform.

"Does that mean he might play?" I asked.

"No, but this way I know what he's wearing."

His second season as the Bears' coach, Mike broke his right hand punching a locker after an overtime loss. Until then, he always wore casual clothes on the sideline, usually a Bears' sweatshirt or a parka, depending on the weather. But when his hand was in a cast, he decided to wear a dress shirt and a tie on the sideline.

"The tie," he says, "keeps me calm."

As soon as the game is over, the tie comes off. But with or without the tie, Mike Ditka is never really calm. In control, yes. Calm, no. That's his style. That's why he's been successful. In a *Sports Illustrated* poll of two hundred NFL players during the 1985 season, Mike finished in a tie with Don Shula and Tom Landry as the coach those players would *least* like to play for.

"I don't know about me," Mike said, "but a guy who doesn't want to play for Landry or Shula has to be a lazy bum."

Dan Reeves took over the Broncos in 1981 after eight seasons with Tom Landry as a Cowboy assistant, the last four as offensive coordinator. With the Broncos, he wisely kept Joe Collier as his defensive coordinator and concentrated on the offense. He's still influenced by Landry, but he also has his own approach.

Bill Walsh put the 49ers together by blending the Shula and Landry types. Walsh wants smart athletes. He doesn't go for tough, physical guys the way Chuck Noll does.

When the Steelers were winning four Super Bowl rings, Noll always had a very physical defense. Much more physical than Shula's or Landry's. On offense, Noll liked a different type of lineman than I did. His linemen couldn't have made my Raider teams, and my Raider linemen couldn't have made his Steeler teams. His linemen were pulling, trapping, running linemen. Mine were more stationary, driving linemen.

The Raiders still look for that type of lineman. Tom Flores has a different personality than I do, but he was an original Raider in 1960, he was a Raider quarterback when Al Davis was the coach, he was on my staff for seven years before succeeding me as head coach. He looks for thick-bodied offensive linemen and strong-armed quarterbacks, just like I did.

Chuck Knox is Vince Lombardi with a little more leeway. He's a fundamentalist. He wants people who will play fundamentally sound football. With him, if you block better than the other team and tackle better than the other team, that's it. You win. Sometimes he's criticized for having a boring offense. He's known as Ground Chuck, a nickname he hates. But he's been very successful no matter where he's been—with the Rams, the Bills, and now the Seahawks.

One reason for Knox's success is that he has always taken several of his assistant coaches with him. Before he took over the Rams in 1973, he had been an assistant coach for fourteen years with the Jets and the Lions, and he never forgot what it was like. He's always taken good care of his assistants. That continuity on his staff has been a big plus.

Of the current coaches, Forrest Gregg is more like Vince Lombardi than any of the others. As Hall of Fame offensive tackle, he played for Lombardi on those Packer teams that won three consecutive NFL titles in 1965, 1966, and 1967, including the first two Super Bowl games. Now he's coaching the Packers after having coached the Bengals to the AFC championship in 1981. When he was hired in Green Bay, he was asked if he would be as demanding as Lombardi had been.

"I'm demanding," he said with a smile, "but I'm not *that* demanding."

Lombardi didn't demand a certain type of player so much as he demanded that a player be *his* type. No matter who the player was or what he had accomplished, if that player was going to play for Lombardi, then there was only one way: the way Lombardi told him. No discussion groups. No meaningful experiences. No vote. He didn't use the word *share* that's popular now, as in "Let's share an idea." Lombardi *told* his players what he wanted. And they did it—or they were gone. Forrest is not as vocal or as outgoing as Lombardi, but he's as tough as Lombardi. Their personalities are different. But he coaches the same way.

Bud Grant has always had a different style. When the Vikings went to four Super Bowl games, his best players were self-starters with pride. Alan Page and Carl Eller were perfect for Bud's style. All-Pros who could get their motors going at 110 mph, play a game, then do the same thing the next week.

Don Coryell is a throwback to the years when the head coach was basically an offensive coach. Sid Gillman was like that as the Chargers' head coach long before Air Coryell arrived. Sid was as innovative a coach of the passing game as football has ever had. With the Chargers and with the Cardinals before that, Coryell has depended on the pass, but at San Diego State he was run-oriented. I know. I was his defensive coordinator there on a staff that turned out four NFL head coaches: Don, Joe Gibbs, Rod Dowhower, and myself.

Joe Gibbs has surprised me. He had been an assistant coach

under both John McKay in Tampa Bay and Coryell in San
Diego, but as the Redskins' head coach he's more like George
Allen. Gibbs believes in experienced players, just like Allen did
when his "Over the Hill Gang" of Redskins went to Super Bowl
VII. Even though he's a relatively young coach, Gibbs believes
in having players who have done it, who have been there, who
won't make mistakes. Rookies, he and George Allen always
believed, make rookie mistakes.

The Best I've Ever Seen

Coaches   George Allen
           Paul Brown
           Weeb Ewbank
           Sid Gillman
           Bud Grant
           Tom Landry
           Vince Lombardi
           Chuck Noll
           Don Shula
           Hank Stram

John Robinson also prefers a specific type of player, especially
at one position. The great tailback.

His first year as the Rams' coach, Robinson traded to get the
second choice in the 1983 draft. John Elway went first, then the
Rams took Eric Dickerson, the great tailback. But even if the
Rams had the first choice, I think Robinson would have taken
Dickerson over Elway. As the Southern Cal head coach for
seven years and an assistant there on John McKay's staff earlier,
he believed in the tailback-oriented running game that SC
used: O. J. Simpson, Ricky Bell, and Charles White running
behind big offensive linemen.

"We're going to keep running and wear the other team down," Robinson has told me. "Things that don't work in the first quarter will work in the fourth quarter because we've worn the other team down."

Bill Parcells depends on preparation. He studies the Giants' opponent, gets a reading, knows what the opponent is likely to do. He's also absorbed ideas from his travels as a coach. He started as an assistant at Hastings College in Nebraska, then he went to Wichita State, Army, Florida State, Vanderbilt, and Texas Tech before being named head coach at the Air Force Academy. Then he was on the Patriots' and Giants' staffs as an assistant. He's an underrated coach. He might turn out to be the best of the new breed.

Raymond Berry of the Patriots is one of the few great players to make it as a good coach. In the twenty years of the Super Bowl, only two teams had coaches who were Hall of Fame players: Forrest Gregg with the Bengals and now Berry.

As a wide receiver for Johnny Unitas on the great Colt teams, Raymond Berry was not a gifted athlete. But he was a hard worker. Forrest Gregg was the same way on the great Packer teams. I think that's why each is a good coach. Through the years, the naturally gifted athletes have not developed into good coaches, but the hard workers have.

Joe Walton is a throwback. Once a tight end with the Giants and Redskins, he moved on to the staffs of both teams as an assistant, then moved to the Jets as offensive coordinator before taking over as their head coach.

Years ago, almost every NFL head coach had been an NFL player and then an NFL assistant coach. But only a few young NFL coaches have that background today: Tom Flores, Mike Ditka, Raymond Berry, Dan Reeves, Joe Walton, Marty Schottenheimer, Rod Dowhower, and Sam Wyche, who got his job as the Bengals' coach because of a playbook he kept in 1968 as a rookie quarterback.

Paul Brown, who organized the Bengals, always kept the playbooks of players who had impressed him. Paul happened to be looking through some of those old playbooks in 1984 when he noticed Sam's.

"I looked at the book," Paul has said, "and he had everything in excellent order. This shows that way back then I had a feeling. He was a student of the game. As a quarterback, he was never a big star, although he did have some very good games, but he was really with it. We really kept close track of Sam down through the years after he left us."

Sam bounced around with the Redskins, Lions, Cardinals, and Bills, mostly as a backup quarterback. He was on the 49ers' staff the season they won Super Bowl XVI, then he was the head coach at Indiana before Paul Brown hired him.

"Sam," said Paul Brown, "was our only choice."

Some owners who hire coaches obviously look for a certain type of coach, just as some coaches look for a certain type of player. But as we all know, owners sometimes make mistakes in hiring coaches, just as coaches and scouts make mistakes in drafting players.

On the Raiders, we had our share of "busts"—players who make you wonder how you ever could have drafted them. Every NFL team has its share of busts, some more than its share.

With the scouting today, with the camps the NFL arranges for players even before the draft, a bust shouldn't happen. But they still do. What we tried to do back when I was coach was not bring in a bust who we thought *might* be a bust. Our philosophy was that we'd rather take somebody we didn't know anything about than somebody we didn't think was our type of player.

"This guy can play in the NFL," our personnel director, Ron Wolf, would say, "but he can't make our team."

If this guy couldn't make our team, it didn't make sense to use a draft choice for him. Draft choices are precious. You only have twelve each year, plus those you obtain from other teams in trades or minus those you deal away. In a good year, maybe half a dozen rookies will make your team—half of your draft choices. If you waste a choice, it decreases your chances. But sometimes you get lucky. In the last round of the 1977 draft, we had run out of players we thought were our type. On a hunch, I phoned my pal John Robinson, then the Southern Cal coach. I asked if he had any players we should draft with our last pick.

"Rod Martin's a better player than anybody who's been drafted in the last five rounds," John told me. "He'll make your team."

Rod Martin developed into an All-Pro linebacker and the Raiders' defensive captain. We were lucky with Rod Martin, twice. Once when we drafted him, and once when we got him back after we had cut him. That year in training camp, we had too many linebackers. When we put him on waivers, the 49ers claimed him. Later, when the 49ers released him, we were looking for a linebacker because of injuries. We signed him.

When the rookies arrived for minicamp, one of the first things we checked was how fast each one could run 40 yards. Then we did it again after the veterans reported to training.

In a game, a player seldom has to run more than 40 yards on any particular play. That's why football timing is always done at 40 yards. At our training camp at Santa Rosa, we timed our players on a heavy grass field that was like a farm. We'd mark off 40 yards, line up the players, one of the coaches would yell "Ready, set, go," and another coach would be looking at a stop-watch. With all the high-tech timing devices around, that wasn't very sophisticated. But hey, this wasn't the Olympics, we just wanted to get an idea of who was really fast, who was fast enough, and who wasn't fast at all.

Some teams time their players in shorts, but I wanted my players timed wearing their helmet and pads. They wouldn't be wearing shorts in a game, they'd be wearing their equipment. I wanted to know how fast they were with their equipment on.

With a lineman, equipment didn't make him any slower than he was. But a cornerback or a wide receiver never seemed to be as fast with his helmet and pads as he had been as a sprinter. I never timed my quarterbacks or my punters or kickers. And as soon as I knew a guy could really play, I didn't care how fast or slow he was. I've seen a lot of guys who had good numbers for the 40, but that didn't mean they could play. Conversely, a lot of guys didn't have good numbers, but that didn't mean they couldn't play. I never cared what Fred Biletnikoff ran the 40 in. I think he did it in 4.8 seconds, not that fast for a wide receiver, but not that slow either.

The best time I ever saw for the 40, in equipment, was 4.4 seconds. George Atkinson ran that as a rookie in 1968, then Cliff Branch, who had been a world-class sprinter, ran it as a rookie in 1972.

Running in equipment on our heavy grass field, that was a true 4.4, not a 4.4 in shorts, not a 4.4 on artificial turf. Over 40 yards, a stride is the difference of maybe a tenth of a second. That meant that all your wide receivers and defensive backs had to be able to run the 40 in 4.5 seconds, maybe 4.6 if they were really quick. If the wide receivers were that fast, ideally the defensive backs who covered them had to be that fast. You always put your fastest defensive backs at cornerback, the next fastest at free safety, the least fastest at strong safety. If you time a defensive back at 4.7 or 4.8, you're talking about a difference of maybe four strides over 40 yards if he's trying to cover a wide receiver. That's enough to turn any coach into an insurance salesman.

Sometimes a running back will be timed at 4.5 or 4.6 in training camp, but by the end of the season he's so beat up, he just can't run that fast anymore. Especially if he plays on artificial turf.

No matter how fast a guy is, if he can't play or if you don't think you can teach him to play, he doesn't have a chance to make your team. But unless a rookie turns out to be a bust, cutting a player in training camp is never easy. Especially an older player. Before the preseason games began, I usually had a good idea who I was going to cut. To test the rookies, I created game situations in practice. That's where I learned all I needed to know. I never used the preseason games as a tryout. Back when I was coaching, we usually had six preseason games—

twenty-four quarters. That wasn't much time. I wasn't going to waste any of that valuable time looking at a player I knew I was going to cut anyway. With only four preseason games now, a coach has only sixteen quarters to assess talent. In my ten years as the Raiders' head coach, the player limit fluctuated from forty to forty-seven to forty-three to forty-five. But no matter what the eventual number had to be, at training camp we discussed it every evening after dinner when I met with my assistant coaches.

"All right," I'd finally say to them, "rate each of your players —in order."

The names at the top of each list hardly ever changed. But the names at the bottom varied from day to day, from practice to practice, from preseason game to preseason game. In choosing, say, a forty-five-man roster, you know you need a basic number of players at each position. Offense: three quarterbacks, four running backs, four wide receivers, two tight ends, eight offensive linemen, one punter, one placekicker. Defense: six defensive linemen, six linebackers, eight defensive backs.

That adds up to forty-three, which leaves two spots for you and your assistant coaches to argue about. Do you keep another running back or another linebacker? Or both? Or the rookie wide receiver with all that speed? Or that experienced defensive back who's not as quick as he once was, but who never makes a mistake? Or that young offensive tackle who needs time to develop? Or that fanatic on special teams?

Each assistant coach will fight for one of his players, but the head coach has to referee the fight, then hand down the decision.

As the cutdown dates approached each week, I always found that the longer I had a player, the tougher it was to cut him. With a young player, I hadn't been around him long enough to be fond of him, or to be fond of what he'd done for me. With a young player I usually sent Ken Bishop, who was on our administrative staff, to tell him to come to my office.

"Remind him," I would tell Ken, "to bring his playbook."

That's when a player knew he was gone, when Ken told him to bring his playbook. But when I knew I was cutting an older player, I did the dirty work myself. I'd phone him in his room or I'd tap him on the shoulder walking back from dinner and ask him to come to my office.

"When you cut me," Ben Davidson, our big defensive end, told me later, "you felt worse than I did."

Game Plans
and
Danish

NOW THAT YOU'VE GOT YOUR roster, it's time to start the season, to play your schedule. Your players should be ready, mentally and physically. They should know their plays on offense. They should know their coverages on defense. They should know their bodies. Now it's a matter of preparing your players, week after week, for the next opponent. Creating the best possible game plan to exploit that opponent, both on offense and defense. Then drilling that game plan into your players in practice.

"You learn during the week, we teach during the week," I told my players. "When you go out there on Sunday, you just react."

When the whistle blows for the kickoff on Sunday, it's too late for them to learn, too late for us to teach. Too late for your players to do anything except react to what develops. But in order to get them to react properly, they must be taught during the week. All their mental alertness has to be developed during

the week. When you succeed in developing that mental alertness in your team, that's when your team is ready to play. It
starts on Tuesday and continues the rest of the week.

Some coaches bring their players in on Monday for meetings,
then give them Tuesday off. I always preferred to give my
players Monday off, to let them rest their bumps and bruises.
But the coaches always worked on Monday.

In the NFL, an assistant coach is really a specialist. He usually
has one group of players to worry about—quarterbacks, running backs, pass receivers, offensive linemen, defensive linemen, linebackers, defensive backs, or special teams. In putting
together a staff, I always wanted assistants who were, first, different from me and then different from each other.

Some assistants enjoy breaking down film. You need one of
those on offense and one on defense. Some are good game
coaches; they enjoy the strategy of the game itself. Others are
good at drills; they help keep your practices sharp.

You need that variety. But more than anything else, an assistant coach has to be respected and liked by the players in his
group. That rapport is important. He's with his small group of
players all the time. In meetings, watching films, at practice.
Being around the players so much, he's got to wear well. If he
doesn't, he'll turn off the players. They'll stop listening to him.

Different positions also demand different types of assistant
coaches. Most defensive players are wild guys and they relate
to a coach who's a little wild. So one of my defensive coaches
was always a wild guy. But for a balance, my other defensive
coaches were a little calmer.

Ollie Spencer, my offensive-line coach, enjoyed lifting
weights with the players. If he was in the weight room, I knew
he was encouraging them to work a little harder than they
would if he wasn't there. And one assistant had to enjoy drawing
up the game plan itself. In putting it together, we always drew
the offensive plays and the defenses on the blackboard. That
way, we could really study them. When we finalized everything, we still had to write it up. I didn't have a secretary. Lew

Erber, my offensive-backfield coach, wrote it up, real neat, and gave it to Ken Bishop to type up. Tom Dahms, my defensive-line coach, did the same with the defensive game plan and Joe Scanella did the special-teams game plan. I never wanted our game plan to come out of a computer. I wanted it all written down by one of our coaches before it was typed up. That way, if anybody had a question, they knew exactly where everything was.

"Hey, where's that double-wing stuff we put in," I might ask.

"Right there on page two," Lew would say. "Top of the page."

Some assistant coaches are consumed with getting a head-coaching job, others are pushed into searching for a head-coaching job, and still others seem to prefer being an assistant coach. Ernie Stautner, the Cowboys' defensive coordinator, has been on Tom Landry's staff since 1966, perfectly happy and a terrific coach. Buddy Ryan had been an assistant coach since 1968 with the Jets, the Vikings, and the Bears before taking over in 1986 as the Eagles' head coach. The day his hiring was announced, Buddy was asked if he felt he was ready to be a head coach.

"Been ready for twenty years," he said.

That's Buddy Ryan, whose Bears' defense in 1985 was the best NFL defense I've ever seen. Even better than the Steel Curtain of Pittsburgh's four Super Bowl championship teams. In my TV travels during the 1985 season, I was in the booth with Pat Summerall at five Bear games. In those five, the Bears never yielded a touchdown. They shut out the Cowboys and the Falcons during the season, then shut out the Giants and the Rams in the playoffs. In the other regular season game, the Jets got two field goals. Now that's defense. Buddy Ryan's defense.

Buddy designed all the Bears' defenses, notably the "46" defense that put eight men up on the line of scrimmage. And before each play, he called a defense from the sideline. To me, the Bears' defense was divided into three parts: Buddy's design, Buddy's calls, and the Bears' personnel.

Buddy won't have as many good players in Philadelphia, at least not right away. But he has a good chance to be successful. With the Bears he had his own domain. As the *head coach* of the defense, he had more responsibility than any NFL assistant coach I've ever known. Even more than Bill Arnsparger, who was Don Shula's defensive coordinator on the Dolphins for many years. Buddy earned that responsibility. He had been on the Jets' and Vikings' staffs that went to Super Bowls III and XI before he joined the Bears.

Buddy was hard on his Bear players. That was his way of motivating them. And it worked. His players hated him at first, but they grew to love him. They changed, but he didn't. When the Bears won Super Bowl XX, the defensive players carried him off on their shoulders.

Now that Buddy is a head coach, his biggest problem might be the adjustment that every new head coach must make after being an assistant coach—dealing with people other than the players. The front office. The media. The functions he has to attend. The criteria for being a good head coach aren't the same as the criteria for being a good assistant. In football, a good assistant coach is in charge of one part of the team, like Buddy was with the Bears' defense, or one group of players. He works with those players. He teaches them. He drills them. He gets them to do what they're supposed to do.

Some assistant coaches are masters at that level. But when the same man is suddenly a head coach, suddenly he's in charge of everything. Some guys just can't deal with that.

It also works the other way. I always thought John Ralston was a good head coach with the Broncos, but I didn't think he was a good assistant. John had to be in charge. The first head coach I ever worked for, Al Baldock at Hancock Junior College, went to San Diego State as an assistant coach, but he didn't like it. Al was geared to be a head coach, not an assistant.

In the NFL, dealing with the media takes more and more of a coach's time each year for the simple reason that each year there's more and more media.

For a coach, time is precious. For that reason, I answered questions from the media at the same time every day—immediately after practice ended. I always took care of every sportswriter, radio reporter, and TV crew who had waited for me, no matter how long it took me. But to be honest, I didn't return all my phone calls. Especially those from the eastern time zone. With a three-hour difference, I figured it was too late for their deadline anyway. And if I answered every call, I wouldn't have had time to coach my team. In those years, the Raiders never had a big media crush until the playoffs or maybe a big late-season game. But no matter how big that crush is, a head coach has to deal with it. He's the primary spokesman for his team.

How long anybody is a head coach, of course, depends on his won-lost record. Which depends on his players. I was lucky. As the Raiders' head coach, I always had good players.

With a bad NFL team, I might have lasted two years and been fired, like so many other coaches. But when the Raiders kept winning, I kept coaching. And the more the Raiders won, the closer our team got. In any sport, success breeds togetherness. But don't be fooled, togetherness doesn't breed success. If a bad team tries to develop togetherness, that's nice; but it's still a bad team. Being together won't make it a good team. Take the Pittsburgh Pirates. When they won the 1979 World Series, they were "family," they were a good team. But when the Pirates dropped out of contention after that, they weren't family anymore. They were a bad team—that's why they weren't a family.

Togetherness usually develops on winning streaks, which are the secret to winning your division, no matter what the sport.

On the Raiders, we were able to put together long winning streaks. Get on a roll and keep it rolling. Some teams win two or three games in a row, but then they get satisfied. They start celebrating, or start thinking they're better than they really are. They forget how they won those two or three in a row—by working, that's how. So now they don't work as hard. Then they lose, but they don't know the real reason why they lost.

Good teams work to get it, then work to keep it. The way the

Bears did when they went 18–1 to win Super Bowl XX, the way
the 49ers did when they went 18–1 to win Super Bowl XIX, the
way the Dolphins did when they went 17–0 to win Super Bowl
VII, the way my Raider team did when we went 16–1 to win
Super Bowl XI.

As a coach, when your team starts a streak going, you don't
let up. Instead, you've got to be tough. You've got to be just the
opposite of the way the players are. When your team wins two
or three in a row, the players' friends tell them how great they
are. But that's when you've got to pound that work ethic into
them. If they win the next game, they'll accept it again the
following week. The more they win, the more they'll accept it.

But even before you see them trying to slide, that's when
you've got to *whap* them back into line.

"You guys have won three games in a row," I would tell my
Raiders. "You all want to take it easy. Hey, everyone wants to
take it easy. It's human nature. But if you take it easy, you're
going to lose."

I knew how they were going to try to take it easy, so then I
threw a few examples at them.

"You don't want to do the tough things anymore because
things have been too easy," I would say, my voice rising. "You
don't want to run after practice anymore. You don't want to lift
weights after practice. You don't want to catch a hundred
passes after practice. You don't want to stay out there with the
special teams. We're going to get our asses beat Sunday because
you guys don't want to do all those things anymore."

Nobody had goofed off at all, but I ranted and raved like
everybody had goofed off. That was my trick. Beating them to
the punch. As soon as a player even considered goofing off, he
thought, He told me I'd feel this way, I better not do it. And if
a guy made the mistake of goofing off, I really had him.

"Look, that's what I was talking about, right there, see that,"
I might say as a wide receiver disappeared into the locker room
as soon as practice ended. "You remember a week ago, when
we were getting ready for Kansas City, he stayed out and
caught a hundred passes after practice. But now he's not. That's

what I was telling you guys in the meeting. Now you see what I was talking about."

Hey, anybody can tell players what they should have done *after* a loss. But by telling them *before* the game, they start thinking about it. Then they don't want to goof off, or they won't because you warned them they would. Either way, they didn't goof off. Which is all I wanted.

It worked pretty well. In my years with the Raiders we had ten winning streaks of at least four in a row—thirteen, ten, nine, seven twice, six, five, and four three times. In contrast, we never lost more than three games in a row, and we only did that twice, in 1971 and 1978, the only two seasons my teams didn't make the playoffs. When we were on a losing streak, I'd try to be gentle with my players. Well, not exactly gentle—I was never gentle with them—but I'd try not to get upset, not to get angry. When you're angry, you say things you don't mean. And when your team is losing, angry words hurt and form scars. So what I would do is become very strategic. Not strategic philosophical, but strategic footballwise.

I'd go back to fundamentals—to footwork, to stance, to formations. I'd talk more about our game plan. That way I knew I would be talking to them in a calm voice.

You can't get upset drawing a play on a blackboard. Who are you going to get upset at, the chalk? Also, by talking about a play, I wasn't talking about a player who might upset me. Just because we had lost, I wasn't going to get soft or become a good guy. I knew my players knew me as well as I knew them, if not better. So when we lost, my way was to talk about things that wouldn't upset me.

At our Tuesday meetings, we would split into offense and defense, then watch the films of our previous game to go over our mistakes. I usually sat with the offense. But watching game films isn't like going to the movies. Watching game films, we didn't munch popcorn. Watching game films, we were going over an exam. With rookies, I sometimes had to teach them how to watch.

"If you miss a block," I might say, "I don't point it out to embarrass you. I point it out so *you* will see why you missed it. Maybe it was your footwork. Maybe you didn't get your hands up."

Jim Otto, our Hall of Fame center, understood that better than any player I've ever known. Instead of being embarrassed if he missed a block, he would ask me to show that play over and over again until he knew exactly what he had done wrong and had corrected it in his mind. He was so concerned about correcting his mistakes, he made it easier for me to convince other players why I kept stopping the film to point out something.

"We watch the good things you do so you can see why and how you did them," I would say. "We watch the average things so you can improve on them, and we watch the bad things you do so you won't do them again."

When we were through watching the films of our previous game, we started watching films of our next opponent in order to familiarize ourselves with their personnel. I always reminded my players of who the other team's players were, and told them about any new players.

"Namath's with the Rams," I told my players in 1977 before we played the Jets. "Richard Todd is their quarterback now."

That might seem unnecessary. But you'd be surprised how many NFL players aren't that aware of changes in another team's roster. The fans keep up with "transactions" more than players do. I'm sure all my players had known that Joe Namath had moved to the Rams, but I reminded them anyway. And as the film went along, I did that with everybody on the team we were about to play.

"This is . . . " I would say. "This is. . . ."

I always identified players by their names. But some coaches prefer to use numbers, like Tom Landry.

"Number 12," Tom will say about Joe Montana. "Watch him roll out here."

Buddy Ryan is another coach who uses numbers. If he were talking to his people about the 49ers' offense, a stranger would think he was talking in some secret code.

"On this play," Buddy might say, "87 goes here, 80 goes there, 81 comes down, and watch out for 33 over here."

Buddy would be talking about the 49ers' two wide receivers, Dwight Clark (87) and Jerry Rice (80), their tight end Russ Francis (81), and their fullback Roger Craig (33). But there's a method to that madness, especially for a defensive coach. Using a number is a way for the coach to avoid creating the aura that a name represents. Especially the name of an established All-Pro player. Somehow a number isn't as alarming as a name.

Yeah, number 87, a defensive back might be thinking, I can cover number 87.

For some players, just thinking about covering a number might be easier than having to think about covering *Dwight Clark*. But on the Raiders, we always talked in names, not numbers. Not only in that Tuesday meeting, but for the rest of the week. I wanted my players to associate somebody's name with his number. Then in our special quarterback meeting on Tuesday after the other players had gone home, I'd go over the opposing team's defensive players again. By name. One by one. Just so the quarterbacks could see them again, get to know them again.

When we went on the field Tuesday afternoon, we corrected the mistakes we had seen that morning on the films. Both on offense and defense. If our pulling guards had trouble getting outside on a sweep, we worked on that. If one of our wide receivers wasn't getting open across the middle, we worked on that. On defense, we checked our pass coverage. If we hadn't covered well against certain formations in our previous game, our next opponent would see that on their films and would use plays designed to beat those coverages.

No matter how small the mistake might seem, I tried to get it corrected right away. If not, it was soon a big mistake. I learned that sitting around with Don McMahon, who grew up in Brooklyn with Al Davis.

If you're a baseball fan, you probably remember Don, a relief pitcher for eighteen seasons with seven major-league teams:

Milwaukee, Houston, Cleveland, Boston, the Chicago White
Sox, Detroit, and San Francisco. He had a 90–68 record, with
153 saves, so he knew baseball. He also knew football. Al had
him scout college players for us. When he was in the office one
day during my first year as head coach, I asked him why a
certain baseball team never got better.

"I'll tell you why," he said. "When a guy makes a mistake, the
manager never says anything to him. So the players start to
think it's okay to make that mistake. They make it in practice,
then they make it in a game. And when the manager still
doesn't say anything, they keep making it again and again."

Hearing that, I told myself, Whatever I do, I'm not going to
let a mistake go untalked-about, I'm going to correct it then and
there. And I did. If a guy dropped a pass or a quarterback threw
an interception, that's not a mistake. That's human nature. But
if somebody lines up offside, or if he lines up in the wrong
formation, or if he goes in motion when he shouldn't—*those* are
mistakes. In my travels as an announcer, I've learned that most
coaches hate those mistakes as much as I did. Somebody once
asked Don Shula if it wasn't a waste of time to bother correcting
a small flaw, but Don didn't seem to understand the question.

"What's a small flaw?" he wanted to know.

When our players left practice Tuesday, they had seen films
of our previous game, they had been made aware of their mistakes. They also had seen films of our next opponent's personnel, and they had been out on the field correcting their own
mistakes.

After practice, my Raider locker room was always open to the
media—newspaper writers, radio reporters, TV crews, whatever.

I never understood why some teams closed their locker
rooms to the media. To me, that always created more problems
than it solved. As soon as a team closes its locker room, some
media people want to get in there just to prove they can. With
our open locker room, some media people didn't even show up.
The only ones who were there every day were the "beat" writ-

ers from the Oakland and San Francisco area papers, the writers who covered the Raiders on a day-to-day basis. They would walk around the locker room, talk to the players, maybe have a cup of coffee. And that was it.

The only big hassle I ever had with writers was over putting players on waivers, which means making a player available to the other NFL teams in the inverse order of the standings. When some teams put a player on waivers, they announce it to the media that day, but the Raiders never did.

To me, waivers was a forty-eight-hour procedure. You put a player on waivers at four o'clock Monday afternoon. Another team could put in a claim for that player until four o'clock Tuesday afternoon. If a team claimed a player, you had until four o'clock Wednesday afternoon to decide if you wanted to recall the waiver. To me, a player wasn't really on waivers until that forty-eight-hour period expired, not at the beginning. When we wouldn't tell the writers who was waived, they always tried to find out. They always considered it a big deal. Even when it involved players who didn't figure to be on the final roster anyway.

"If you didn't write about the guy when he was here," I used to ask, "how come it's such a big deal when the guy is cut?"

I didn't care if the writers knew which players we put on waivers, or even if their readers knew. But it was a little game we played with every other team, just as every other team played it with us. Sometimes we were trying to get a player through waivers without anybody claiming him so we could put him back on our roster later. Or if a player was claimed by another team, we might reclaim him, then try to negotiate a trade with the team that was interested, possibly getting a draft choice in exchange for that player instead of losing him for free. If the other teams knew what we were trying to do, they could disrupt our plans. That's why we tried to keep secret which players we had put on waivers until the forty-eight-hour period expired. But every so often some of our "beat" writers would discover which players we had put on waivers and write about it. One year Jim Street of the *San Jose Mercury* somehow found out which players had been put on waivers and listed their names in his newspaper. When he came to practice the next day, I confronted him.

"Get out," I yelled. "You're not going to get your information both ways. If you're going to get it from the outside, like you got those waivers, get it all from the outside. If you're going to get it here, get it all here. This isn't a smorgasbord."

I was wrong. I should have let it go. Jim Street had just switched to covering the Raiders after covering the 49ers for a few years. Jim's a nice guy and a good writer. But when you're a coach, waivers are important. And if I were to coach again, I'd probably feel the same way.

Injuries are even more important. Not only to a coach, but also to the NFL office, which now requires every club to file an injury report on Wednesday and update it on Thursday.

In the report, every injured player must be listed regarding the likelihood of his playing the next game—probable, questionable, or doubtful. But the injury itself could remain a little vague. I always reported an injury as "knee" or "ribs" or "shoulder," but I never identified which knee or which ribs or which shoulder. If one of your running backs had sore ribs on his right side, you didn't want the defensive players on your next opposing team to have that information. If they did, they would bury their helmets in those ribs. You might as well draw a red bull's-eye on those ribs. But the difference between an injury and natural soreness can be tricky. Sometimes what appears to be a real injury would prove to be soreness later. And sometimes what appears to be soreness is a real injury.

I learned that the hard way in 1969, my first year as the Raiders' head coach. Late that season our fullback, Hewritt Dixon, got banged up and couldn't practice. But it wasn't anything serious. Just some heavy soreness.

I assumed that Hewritt would be able to play on Sunday, so I didn't put him on the injury report. When it was time to update the report, I still expected him to play. But on Sunday he couldn't play. Suddenly we had a fullback who couldn't play who had not even been mentioned on the injury report that week. Even though the AFL did not actually merge with the NFL until the 1970 season, we had to answer to the NFL office. The next day I got a phone call from the NFL office asking why Hewritt Dixon had not been on the injury report.

"I thought he was going to play," I said.

Several days later I got a letter from Commissioner Pete Rozelle telling me that since this was the first time I had filed an incomplete injury report, and I was a rookie coach, I was excused. But if it happened again, not only would I be fined, but I might be required to appear at the commissioner's office in New York, and possibly have to take a lie-detector test about filing a false injury report. After that, my reports included anybody with any injury, even a hangnail.

Different players recuperate from injuries differently. The human body is made to play ten, twelve games a season—that's all. More than that, you're stretching a body's vulnerability to injury, young or old.

The guys I really worried about were those who joined an NFL team after playing in the USFL in the spring and early summer of the same year. That's twelve straight months of pro football. When the Bears won Super Bowl XX, their right guard, Tom Thayer, had come over from the Arizona Wranglers. That same season Bart Oates, the Giants' center, who had come over from the Baltimore Stars, was another who had played twelve straight months.

After twelve straight games, a rookie's body is telling him that it's basketball season but his NFL coach is telling him the football season has four more games. And if their team makes the playoffs, anywhere from one to four additional games.

With an older player, early in the season he's sore on Monday and Tuesday but by Wednesday he's able to practice. As the season progresses, he's still sore on Thursday, then on Friday, sometimes even as late as Saturday, and sometimes he never stops being sore. By the end of the season, some older players are so banged up with bruises, contusions, and sprains that they really don't do much in practice. But on Sunday they play. And usually they play well.

Some players won't have an injury treated when anybody else is around. Kenny Stabler was like that. In recent years I learned that Jim Brown was also that way.

Instead of going to the Raiders' trainer's room for a whirlpool after practice, Kenny went home. When all the other players had left, our trainer, George Anderson, would phone Kenny, who would drive back. Jim Brown treated himself at home. He didn't want *anybody* to know that he was hurt. He figured that if even the trainer or one teammate knew, then somebody on the other team might know. And if the other team knew, their tacklers might try to gang up on him, hoping to reinjure him.

In our offensive meeting Wednesday morning, I went over what all the opposing defensive players did in certain situations —the fronts they used, the coverages they used. I always wanted my players to understand who the opposing players were and what those opposing players did before I let them know what we were going to do.

Watching those films, I sometimes challenged one of my players, reminded him that he had to do his job if we were going to run a play successfully. In those years, the Steelers always were the team we had to beat. Whenever we played the Steelers, the films from their previous game would show Joe Greene barreling through the right guard and nailing the ballcarrier. As soon as I saw that, I would stop the film and stare at George Buehler, my right guard.

"George," I would say, "unless you can get Joe Greene blocked, we don't have a chance to run there. You've got to block him."

George got the message. So did all our other offensive linemen. Against that Steel Curtain, your offensive linemen had to get off the ball, they had to know what the man across from them was going to do. We had been working on what we do for weeks, maybe months. We should know all that. But that other team was new to us.

That other team. That's what complicates your thinking. As a coach, I can't draw up a running play until I know the defense. Since the other team has several different defensive alignments, I have to draw up that play against each of those alignments. With a pass play, I have to draw it up against each of their coverages. On a run, I've got to get everybody blocked. On a pass, I try to spring somebody open. In our defensive game plan, we try to devise alignments and coverages that will confine our opponents' offensive thinking.

While the offense was meeting, the defense was getting its game plan. On the field Wednesday afternoon, we mostly worked on defense.

Our offense would use the plays we expected our opponents to use—running plays, passing plays, all the situations. When we were satisfied that our defense knew as much as it could about what the other team would do, our offense would practice for maybe half an hour. Nothing special. Just our usual running plays, our usual passing plays.

In our quarterback meeting Wednesday night, we gave the quarterbacks the game plan. Oooh, the game plan.

Some people talk about a game plan like it was a document snatched from the CIA's files. But it's just a list of running and passing plays that we believed would work against the opposing team, depending on the situation and the area of the field where we had the ball—first-down plays, second-down plays, third-down plays, short-yardage plays, goal-line plays, maybe a reverse we thought might work, maybe a new bootleg play.

In the NFL, most game plans aren't much different, but the philosophy of each always is.

When the Packers were winning all those NFL championships under Vince Lombardi, their game plans reflected his philosophy that the Packers were going to do what they did best and defy the opposing defense to stop them. Then there's Bill Walsh's philosophy with the 49ers now. Bill scripts at least the first twenty-five plays the 49ers will use. One after the other, in order. When the 49ers won Super Bowl XIX, he scripted plays into the third quarter. Eventually, I'm sure he'll script the whole game.

Bill's reasoning is that his 49ers usually started out like gang-busters with their script. But after the script ran out, the 49ers struggled. So he kept adding to the script.

Tom Landry doesn't have a script as such. But he's got all the Cowboy plays categorized on a sheet of paper. As the game goes along, he adjusts to what's happening. He sends in whatever play fits the situation.

Don Shula is big on scripting the first series. I don't know if there's a stat for it, but I have to believe the Dolphins score more on their first series than any other NFL team.

I used to script certain Raider plays. Starting points, I called them: the first short-yardage play, the first pass inside the 20, the first goal-line play. But unlike most coaches, I never scripted the first play of our first offensive series. Some coaches like to start off with a fancy-dan play that might fool the opposing defense. But my quarterbacks knew that all I ever wanted to do on the first play was give the ball to our fullback and let our linemen fire out. Now that I think about it, I guess I did script the first play but it was usually the *same* play: our fullback up the middle.

Back when I was an offensive lineman in college and high school, I hated to start the game with a fancy-dan play. Here we were, all fired up by the coach to go get 'em, but he didn't give us a play to let us do that. Instead, he gave us something that had me pulling or blocking down.

On the first play, I just wanted to tie into my man. Let him take his hacks at me, let me take my hacks at him. As a coach, that's all I wanted to let my linemen do. To me, the first play was never more than "Hey, let's get the game started, let's get our uniforms dirty, let's get some sweat going." If the game was going to last sixty minutes, the first play wasn't going to be that important anyway. No team ever won a game on the first play.

I'm not really superstitious, but Wednesday nights I tended to be a little more superstitious than usual. If my coaches and I had stayed until two in the morning on Wednesday finalizing our offensive game plan and then we had a good game on Sunday and won, I made sure we stayed until two in the morning the following Wednesday.

Even if we were finished by midnight, I'd think, Hey, last week we stayed until two in the morning and we won, so let's not change anything. I felt a little guilty having my coaches hang around to watch films we'd seen twenty times already, but I still did it. As a coach, you really never know why you won. You really never know what you did last week that you dare not do this week. If you decide not to watch films until two in the morning, for all you know that was when you learned something that helped your team win. Or if you had a long practice Thursday, maybe that was it. Instead of taking a chance on picking the wrong thing not to do this week, you don't pick anything. You do everything the same.

"Tom Flores and I used to bitch about staying late," John Robinson, my backfield coach one year, told me recently. "But now that we're both head coaches, we do the same thing."

No matter how late I stayed, I hardly ever slept on the office couch, I always went home. But some coaches sleep at their office all the time, like Dick Vermeil did before he resigned as the Eagles' coach on the grounds that he was "burned out."

During the week, Dick would stay watching films by himself until three or four in the morning. Then on Wednesday night he'd sleep on the couch. When the Eagles won on Sunday, he didn't dare not sleep on the couch the following Wednesday night. Next thing he knew, he also was sleeping there Monday night and Tuesday night. Joe Gibbs does the same thing now. He does it because he did it the two seasons the Redskins went to the Super Bowl. He doesn't dare *not* do it.

Thursday morning we gave the game plan to the entire offense, then we went through it in practice that afternoon.

In studying for my master's degree in education at Cal Poly,

I learned that one of the most important tenets of teaching is repetition. Tell your class over and over what you want it to learn. As a coach, I applied that same principle. Show the players the game plan on paper. Show it to them on film. Then show it to them on the field. I always used our two practice fields Thursday afternoon: one for pass plays, one for running plays. I never practiced the passing plays and the running plays on the same field. Passing and running are two different games. I wanted my players to feel that difference. And when we practiced our goal-line plays, I took them down to the goal line itself.

"All right," I'd yell, "here it is, here is where we either get it in the end zone or we don't."

In golf, you drive for show and you putt for dough. In football, you play in the middle of the field for show and you play at the goal line for dough. Down there you turn up your engine. Six points for a touchdown are twice as many as three points for a field goal. To me, the players' attitude at the goal line was more important than the plays we used. Down there football is a different game. Everything has to be done shorter and tighter. Every pass receiver has to work within the 10 yards of the end zone. Everybody is packed into a small space, like in a free-for-all.

"Are *you* going to score?" I'd yell at the offense, then turn to the defense. "Or are *you* going to stop 'em?"

If the offense got in, they cheered. If the defense held, they cheered. Whatever happened, one unit was fired up because they did their job and the other unit was pissed off because they hadn't done theirs. Either way, everybody was taking his job seriously. When they were on the goal line in Three Rivers Stadium or Mile-High Stadium, they had to take it seriously. And that's what we were getting ready for.

You don't see all that rah-rah stuff on the goal line in the fourth quarter. When a team starts to get tired in the fourth quarter, that's when its true discipline comes out.

Third-and-two down near the goal line, that's when you can't make a mistake. But that's just when some teams jump offside. Now it's third-and-seven, a big difference. The players on that team might all wear ties and sportcoats, they might look good on the airplane and look good in the lobby of the hotel. But they're not a disciplined football team.

Hey, if a player wears a tie and sportcoat, if he has a nice haircut, if he likes milk and apple pie, that's nice. But if he jumps offside, he's an undisciplined football player.

Some people think the way a player talks is a tipoff as to whether he's disciplined or not. They hear a young player say "Yes sir" or "No sir," and they think that just because he sounds like he's at West Point or Annapolis or the Air Force Academy, he must be disciplined. And when they hear a young player say "Yeah," they think he's undisciplined. But believe me, the guy who says "Yeah" can be a disciplined football player. And the guy who says "Yes sir" and "No sir" can jump offside near the goal line.

"Discipline," I used to tell my players, "this is what discipline is in football. You don't jump offside. If we're running out the clock, you don't go out of bounds. If we're on defense and trying to stop the clock, you keep the other team from going out of bounds."

Sometimes the other team's player is too strong or he has too much momentum to be stopped from going out of bounds. That's a physical situation. I always accepted that. But not a mental mistake. I never accepted a mental mistake. Like if my player didn't know enough to make sure the other team didn't get out of bounds. Or a running back lining up in an illegal formation. Or a piling-on penalty long after the play was over. All those things are just stupid. And if any of them happen near the goal line, it's even stupider. That's why we worked so much down near the goal line in our Thursday practice, our big rehearsal for the offense.

Years ago, back in the early sixties and before, coaches worried about spies sneaking in to watch practice, or looking through binoculars from a nearby building. By the time I joined the Raiders' staff in 1967, the film exchange had pretty much ended that. But the older coaches still worried.

As the Rams' and Redskins' coach, George Allen always had

his practice field patrolled by a security guard who was known as 007, but George was not above suspicion himself. At a Cowboys' practice before a Rams' game, Tom Landry noticed a yellow Chevrolet parked nearby and realized it had been parked there the day before. He sent an aide to check out the occupants, but they zoomed away. When the Cowboys traced the license plate, they discovered it was a rental car hired by a Rams' official. In the days before the Packers were to play the Rams in a 1967 playoff game, Vince Lombardi took his team inside Lambeau Field rather than using their open practice field.

"No visitors at practice," Vince decreed.

"What about the writers?" a Packer aide asked. "What should we tell the writers?"

"That we're putting in the single-wing," Vince said.

Whenever a helicopter rattled above a Jets' practice before a Raider game, Weeb Ewbank thought Al Davis hired it so a spy could check out any new plays. But as the Raiders' coach, I never got any information from spies and I don't think any other team spied on us. I always figured that even if the other team knew our plays, it still didn't know when we were going to call them.

In our Friday meeting, we concentrated on special teams. That was their day, just like Wednesday was for defense and Thursday was for offense. When we went out to practice on Friday, we went over all our special-team situations. Even the extra point. *Especially* the extra point.

I know, the extra point is supposed to be automatic, but it's not. During the 1985 season a total of twenty-seven extra points were not made for whatever reason—a bad kick, a blocked kick, a bad snap, or a bad hold. One reason, I've always thought, is that for some offensive linemen, the extra point is an anticlimactic play.

Hey, we just got a touchdown, someone thinks, I'll just lean on my man during the extra point.

They line up, he leans on his man and *boom*, his man gets an arm up high enough to block the extra point. Now, instead of getting 7 points, your team only gets 6. The extra point is just that, an *extra* point, a bonus for having scored a touchdown. But now it's been wasted, just because a lineman decided to celebrate a touchdown by leaning against his man. That's why the Raiders practiced extra points. Practiced them in training camp. Practiced them every Friday during the season. Practiced them with all the other players watching.

"All right," I asked the others, "pick out the best rusher on this kick."

Now it was a contest. Now it was serious. Now the rushers were trying to get up in the air to block the kick. Now the linemen were trying to drive the rushers back, prevent them from getting a hand on the ball. I didn't put as much emphasis on our kickoff coverage or our punt coverage, or our kickoff returns and our punt returns. I just turned my controlled fanatics loose on those special teams. I didn't put as much emphasis on our field-goal unit. That was for 3 points. They paid attention for 3 points. But the extra point was different both ways: preventing the other team from blocking our kick and trying to block the other team's kick.

"I want the best extra-point team in the league," I would yell in training camp. "And the best extra-point block team."

Saturday we reviewed everything out on the field where we would be playing on Sunday, either in the Oakland Coliseum if we were playing at home or in the other team's stadium if we were on the road. When we traveled, our chartered jet left the gate at the Oakland airport at the time listed on the itinerary, regardless of who wasn't there.

"The plane leaves," I always told my players, "whether you're on it or not."

If anybody missed the plane, he had to get to the road game on his own. Buy his own ticket. Pay for his own cab. Plus, he knew he would be fined. No excuses were accepted. If he had a flat tire driving to the Oakland airport, hey, it didn't make any difference. Either he was on the plane or he wasn't. On our charter, I never made my players dress up with a jacket and tie, but I did make them respect the people along the way—the flight attendants, the waiters or waitresses in the hotel. Anytime I see anybody bullying people who are serving them, it really pisses me off.

With the reputation the Raiders had as "renegades," some people probably thought Attila the Hun's army had arrived. But in my ten years as coach, I don't ever remember being told about a problem between any of my players and the people along the way.

Traveling with a football team, most things are the same: the chartered jet, the buses, the hotel. But each stadium is different, often quite different. Your team should always fit your own stadium. My years in Oakland, we had a soft, slick grass field. It was so slick that Al Davis was often accused of having the field watered down to slow up the visiting team. Hey, nobody watered it down. Nobody had to. The field was below sea level. Oakland's inner harbor and San Leandro Bay were nearby. When the tide came in, the water table under the Coliseum would rise just enough for the grass to be slick.

Visiting teams used short cleats on their football shoes. But we knew better. On that slick grass, we had our players wear long cleats.

We also built our team with our field in mind—bigger, heavier grass-type players rather than smaller, faster artificial turf-type players. When we were on the road, we naturally preferred fields that were similar to ours. But not quite as slick.

Both then and now, the best football field in the NFL is Lambeau Field in Green Bay, named for Earl "Curly" Lambeau, who organized the Packers in 1921 and coached them for nearly thirty years.

If you want to know how a football field should be built, just look at Lambeau Field. First of all, it's strictly a football field— no baseball, no soccer. Its front-row seats are along the sidelines and behind the end zones. Every seat in its 57,000 capacity is a good seat. Finally, it's got real grass that doesn't turn to mud in the rain and doesn't fall apart after a few plays. Any player can do what he does best on that grass, and any team can do what it does best. My Raider teams played there three times and won there three times, in 1972 and 1978 and also in the 1971 preseason. Since then I've done a few TV games in Green Bay and the field has always been the same: perfect.

I like RFK Stadium in Washington. Its grass isn't as good as Green Bay's, but it's good. Mile-High Stadium in Denver has good grass, but you always have to worry about the weather there. At the kickoff it might be sunny and warm; by the fourth quarter it might be snowing.

Most of the stadiums in warm-weather cities have good short grass: the Los Angeles Coliseum, Anaheim Stadium, Jack Murphy Stadium in San Diego, the Orange Bowl in Miami, Atlanta Stadium, Tampa Stadium. Candlestick Park in San Francisco has good grass, but the wind blows in circles. Shea Stadium, where the Jets used to play, had that same circular wind along with a hard field with hardly any grass, especially late in the season. Cleveland's Municipal Stadium gets hard when the weather gets cold. But playing in Shea or in Cleveland is still better than playing on artificial turf.

Of the stadiums with artificial turf, Giants Stadium and Texas Stadium are the best, but as you may have gathered, I don't like artificial turf. In Busch Stadium in St. Louis early in the 1973 season, the turf was so hot, my Raider players got blisters on their feet, right through their shoes. In the Houston Astrodome, the turf was always the worst, hard and scruffy. It scraped the skin off your arms. And in a dome, the noise always stays inside.

I miss the old ballparks. They weren't as spiffy as the new stadiums, but they had grass and they had charm. We once played the Patriots in Fenway Park with that big green left-field wall. Our locker room was behind the third-base dugout. Before the introductions, we got jammed up in the little tunnel to the dugout. I was all hunched over, with water dripping down on me. But all I could think of was that when Babe Ruth played there with the Yankees, he walked through that same tunnel.

I miss Municipal Stadium in Kansas City, Wrigley Field in Chicago, and Metropolitan Stadium in Minnesota; hey, I even miss War Memorial Stadium, in Buffalo, where you had to run a gauntlet of screaming fans to get to and from the field.

The visitors' locker room in War Memorial was up a rickety wooden staircase. When you went out for the warmup, you had to go down those stairs, then past hot-dog stands that were so close you could grab a mustard jar. Dozens of Bills fans were waiting to let you have it. On the way back from the warmup, you had to do it again. Then when it was time for the kickoff, out you went again. Back in at halftime. Out again for the second half. Then back in after the game. Every time those fans were waiting for you.

"You bums!" they would be yelling, along with a few other choice phrases.

Life's like that on the road. The first time the Raiders went to Pittsburgh, in 1972, we were practicing on Saturday at Three Rivers Stadium when a Steelers' groundskeeper wandered over near our huddle. His name, I learned later, was Steve "Dirt" Dinardo, a short heavy guy who had been with the Steelers and the baseball Pirates back when they both played at Forbes Field. He had a voice you could hear in a blast furnace.

"Ha, ha," he started out saying that day, "Joe Greene will eat you guys for lunch."

I spun around. Hey, when a team is practicing, nobody is supposed to bother them, but here was this guy in blue coveralls heckling my team.

"Where's security?" I yelled.

"Forget security," he said.

"Get out of here," I roared. "Stop bothering us. Get off the field."

"This is my field," he said.

By now, he was laughing, which got me and my players laughing. From then on, whenever we went to Pittsburgh, we knew Dirt Dinardo would be heckling us at our Saturday practice. We got to enjoy it as much as he did. One time when we arrived at Three Rivers for a Saturday practice, I found a pair of blue coveralls in my locker. Attached to them was a note:

> John, these are for you, because after you get your ass beat tomorrow, you're going to get fired. Then you'll have to go to work like the rest of us.
>
> [signed] *Dirt*

I loved it, especially when we didn't get beat. But even with Dirt hanging around, we always had a good Saturday practice. We lined up our defense against our simulated Steeler offense, starting on the Steeler goal line. We worked our defense against all the plays the Steelers were likely to use to get to their 10-yard line, then those they were likely to use from their 10 to their 20, then from their 20 to midfield, then down to our 40, our 30, our 20, our 10, and then at our goal line.

After that, we lined up our offense on our own goal line against our simulated Steeler defense. But instead of telling my quarterback what to call, I just gave him the situation. He called the play.

If we were on our own 3-yard line, Kenny Stabler always knew to call a running play that was likely to get us at least to the 5-yard line. That way, if we had to punt, Ray Guy could set up in his usual 15 yards—5 yards plus the 10 yards of the end zone. If we had to punt with the line of scrimmage at the 2, he would have only 12 yards. That's a big difference. The snap is shorter, the spacing of our blockers is tighter, and the timing for Ray has to be quicker.

Once we got out from our goal line, we did the same thing we did with the defense: use our best plays to get from the 10 to the 20, then out to midfield, then down to their 40, their 30, their 20, their 10, and their goal line.

No matter how good the Saturday practice was, I was never really satisfied. "Oh, wait," I'd always yell, "one more thing, if they . . ." This was our last rehearsal. It had to be good. It had to be complete. When we had gone through all the plays in our game plan, and maybe a few that weren't, that was it. Except for the punters and the placekickers. They always loosened up at the end of the Saturday practice.

For most of the team now, the hay was in the barn. But not for the coaches and the quarterbacks.

Saturday night at the hotel, either on the road or at the Hilton in Oakland if we were playing at home, we always gathered in my suite for a meeting. It started at about 7:30 and ended at 11:00, the curfew time when our players had to be in their rooms. Not asleep, but in their rooms. When the assistant coaches and the quarterbacks drifted into that 7:30 meeting, they were usually talking about that day's college scores. But we soon got down to why we were there. I'd turn on the projector and show game films of the opposing team's defense.

"All right," I'd say to Kenny Stabler, "give me all our starting points."

He would rattle off the first play we wanted to use in every situation: deep in our territory, midfield, down at the other team's 20-yard line, short-yardage, goal line. Those plays varied from week to week, depending on the other team's personnel. But one thing seldom varied: When we ran, we usually kept running to our left behind Art Shell and Gene Upshaw until the other team stopped us. And even if the other team stopped us, we'd try running there again to see if they really stopped us or if they just happened to luck into it. If we decided the other team had really stopped us, then we'd try to figure out why they stopped us and how we could do something else to take advantage of their adjusted defense. If they never stopped us, we'd just keep running there the whole game.

I always dragged out that Saturday night meeting. For me, it was always more of a hangout, something to do to kill the loneliness.

I never took Virginia or our boys, Mike and Joe, on a road trip. I never liked to go out to dinner on the road, or to look up old friends. With a game to coach the next day, I was in no mood for socializing. Even now, in my TV travels, I never go out the night before a game. I prefer to order room service just like I did during those Saturday night meetings. For me, watching game films was always a form of relaxation.

"Hey, look at this," I was sure to say at our Saturday-night meeting. "I didn't notice that before."

I sometimes kept watching films long after the quarterbacks went to their rooms. Long after the assistant coaches went to check their players' rooms. Long after some of the players had knocked on my door for the Danish pastry, one of my few superstitions. My first year as the Raiders' coach, I started having Saturday-morning meetings with my assistant coaches and my quarterbacks because our preseason games were on Saturday night. In the morning, you eat Danish and drink coffee, so that's what I ordered from room service for everybody: a big tray of Danish pastry and a big pot of coffee.

When the season started, I figured, hey, don't change a winning order. Even though the meeting now was Saturday night, I kept having Danish and coffee sent up.

But who has Danish and coffee at night? Not my assistant coaches, not my quarterbacks, not even me. After a while, some of the players learned that all that Danish was just sitting there. After the assistant coaches and the quarterbacks left, some of the players would come to take the Danish to their rooms. My superstition about the Danish and coffee, I discovered later, turned into a Raider tradition. During the 1983 season, I was in Los Angeles to do a Raiders-Giants game. After the Raider practice at the Coliseum on Saturday afternoon, I went up to Tom Flores' room at the Beverly Wilshire, where the team was staying that night. Tom, of course, had been my quarterback coach and my receivers coach the last seven seasons I was the Raiders' coach. We talked about old times, we talked about his Raider team, which would go on to win Super Bowl XVII that season, then I looked at my watch.

"Hey," I said, "it's time for your meeting. I better get out of here."

Just then, there was a knock on the door. Tom answered it, then swung the door open to let a room-service waiter roll in a big cart with Danish and coffee on it.

"You're still having Danish and coffee sent up," I said.

"Yeah," Tom said, "and nobody eats it now either."

On the
Sideline

NOT EVERYBODY ATE AT OUR pregame meal Sunday morning. Fred Biletnikoff would sip a cup of coffee and smoke a cigarette. Others might just have toast and tea. But most players knew they needed some fuel. My first few years as coach, they usually had orange juice, steak and eggs, toast, and coffee, tea, or milk. But when nutritionists started touting carbohydrates, some players asked for pancakes or waffles, even spaghetti. My last few years as coach, I decided the players could ask for whatever they wanted. Some still ordered steak and eggs; others preferred pancakes or spaghetti. And then one Sunday morning I happened to be standing near Dave Casper as he looked up at the waitress.

"I'll have a banana split," Dave said.

If that's what stoked my All-Pro tight end, I didn't care if he had two cherries on top of the whipped cream. But no matter what my players had at our pregame meal, they always sat down to eat exactly four hours before the kickoff. For a Sunday game, that meant we might eat at 8:00 or 9:00 or 10:00 or 11:00, depending on what time zone we were in. But on Sunday, at least we ate in the morning. When we had a Monday night game, we would eat as late as 5:00 in the afternoon if we were in the East, or 2:00 in the afternoon if we were in California.

Sitting around all day Monday before those nine o'clock games in the East was the longest and toughest wait. I don't know of anybody in football who doesn't prefer getting up around 8:00 in the morning, having your pregame meal at 9:00, and having the kickoff at 1:00 in the afternoon.

Whatever time the kickoff was, my players had to be in our locker room two hours before. But some players were what I call "early birds," those who left the hotel right after the pre- game meal. Instead of waiting for the buses, they would take a cab to the stadium just to hang out in the locker room. Play cards. Try on different shoes. Get new laces in their shoulder pads. Get their ankles taped early so they won't have to wait later on. Maybe take a nap. Anything to be in the locker room.

My first few years as the Raiders' coach, I was very hyper in the locker room before the warmup. I couldn't sit still, couldn't keep quiet.

"Hey, on that sweep," I might say to Gene Upshaw. "On that sweep, you've got to remember that the linebacker will try to slide."

Gene knew that better than I did. He didn't need me to remind him. But the moment I saw him in the locker room, I had to remind him. Almost every player I saw, I had to remind him of something. By being so nervous, I made some of my players nervous, especially my young players. It got so that my young players avoided me during the hour or so we were all in the locker room before the warmup. Looking back, I think I changed during the 1973 season, when I decided that Kenny Stabler was our quarterback. In his five previous seasons he had started only two games, so he was likely to be more nervous than I was. To keep him calm, I had to appear calm myself. Instead of taking a chance on reverting to being hyper in the locker room, I didn't go into the locker room. At least not where the players were.

I'd change clothes in the coaches' room, then go outside. I might sit in the stands. If we were playing in Oakland, I might wander up to the press room for a quick cup of coffee. Anything to stay out of the locker room.

In those hours before a game the team doctor is in the trainer's room checking out the players who had been on the NFL injury report as probable, questionable, or doubtful. Not just any doctor can do that. You need an orthopedist who understands football and football players, who can evaluate whether a player is hurt or injured. That might sound the same, but it's not. When you're hurt, you can play. Maybe you'll have to play in pain, but you can play, you can do your job. Some players have a greater tolerance for pain than others—that's an individual thing. But when you're *injured,* you shouldn't play. If you play when you're injured, you're going to injure yourself even more, and you're going to weaken the team because you really can't do your job.

The difference between being hurt or injured is the decision the doctor must make. Like most teams, the Raiders had two team doctors: an orthopedist, Dr. Robert Rosenfeld, and a general practitioner, Dr. Donald Fink. But once a doctor makes his decision, that's it. I don't know of any coach who ever overruled a doctor's decision. I know I never did.

During a game, your doctor is right there on the sideline, ready to hurry out to examine a fallen player. Anytime a player is down, his head coach is also allowed to go out there, but he seldom does—on doctor's orders. I learned that my first year as the Raiders' head coach after I rushed out there a few times.

"I'd appreciate it," our orthopedist said to me, "if you didn't go on the field every time somebody's hurt. If the player sees you out there, he'll say he can play, no matter what."

After that, I picked my spots—once or twice a season, if that. I learned that groggy players are like groggy drivers. If a player gets knocked out, when he comes around, the doctor will test him by holding up two or three fingers, sometimes just one.

"How many fingers," the doctor asks.

"Two," the player will usually answer.

It's like what my Pleasanton neighbor, Carl Marsh, a California state highway patrolman, always told me about people who are stopped on suspicion of drunken driving. Whenever those people are asked if they've been drinking, they all have the same answer.

"Just a couple of beers," they say.

When a football player comes around after having been knocked out, he just sees a couple of fingers. But when a player is injured during a game, he's usually the worst judge of his condition. Most players will say, "I can go back, I'm all right, I can go back." If the doctor doesn't let them, they stomp around like little kids. Sometimes they'll even succeed in sneaking back into the games. To prevent that possibility, the Giants came up with the best solution. Hide the player's helmet. No matter how goofy a player is after his bell is rung, he won't try to sneak back into the game without his helmet.

But the Giants' players soon got wise to that trick. One time when Joe Morris got knocked dizzy, he sat on the bench with his helmet jammed between his legs. Nobody was going to hide *his* helmet.

Once a player takes a shower and the soreness sets in overnight, he usually realizes the doctor was right. Having an X-ray facility in every NFL stadium has made it easier for the doctor. When you see a player going to the locker room during a game, chances are he's about to be X-rayed. If a fracture or even a hairline fracture shows up, a player won't argue anymore. I even needed an X-ray once. At halftime, I was so pissed off at the way we were playing, I punched a blackboard. I didn't let on how it hurt, but during the second half it started swelling up and by the time the game was over, the middle knuckle on my right hand really hurt. I showed it to Dr. Fink, who took me to the X-ray machine.

Sure enough, my knuckle was fractured. I was hurt, but not injured. I was able to coach in pain.

Another of my pregame rituals was to visit the officials in their dressing room. I went there to make the opposing coach think I was trying to con a call from the officials. Sometimes I was, especially if the other team's offensive linemen had been getting away with holding in previous games. Or if that officiating crew had made a bad call the last time it worked one of our games.

"That pass interference call in Denver," I might say. "McNally told me you guys blew that one."

I wanted them to know that *I* knew that Art McNally, the NFL supervisor of officials, had agreed with me when I complained about that call. Another reason I visited the officials was to check my watch with theirs. Wherever I was in the stadium before a game, I would glance at my watch every few minutes. I had to be back in the locker room in time to go out on the field with our first group of players to warm up —our kicker along with his holder and snapper, our punter, our return-men, and anybody else who wanted to go out early. I'd stay out there when our whole squad was warming up, watching if our banged-up players were running easily, and having an assistant coach watching how the other team's banged-up players were running. The year we went to Super Bowl XI, we didn't know if Franco Harris or Rocky Bleier would play for the Steelers in the AFC championship game. Franco's ribs had been banged up the week before in Baltimore, and Rocky had a bad ankle.

During the warmup, Franco just stood around. Rocky tried to run, but he was hurting. That made a big difference.

Without both Franco and Rocky, about all the Steelers had was Terry Bradshaw, which was enough of a worry. Without those two running backs in there, we knew we could gang up on Terry, because he was the only way the Steelers could hurt us. But just because a player stands around during the warmup doesn't mean he might not play. During the 1983 season, I was at a Bear game in Tampa when Walter Payton was listed as "probable" because of a leg injury.

"We'll see how Walter runs in the warmup," Mike Ditka told me. "Then we'll know if he can play."

In the warmup Walter not only didn't run, he just stood on the sideline in his Bears' warmup jacket and watched. I figured no way Walter would play. But when the Bears' offense trotted onto the field, Walter was there. By the time the game was over, Walter had rushed for 106 yards. But when our warmup was over, I always went back into the locker room and stayed in my coaches' office until it was time for me to talk to the team, just before the introductions.

"If we kick off, stay in your lanes," I might say. "They ran it back all the way last week. And if we receive, I want a middle return."

Depending on our opposing team, I always reminded them of something. Against the Dolphins, I reminded them that Don Shula always came at us with his best plays on the first series but if the Dolphins get a quick touchdown or a quick field goal, it didn't make that much difference.

"One touchdown or one field goal," I always said, "isn't going to beat us."

I also reminded them that if our defense stopped the Dolphins on that first series, it didn't make that much difference either.

"Just because we stop 'em once," I always said, "we still haven't done anything."

If none of this sounds like a pep talk, you're right. I always believed that you got ready on the practice field during the week, not with a pep talk in the locker room. You can't expect players to respond to a coach who asks them to "Win one for the Gipper" every week. Hey, not even Knute Rockne did that. Just about everybody in football has heard about Rockne's famous "Win one for the Gipper" speech. But he didn't use that speech until eight years after George Gipp died. Gipp was an All-America halfback at Notre Dame in 1920, the nation's outstanding college player. Late in the season he suddenly died of pneumonia. Several days earlier Rockne had visited him in the hospital.

"Someday in a tough game," Gipp is supposed to have told Rockne, "ask the players to win one for the Gipper."

Rockne saved that request until the 1928 game with Army at Yankee Stadium, which Notre Dame won, 12–6, the perfect ending for the perfect pep talk. And if somebody like George Gipp had asked me to have my team "win one" for him, maybe I would've—at the right time and the right place. But mostly, I found that the bigger the game, the less I had to say in the locker room. If my team wasn't ready to play, nothing I said would help. And if my team was ready to play, whatever I said didn't make much difference. Before all our big games and especially before Super Bowl XI, about all I did was open the door and get out of the way.

"All right," I would say, "we've waited for this one. Let's go out there and get it."

Sure, football is an emotional game. Sure, football has to be played emotionally. And your players better play it that way. But in order to perform emotionally, players must be prepared mentally. On a Saturday night before a game, a player should feel he knows everything he has to do on every play, and knows everything the opposing team is going to do on every play. If he knows all that, he'll sleep well. If he doesn't know all that, he won't.

If he's prepared mentally, that allows him to be emotional in Sunday's game. If he's not prepared mentally, if he doesn't know which guy to block or which guy to cover, emotion isn't going to do him any good.

Just because players come charging out of their locker room whooping and hollering doesn't mean they're emotionally up. Some college and high school teams run out on the field and jump up and down, pound each other, and that's more contact than they have in the game. Maybe all that excitement is a carryover from what the coach told the team in the locker room. But whatever he told them, it's not going to last much beyond the opening kickoff. Tough games are won or lost in the fourth quarter, not on the opening kickoff. The fourth quarter is when you need guys to dig down, to play when they're tired, to use the energy they saved by not whooping and hollering earlier.

I learned about false emotion in practice. In the years before the Raiders started filming practice, I gauged how good a practice we had by how much noise the players made. The more noise, the better the practice. The quieter they were, the worse the practice. Or so I thought.

After we started filming practice, I realized my gauge was wrong about half the time. In studying the films, I noticed that sometimes the players were quiet because they were concentrating so hard, and those turned out to be a good practices. I also noticed that sometimes when they made a lot of noise, they weren't concentrating, and those turned out to be bad practices. But we also had good practices with noise and bad practices without noise.

The moment the ball is spotted after the kickoff return, the game situations start—either on offense or defense.

No two football games have ever been exactly the same. No two situations have ever been exactly the same. Even if the down-and-distance situation is the same, the field position is different. Or the opposing defense. Or your offensive personnel. Or the score. Or the time remaining. Learning how to deal with all those different situations takes time, especially for a young head coach. I was only thirty-three my first season as the Raiders' head coach, the NFL's youngest head coach at the time. Not only that, I'd only been a head coach for two years at Allan Hancock Junior College in Santa Maria, California, before going to San Diego State as defensive coordinator for Don Coryell, and then to the Raiders as their linebacker coach. So to give myself a cram course in NFL game situations my first few years as the Raiders' coach, I went to high school games.

That's right, high school games. Friday night I would take

Virginia and the boys to whichever local team in Pleasanton was playing at home, either Foothill High School or Amador High School.

If the Raiders were playing the Chargers on Sunday, I would pretend that, say, Foothill High were the Raiders and their opponents were the Chargers. When the Foothill offense had first-and-ten at their 34, I would be thinking what I would be doing on that down and distance in that field position. Not that the personnel or the strategy were the same, but the situation was. Maybe it was third-and-three at the other team's 31-yard line, what pass play should we use? Or if it was fourth-and-one, at their 27-yard line, should we try for a first down or go for the field goal? Or if Foothill was on defense in a third-and-eight at midfield, what pass coverage should we be in?

The more I did that at high school games on Friday night, the more I found that when those situations developed on Sunday afternoon, I had been there before.

That's the whole idea: to have been there before. When you think about it, that's all experience is. Even though I had only been watching a high school game, I still had been there before. After a few years, I stopped going to the high school games. Not that I knew everything, but I knew I didn't need to do it anymore. By then I had been there before on the Raiders' sideline. I remembered situations in other games or I remembered situations I had seen in game films. By then, I was an experienced coach.

No matter how experienced a coach is, no matter how good his team's practices have been all week, sometimes a team starts out flat.

It's not necessarily anybody's fault. Sometimes it just happens. You go out there and you can't get your offense going. You try this and you try that, but nothing works. Sometimes the opposing team makes you flat. No matter what you try, they shut you down. Whenever we played the Dolphins, it seemed like we started out flat. But that was because Don Shula's defense made us flat. Even if we popped the Dolphins with a good pass play, they would make an adjustment. The next time we tried that play, *bang,* they might be coming back at us with an interception.

Now you try something else. No good. So you try another play. No good. And another. No good. Now you're punting.

It's like being in a maze. You're searching for a way out, but you can't seem to find it. In some games, you never do. But in most games, you usually find something.

"The toughest score to get," George Blanda once told me when I was an assistant coach, "is always the first score."

I enjoyed talking strategy with George because he was our backup quarterback as well as our kicker. He always talked more as a quarterback than a kicker. After he mentioned how the first score was always the toughest, I became more aware of the first score. George was right. The sooner you got those points on the board, whether they were for a touchdown or a field goal, the easier it was to put more points on the board. As a head coach, I always coached that way. Get the first score. If you get it early, it opens the gates. But if you don't, you might spend the whole first half trying for it. Anytime you don't have any points on the board by halftime, you know you're in for a struggle.

What goes on at halftime isn't what most people think. To begin with, you only have fifteen minutes from the time the first half ends until you're lining up for the second-half kickoff. By the time your players get into the locker room, grab something to drink, take a leak, then sit down at their lockers, you've got maybe five to seven minutes before you go out on the field again. So there's no time for a fiery talk, not if you want to use your time the way you should use it: to prepare your team mentally for the second half.

Your locker room is divided into offense on one side, defense on the other. Each unit has its own blackboard. While the defensive coaches are putting on their blackboard what the opposing team was able to do and why, the offensive coaches are putting on their blackboard the new plays to use in the second half. They're also looking at the Polaroid photos, taken from the press-box level or maybe from the stadium roof, of the various coverages the opposing defense used. By halftime all those photos have been separated into various down-and-distance situations—first down, second down, third down, short yardage, goal line, runs, passes, the different defensive fronts, and pass coverages.

"Show me," I might say, "what that third-down blitz with the seven defensive backs looked like."

I had an opaque projector that would blow up that Polaroid photo on a wall so my quarterback could really see what that blitz looked like.

"When that defensive tackle goes to his left, it's not an overload," I might say. "But if he doesn't, it's really an overload."

With a Polaroid photo, you can tell. That photo is snapped as the defensive players take their first step. That's important. Before the ball is snapped, a free safety might line up in the middle of the field. But at the snap, he'll go to the weak side, which is where he knew he was going all along. On defense, a player's first step never lies. Out there on the field, an offensive player might not know exactly what happened. At the snap, a play is like an automobile accident. Things happen so fast, nobody knows for sure what's happening. But those Polaroid photos know.

"So the next time we're inside the twenty," I might tell my quarterback, "run the ninety-four corner with a K-sixteen."

Kenny Stabler was great at storing that information. In our talks at halftime, I would give him some new plays for various situations. The next time we're inside the 20, the next time we're in short yardage, the next time we're near their goal line, the next time we have third-and-long. He'd nod, put his helmet on, and go back out for the second half. The next time those situations developed, *bang*, he would call that play as if I had just whispered it in his ear.

Adjusting to what the other team has done to what you did, that's what you do at halftime. When the second half starts, it's usually easy to spot an adjustment. As soon as a team gets the opportunity, it's going to do what it talked about at halftime. Maybe even on the first play.

During the 1984 season at RFK Stadium, the Cowboys kicked off into the end zone at the start of the second half. After the Redskins lined up at their 20-yard line, Calvin Muhammad took off on a deep pattern and Joe Theismann hit him with a long pass for an 80-yard touchdown. *Boom,* just like that, the Redskins suddenly had a 24–7 lead—now that's an adjustment—and the Cowboys never recovered. The year before at RFK, the Redskins had blown a 20-point halftime lead as the Cowboys rallied to win, 31–30. The Redskins weren't going to let that happen again.

Whatever our offensive problems were, I never believed in taking what the other team gives you.

If the other team gives you the short pass, it's because it wants you to take the short pass. And that means it *doesn't* want you to go for the medium or long pass. But if you take what the other team gives you, chances are you're taking what you don't want.

I believe that on offense, you find a way to take what you want. That you dictate your offense. That you don't let the other team's defense dictate your offense.

If our offense is in a third-and-twelve situation, it doesn't do us any good to take the 6 or 8 yards that the other team is giving us. We've got to go get those 12 yards. Too many teams surrender on offense by taking what the other defense gives them. That's why you see so many quarterbacks throwing to their backs in a third-down situation. Those teams are taking what the other defense is giving them—the short pass. Sometimes a good running back will turn that short pass into a first down. But more often than not, he'll be stopped short of a first down. Which is exactly why the other defense gave them the short pass.

No, you try to take what *you* want to take, not what the other team wants to give you.

Defensively, sometimes you can take what the other team

doesn't want to give you, if you have somebody who knows how to break the other team's wig-wag code for sending in plays from the sideline. Most coaches prefer to use a substitute as a messenger to the huddle. But some teams have an assistant coach wig-wag the plays, using different arm and hand signals. David Humm, one of our backup quarterbacks, had a knack for breaking the other team's code. Now some teams match films of the wig-wag signals with the formation and the play, and from that they try to decipher the signals.

Even if you know the other team's play, you don't have much time to alert your defense to what it is. And if you misread the wig-wag and alert your defense to the wrong play, *boom,* the other team might get 6 points.

On offense, I never used wig-wag signals. I preferred to *talk* to my quarterback, usually on the sideline between our offensive series, but I wasn't the only one talking to him. As soon as Kenny Stabler came off the field, he would get on the phone to Tom Flores, who was upstairs in a booth on the press-box level. Even if we had just scored a touchdown, Tom would have some thoughts for him.

"On every third down, they're blitzing," Tom might say. "And on every first down, they're using man-to-man coverage."

Except for Tom, none of our other coaches were allowed to talk to Kenny on the sideline. And even when Tom talked to him, Tom couldn't *order* Kenny to call a certain play. Tom could only *suggest* a play. When it was time for the other team to punt, Kenny would sidle up to me on the sideline. That's when I might give him a play to use. Not necessarily to see if the play will work, sometimes just to see how the other team reacts to it. That's how you set up a play for later on. But later on you use a play that looks the same as that previous play, maybe drawing the free safety into the same area he hurried into before. Only this time your wide receiver cuts into the open area the free safety had just vacated.

As the second half develops, you wind down to where the game is going to be won or lost. Often in the last two minutes.

Time-out, two-minute warning. As hectic as it was, that was

always the most fun in coaching for me—working a close game on the sideline in the last two minutes, especially a big game. Now all that time we spent practicing our two-minute drill was about to pay off; it wasn't something we did as an afterthought. In fact, we practiced it more than we did most of our other stuff. I've always thought that most teams worked in the middle of the field more than they worked on their two-minute drill. But the two-minute drill is more important. That's when you can win a game that you maybe should have lost.

Turn two or three games around in the last two minutes and you turn your won-lost record around. Instead of 8–8, now you're 10–6 or 11–5—and you're still employed.

As those last two minutes tick off, you're always reminding your players of something. Your team is losing by 4 points, you've got the ball at the other team's 29-yard line, first-and-ten, with fifty-three seconds remaining, and your quarterback is walking over to you during a time-out. That's when everybody in the stands and everybody watching on TV thinks you're giving him a play. But the first thing I always did was remind him of the down and distance.

"First-and-ten at the twenty-nine," I would say. "Only fifty-three seconds. If there's nobody open on this pass, throw it away."

Or if it was third down at the 29, I would remind him that being 4 points behind, we weren't going to go for the field goal on fourth down.

"Third-and-ten at the twenty-nine," I would say. "But if we don't get the first down here, we'll go for it on fourth down."

That might seem unnecessary. But a quarterback is so caught up in the game, he might be thinking about where the free safety will be on the next play instead of what yard line we're on. Or what down it is. Or even what the score is. So he's got to be reminded. If you give him a play in that situation, you tell him the play and the formation. You remind him that if he doesn't get the first down on third down, he'll have another chance on fourth down. That way he won't try to force a pass and maybe have it intercepted.

Remind, remind, remind—that's what a head coach should be doing in those last few minutes.

If your team is ahead and you've forced the other team to punt, you're now hoping to run out the clock in the last few seconds. That's when you have a reminder for your fullback before he runs onto the field with the rest of your offense.

"Hold the ball and go down," I would say. "Don't fight for yardage. Just hold the ball and go down."

That might also seem unnecessary, but a fullback's nature is to be aggressive. To fight for yardage. To squirm and scratch for inches. And that's when he's most likely to fumble. When your team is running out the clock, the worst thing your fullback can do is fumble. So you remind him *not* to fight for yardage now, you remind him to go against his nature and fall down.

On defense, the same thing. If we had to get the ball back, I'd remind Willie Brown, my defensive captain, to remind the other defensive backs what to expect, and I'd remind my middle linebacker to remind the other linebackers and the defensive linemen what to look for.

As a coach, you need to be aware of having the right players in there in the right situation. You don't want a cornerback who can't run because of a bad ankle or a linebacker who can't tackle because of a sore shoulder. Depending on whether you're ahead or behind, you have to keep reminding your players whether to keep the ball or the opponents' ball in bounds to kill the clock or to get the ball out of bounds in order to stop the clock.

"Stay in bounds now," I used to yell when we were trying to kill the clock. "Stay in bounds."

When we wanted to stop the clock, I would yell, "Get out of bounds, get out." My players knew to do that as well as I did, but I kept reminding them anyway. On that sideline in the last few minutes, especially in the last few seconds, you can't assume that your players will remember everything you told them a few days ago in practice or maybe even a few minutes ago right there on the sideline. You keep telling them.

Remind, remind, remind.

In a goal-line or short-yardage situation, I would always send in a play, either during a time-out or with a substitute player. To me, a goal-line situation was a first down anywhere inside the 10-yard line, or a second down inside the 5-yard line, or a third down inside the 2-yard line. To me, a short-yardage situation was a third-and-two anywhere else on the field. If we had third-and-three, to me that was a passing situation.

If we weren't in a goal-line or short-yardage situation, I may or may not give my quarterback a play late in the game.

Sometimes I gave him two or three plays. All the more reason to remind him of the down and distance. If we needed 10 yards on third down for a first down, I didn't want him throwing a 7-yard pass. With some quarterbacks, if you don't remind them of the down and distance, they might throw the ball without looking for the first-down marker.

Other times I wouldn't give my quarterback a play. At least not until I asked him what he had in mind.

If we were on the same wavelength, I'd rather have him call what *he* wanted to call rather than have him call what I wanted him to call. No matter how you slice it, when a quarterback calls a play out there in the huddle with his running backs and his receivers and his linemen, all those offensive players think of it as "our" play. But when a play comes in from the sideline, whether it's from the head coach himself or from upstairs where the assistant coaches are, the offensive players all think of it as "their" play, meaning those who sent it in.

If you're ahead, you remind your defense to go into what most people call a "prevent" defense. You put three pass rushers on the line with your eight other players off the line. Of the eight, as many as six or seven might be defensive backs. If it's successful, meaning as long as you win the game, hardly anybody notices you were in a prevent. But if it backfires and you lose, everybody notices.

I used the prevent, but I didn't like to. I didn't even like the word. It's a dangerous word for the defensive personality. Of all the words you use in coaching football, prevent doesn't fit. Run, block, tackle—each is an aggressive, positive word. But prevent is reluctant, negative. I always worried about the connotation of words. And whenever I heard the word *prevent*, it seemed like it sucked all the aggressiveness out of a player's body. So whenever I had my defense play what other people called the prevent, I wouldn't call it that.

"All right," I'd yell, "let's loosen up out there."

Other times I'd yell, "All right, let's back up a little," or "All right, give me some slack out there." But no matter what I called it, I still didn't like what it meant. Tell your defense to "loosen up," meaning give the other offense the short pass to run out the clock, and your defense starts to loosen up mentally. And whenever I heard the phrase "loosen up," I remembered a story one of my assistant coaches, Paul Roach, told about coaching a North Dakota high school team. One of Paul's cornerbacks got hurt, so he put in a sophomore who had hardly ever played before. On one of his first plays, the sophomore lined up too close to the wide receiver he was covering.

"Loosen up," Paul yelled from the sideline. "Loosen up."

The next thing Paul knew, the sophomore started to do jumping jacks out there on the field—jumping and clapping his hands over his head, like schoolkids do to loosen up in phys. ed. class.

"No, no, no," Paul yelled. "Just back off the receiver."

By now, the poor kid didn't know what he was supposed to do. And in their own way, defensive backs in the NFL don't always seem to know exactly what to do in a prevent defense. They know they're supposed to give a receiver a little more room than usual. But how much is a little? And how much is too much?

In a prevent, sometimes your three pass rushers aren't always as aggressive as they should be.

In the 1972 playoff game we lost to the Steelers on Franco Harris' "immaculate reception," we were ahead, 7–6, with only twenty seconds remaining. The Steelers had the ball on their own 40, but it was fourth-and-ten—their last chance. Looking at the films later, I got the impression our three pass rushers figured that our defensive backs would knock down Terry Bradshaw's long pass. They chased Terry out of the pocket, but they didn't go after him hard.

You know the rest.

Terry's pass sailed toward his halfback, Frenchy Fuqua, who went for the ball along with Jack Tatum, our free safety. The ball rebounded off one of them (even after all the films I've seen, I'm still not sure which one) and floated back toward Franco Harris, who reached down, caught the ball at our 42 and ran untouched into the end zone for a 60–yard touchdown with five seconds remaining on the clock.

We lost, 13–7.

Win or lose, I never said much to my players after a game. I'd remind anyone who got banged up to see the doctor, and if we were on the road I'd remind them what time the bus left for the airport. That's about all. I learned early, especially when you're upset after a loss, not to jump on a player. He's just as upset and he might say something back. You find yourself using words you don't mean, and he's using words he doesn't mean. Then you spend all day Tuesday apologizing to each other.

As soon as I finished talking to the players, I went outside to talk to the media, usually in a little room off the locker room.

Over the years I got to know what questions to expect, especially after a loss. Why did you take the field goal in the third quarter? What did the other team do to take away your running game? Why couldn't you stop their passing game? So even before I opened it up to questions, I would try to answer those I knew would be asked. What some coaches don't seem to understand is that the media isn't second-guessing them about why a decision or a certain play didn't succeed. All the media wants is your explanations to questions that your team's fans are probably asking. I always preferred to be asked those questions and to be allowed to give my explanation.

I stayed there as long as any of the media had questions to ask, but they usually hurried into the locker room to talk to the players.

Win or lose, I expected my players to answer the media's questions just like I did. I never had much respect for a player who stood there in the glory of a win but hid in the trainer's room in the embarrassment of a loss. You stand there either way. I can understand someone who's shy and never talks to the media. I don't agree with that, but I can respect that player more than I can a player who spouts quotes when his team wins but who disappears when his team loses.

No matter what happened in a game, I never second-guessed myself about a decision. I never looked back because as a coach, you should always be looking ahead.

On the sideline, you have to be thinking ahead so much you hardly have time to think about what is going on at that moment. Things are happening quickly. You have to get a play in or a player in. Or you're deciding whether to punt or go for the first down, or if you're down near the goal line, whether to kick a field goal or go for a touchdown.

All those decisions are made, *bang,* let's do this. You don't have much time to think about it. Sometimes only a matter of seconds. Whatever you decide is based on your best judgment at the time. That's all you can go by. Your best judgment at the time.

To go back and second-guess yourself doesn't do you any good. It's an exercise in futility. Whatever you decided, if it didn't work out, that's it. That was your decision. And you only get one chance to make that decision. All your second-guesses don't mean anything. Even if they did, who's to say your second-guess would turn out any different. Dick Howser explained that best while managing the Kansas City Royals to the 1985 World Series championship.

"I never second-guess myself," Dick said, "because nobody has yet proved to me that the second-guess would work."

That's the way football coaches and baseball managers think. The good ones, anyway. Not long ago I reminded my boyhood pal John Robinson about the time my mother offered me $25 to paint our back porch. I hired John to do it for $10.

"You got ten dollars and I kept the other fifteen" I said.

"Yeah," he said, laughing, "but I got my ten dollars."

That's a coach's thinking. You live with what you do. You make a decision to paint a porch for $10, you live with it. In a football game, if you make a decision to run a sweep on third down and you get outsmarted by the defense, you live with it. If you look back, you're thinking behind instead of thinking ahead. That's how a coach loses confidence in himself.

Not that I didn't learn from my mistakes. Anytime a play didn't seem to be working as well as it had in other games or in other seasons, we'd check to see how that play had worked, say, the last ten times we used it. If we discovered that we only averaged 2.2 yards with that play, then I would put together a film strip of those ten times. If new defenses had minimized the effectiveness of that play, we'd throw it out.

To me, that's not a second-guess, that's going back and finding something you were doing wrong and correcting it so you don't do it again. To me, a second-guess is saying to yourself after the game, "I should've taken the field goal at the 1-yard line instead of going for the touchdown." But who's to say the field goal would have been good? Maybe the snap would've been fumbled. Maybe the kick would've been wide. Or if you say to yourself, I should've gone for the touchdown at the 1 instead of taking the field goal, who's to say your offense would've scored the touchdown? Maybe the ballcarrier would've stumbled. Maybe the quarterback would've fumbled the snap.

I always knew what my decision would be in that fourth-down situation long before that situation developed.

On the way down the field, I knew from the score and the time remaining in the game whether I would go for the touchdown or take the field goal, whether I would go for the first down or punt. Say it's third-and-five for a touchdown or a first down. If you know you're going for it on fourth down, then you've got two plays to get those 5 yards. But if you know you're *not* going for it on fourth down, then you've got one play to get those 5 yards. And that affects what play the quarterback calls, or what play you send in. It also affects what plays you used on first down and second down.

That's why it's important to know what your decision will be as your team moves down the field. Against some teams, I knew what my decision would be even when my team was practicing during the week.

In the years when the Chiefs had Buck Buchanan and Curley Culp on their defensive line and Willie Lanier at middle linebacker, I never hesitated to take the field goal. When we were going against those tough Bronco defenses that got tougher the closer you got to the goal line, I never hesitated to take the field goal. And my players knew that. I'd have told them that at practice earlier in the week.

"When we get down there," I would say, "we got three shots at it. If you leave the ball on the one-yard line after three shots, don't look over to me like you want to go for it, don't shake your head when the kicker runs on. You had three shots."

Your emotions and your greed for points want that touchdown. Against some teams, if you think your offensive line can get a push in there to let your fullback score, you go for it. But against a team with a tough defense, your judgment as a coach tells you to take the field goal. If you get it, now you've got 3 points. Your fans think you've given up 7—a difference of 4 points, which can be a big difference in a game. But nobody can prove that you would've gotten the touchdown if you'd gone for it.

Decisions, decisions. But that's the fun of football. That's the fun of coaching.

Every so often I'll hear somebody say that Vince Lombardi couldn't coach now, that he couldn't cope with today's player. Don't you believe it. Tom Landry and Don Shula were coaching in the NFL back when Vince was, and they're able to cope with today's player. What makes a good coach is his ability to adapt to different players, to motivate them and get along with them. Vince Lombardi did that. George Halas did that. Knute Rockne did that. Amos Alonzo Stagg did that. And lots of others did that.

Hey, once a good coach, always a good coach.

About the Authors

JOHN MADDEN is a CBS commentator on their Sunday NFL games. Former head coach of the Oakland Raiders, he lives in California and New York with his wife, Virginia, and their two sons, Mike and Joe.

DAVE ANDERSON, a Pulitzer Prize–winning sports columnist for *The New York Times,* is the author of fifteen books. He lives in Tenafly, New Jersey, with his wife, Maureen. They have four children—Stephen, Mark, Mary Jo, and Jean Marie.